THE EVIL IMAGINATION

THE EVIL IMAGINATION
Understanding and Resisting Destructive Forces

Roger Kennedy

PHOENIX
PUBLISHING HOUSE
living the mind

First published in 2023 by
Phoenix Publishing House Ltd
62 Bucknell Road
Bicester
Oxfordshire OX26 2DS

Copyright © 2023 by Roger Kennedy

The right of Roger Kennedy to be identified as the author of this work has been asserted in accordance with §§ 77 and 78 of the Copyright Design and Patents Act 1988.

All rights reserved. No part of this publication may be reproduced, stored in a retrieval system, or transmitted, in any form or by any means, electronic, mechanical, photocopying, recording, or otherwise, without the prior written permission of the publisher.

British Library Cataloguing in Publication Data

A C.I.P. for this book is available from the British Library

ISBN-13: 978-1-91269-129-6

Typeset by vPrompt eServices Pvt Ltd, India

Printed in the United Kingdom

www.firingthemind.com

Contents

About the author	vii
1. Terrains of evil	1
2. The science of evil	35
3. Psychoanalysis and evil	69
4. The philosophy of evil	103
5. Journeys to evil: the Holocaust and British-American slavery	131
6. Shakespeare and evil—a dagger of the mind	167
7. Final comments—resisting evil	185
Endnotes	195
References	209
Index	219

About the author

Dr Roger Kennedy is a consultant child and adolescent psychiatrist and an adult psychoanalyst. He was an NHS consultant in charge of the Family Unit at the Cassel Hospital for nearly thirty years before going totally into private practice twelve years ago. He was chair of the Child and Family Practice in Bloomsbury and is still a director there.

His work includes being a training analyst and seeing adults for analysis and therapy, as well as children, families, and parents at his clinic. He is a past president of the British Psychoanalytical Society, and is well-known as an expert witness in the family courts. He has had fourteen previous books published on psychoanalysis, interdisciplinary studies, and child, family, and court work, as well as many papers.

CHAPTER 1

Terrains of evil

There are many terrains of evil, too many. How often one has heard the refrain "never again" after yet another series of genocidal killings or other acts of extreme cruelty have come to light. Yet there are always new instances of dehumanising human cruelty involving what I will describe as the "annihilation of the human subject", where human otherness and agency is psychologically denied and/or physically eliminated. At such times, the human subject becomes invaded by the other, subject relations are cancelled, and there is a denial or destruction of the gift of otherness with the carrying out of evil acts such as organised killings, rape, child abuse, slavery, and other violations of the subject. This notion is like that of Kathleen Taylor's term "otherization", which "expresses the sense of creating an increasingly impassable social gulf between Us and Them".[1] However, my emphasis is more on the nature of the attacks on the human subject, driven by destructive ideas and fantasies, or what we could call an "evil imagination", which result in, or are a consequence of, "otherization", when humans become subject *to* excessively cruel external forces rather than subject *of* their own actions.[2]

I will consider what leads to the committing of evil acts, and what are the individual and social circumstances that make such acts more likely, and whether one may be able to reduce the risk of evil acts being repeated. A main theme is that evil is here to stay, it is part of our landscape, and there should be ways of minimising or resisting its impact, but that this requires that one must try to understand evil, how it affects people and how it shatters world views and trust in others. I strongly believe that if we do not understand evil and the evil imagination, we will be ill-equipped to root it out from its various sources and thus minimise its impact in the future.

Seeing the crater from the destruction of the Twin Towers, or the piles of dead children's shoes at Auschwitz, or images of ships' holds where West Africans were piled in en route to slavery and physical and social death, or remnants of the killing fields of Cambodia, or current atrocities in the Russia–Ukraine war, the observer is made aware of the obliteration of human lives, a cold and unfeeling destructiveness. Observing the storming of the US Capitol in Washington reminds us of the ongoing risk to democracy of uncontained mob violence. With the reality of despairing victims of modern slavery, continuing genocides, persistent racism, the uncovering of ongoing child sexual abuse and sexual exploitation in its various forms, we continue to be faced by the "dark" side of human nature. One may reasonably think the modern world has failed to provide a safe haven against the worst outbreaks of human destructiveness. Compare these despairing images to the excitement of discovering ancient fossils of the footsteps of early mankind embedded in an African rock. With the latter, one can feel somehow an emotional link with our ancestors and reassured that there is another more positive side to humankind inscribed in our natures from ancient times.

The book explores with the help of a psychoanalytic perspective both a positive image of what makes for a decent society as being able to provide what I shall discuss as a "home for otherness", where human diversity and difference are both tolerated and promoted and resistance to evil is possible, while at the same time recognising that this is impossible without facing head-on as a harsh reality that human actions are regularly destructive of the links between fellow humans. I shall be looking at the nature of this harsh reality, at various narratives of evil, and which ones may be relevant in trying to overcome contemporary societal challenges, and how past atrocities and their accompanying traumas continue to haunt present-day societies, preventing or at least constricting attempts to promote respect for otherness.

I would suggest that part of the way that one can resist evil in its many guises is to have a clear image of what a decent society consists of. One of the lessons of history is that dangerous and destructive ideologies can take over a society when that society is in crisis, or lacks just institutions, or lacks a positive counterbalancing vision. Another lesson is that destructive ideologies are often adept at distorting or denying history for their own purposes, and that a painstaking reconstruction of past evils and the working through of their continuing impact on the present usually requires considerable emotional courage and persistence, essential elements in creating a decent society.

In this introduction I shall offer a general view of the territory to be covered from a multidisciplinary viewpoint before examining issues in more detail. The latter will consist firstly of a review of the science of evil, including evidence from neuroscience and social psychology, then psychoanalytical studies of individuals and groups, and next an overview of some of the main themes of the philosophy of evil. These opening chapters, along with the addition of information from historical and social studies, will inform an understanding of evil in action through examining the nature of genocide, with a focus on the Holocaust and what I have called the "Nazi Imaginary", the way that German society created an imaginary political community with which millions of ordinary Germans identified. I will also consider the evil practices of British-American slavery. I call the latter by this mixed title as, though slavery was not a British invention, and the West African–Atlantic trade in slaves involved several European and African nations, one can argue with good reason that it was the British who had a main role in institutionalising slavery for its vast profits and laid the basis on which the US then established its own institution of slavery.

A main reason for focusing on both these areas is their continuing relevance for understanding contemporary society and issues. The Nazi past continues to disturb, and as Mary Fulbrook writes,

> … its resonance seems if anything to be growing with time … The Holocaust has become a defining feature of contemporary self-understandings and values, and the more generic notion

of genocide has become a controversial catchword for mass violence in a wide range of contexts.[3]

While, as Paul Gilroy argues,[4] the politics and social fabric of Western society, reliant as it was on slavery as a foundation of economic wealth, continues to be haunted by the inability to process the harsh reality of slavery and its continuing after-effects. Current arguments about whether to display statues of past influential figures whose wealth and standing were reliant on the proceeds of the slave trade are just the tip of this particular iceberg.

I will also discuss how Shakespeare's evil characters encapsulate how the evil imagination can develop and take over a person's inner world, revealing "a deep, poetic, psychology or metaphysics of the birth of evil",[5] and how people can become "bewitched" by evil into performing or colluding with dreadful actions.

The final chapter will summarise the main themes and will also look at those who have resisted evil and what we can learn from them if we are to have a society that can resist the forces of evil in the future.

What is evil?

The term evil has a long history, much of it connected to various religions, some aspects of which remain relevant even in a predominantly secular age. Evil in the religious tradition often involves some sort of rebellion against God or the gods and includes some kind of war against the moral order and the forces of goodness, offering instead an alternative moral universe, where sin, or indulgence or the exercise of power is given free reign. Redemptive religions such as Christianity would even seem to require the existence of evil and unrighteousness so that humanity can then be redeemed by faith.

Much theological thought has then gone into puzzling how an all-powerful God could allow the flourishing of such an alternative moral dimension, and the existence of intense human suffering and moral evils—the so-called problem of "theodicy". Whether or not there is any answer to such a dilemma, this very issue has led to complex and deep moral thinking which remains relevant. For example, the thought of Kant, which I shall discuss later, provides some key themes relevant for understanding human evil.

Kant tried to incorporate religious thinking within the boundaries of reason. For him, the overwhelming evidence from observing human behaviour and from introspection is that all humans have an innate propensity for evil, rooted in human nature, or what he called "radical evil", and for which the human will is responsible. However, we can overcome this propensity by taking responsibility for our choices. To become a morally good person, however, "… it is not enough to let the germ of good which lies in our species develop unhindered; there is in us an active and opposing cause of evil which is also to be combatted".[6]

Kant describes how one has to constantly work against the assaults of evil and keep armed for the battle on behalf of human freedom.[7] In order to fight such evils as envy, addiction to power, avarice, and their malignant associations, which arise as soon as humans come together in groups, he proposes the setting up of an "ethical community", or a "people of God", united in accordance with the principles of virtue. Such a community, which can only be realised for him within the framework of a Church, strives for a consensus of all human beings in order to establish an ethical whole. He opposes the notion of a people of God with those united together in a bond to propagate evil.

As Peter Dews discusses,[8] Hegel points out that there is a significant dilemma with the modern notion of morality as it increasingly places the onus on the human subject to determine what is good and what is evil, but unlike the religious framework, provides no stable criterion for distinguishing between the two. As a consequence of the increasing growth of the notion of subjective freedom, the potential for devastating outbreaks of evil doing also grows. Hegel then looks at what social organisations can minimise this danger, proposing, for example, a "community of faith" which accepts all its members as equal in their infinite worth and freedom.

Without the religious framework underlying ethical thought there is a gap in our approach to understanding evil. Religion can provide a "home" for ethical thinking without which there is a risk that our moral compass becomes adrift, leaving a spiritual void. The danger then is that this void can be filled by some apparently tempting ideology, promising material or other benefits. However, organised religion can hardly be said to have prevented human atrocities; indeed, many wilfully violent and destructive acts have been undertaken in the name of religion.

The notion of a violent Christian war only developed gradually and then became legitimised when Christianity became the official religion of the Roman Empire in the fourth century. Augustine

> suggested it might be legitimate to use a sinful act, violent war, to fight sin provided the act was performed with right intent, in a good cause—defence, protection, or restitution of property or rights—and under legitimate authority. A key text was Romans 13:4: "for he beareth not the sword in vain: for he is the minister of God, a revenger to execute wrath upon him that doeth evil".[9]

War increasingly became a central social institution defining cultural activity, with its own aesthetics and moral code, as can be seen during the various Crusades. It was "the central proving ground for aristocratic personal virtue and public status as well as the prime mechanism for political power and economic reward … Violence became as embedded in western Christian culture as its antithesis, monastic vocation."[10]

As the Crusades and modern religiously motivated acts of violence, such as terrorist attacks, reveal, faith held under certain conditions can lead to evil, for example, when one faith is felt to be threatened by another faith, attacks on one's faith can be seen as threats to a group's identity, and holding a faith tends to promote those who will defend that faith against other faiths.[11] Of course, one must not confuse religious faith with ideological fanaticism.[12]

It is usual to distinguish natural from moral evils—with the latter corresponding to humanly inspired evils and the former being earthquakes and other disasters which occur without direct human intervention. In the eras dominated by religious thinking natural evils would be understood as, say, punishments for man's sins. But it is not always that easy to distinguish between natural and moral evils; there is sometimes an overlap. For example, the COVID-19 pandemic could be seen as a natural disaster yet may have arisen as a result of human error or negligence. In addition, how we deal with natural evils may well have different outcomes depending on the quality of human decision making, for example, in how the COVID-19 pandemic has been handled with regard to cautionary measures and their relaxation, and how this is judged against risks to life. So even natural evils can merge with moral evils in some way. Indeed, one could say that the human world is embedded in the natural world; though the two orders are different, they touch and merge at various points.

A secular definition of evil, or what I would call the "spectrum of evil", involves a whole range of extreme forms of intentional harm to others, with accompanying suffering and psychological damage and trauma experienced by those on the receiving end of such destructive acts—including intended malice or indifference to suffering, from the active perpetrator to the passive but complicit bystander to evil actions. The most destructive actions involve enduring and significant harm and usually involve the wilful destruction of human beings, either physically or psychologically, often with the excessive misuse of power over the receiver of such actions. I shall be arguing that there is a particularly strong thread linking many such actions, that they involve the attempt to *annihilate the human subject* and *obliterate human agency* as well as corrode *intersubjective relations*, subject to subject relationships. This means that evil not only destroys the subjectivity of the victims, with the attendant loss of dignity, agency, and even their life, but also provokes a transformation in the subjectivity of the perpetrator who loses, passively or actively and to a greater or lesser extent, the capacity for empathy with others; the consequence of this erosion of empathy is that *otherness* becomes a source of prejudice and in extreme cases social and/or physical death. Sometimes, as I shall describe, the annihilation of the subject is accompanied by or motivated by the fantasy of psychic rebirth following death, as can be seen in some serial killers, terrorists, and as part of the Nazi ideology of creating a new society cleansed of non-Aryans. In the Nazi ideology history was also erased and then reconfigured; exterminating the Jews would bring apocalyptic deliverance, eliminating any debt to the Jews as the people of the Bible and building a society that owed no historical or moral debts to the Jews, whom they saw at the same time as immensely powerful, the source of all evil, of both capitalism and Bolshevism.[13]

Evil concerns not merely wrongful actions, but those which are very wrong and usually elicit consequently a horrific response. In concrete terms, a person or groups of people undertaking an evil act try to limit the other as subject in extreme ways, by attempting to confine, kill, hurt, freeze, control, and violate them physically and/or emotionally, that is by all ways of eliminating or annihilating the other as subject, where the other's presence is not "welcomed". Evil in its various forms tries to constrict the other as subject, tries to destroy intersubjectivity, or, in Martin Buber's terms,[i] tries to make the I/Thou relationship into a predominantly I/It relationship.[14] Evil involves the breaking of ethical bonds between people, eviscerating the life of others, the complete opposite to the respect for others as imagined in Hegel's community of faith or Kant's ethical community. Evil arises, as Emmanuel Levinas describes, when the ethical imperative that binds us to the other is deliberately violated.[15]

As a concrete illustration of this process, a vivid if horrific example (one of many) can be viewed in Claude Lanzmann's documentary *Shoah*, when a survivor described how inmates at one of the extermination camps had to collect and burn dead bodies of fellow inmates. The guards would severely punish anyone who called the people being burnt victims or corpses; they were either *Figuren* (figures) or *Schatten* (shit). Even in death the dead were deprived of their subjective presence.

Michael Stone, in his book *The Anatomy of Evil*, a study of violent criminals, has a useful working definition of evil actions that captures the degree of harm intended by them. They must be breathtakingly horrible, involve malice aforethought or evil intention usually preceding the act, a degree of suffering in the victims which is wildly excessive, and the nature of the act will appear to be incomprehensible, or at least be beyond the imagination of ordinary people in the community.[16]

John Kekes defines three essential elements of evil actions—"the malevolent motivation of evildoers; the serious, excessive harm caused by their actions; and the lack of morally acceptable excuse for the actions".[17] This definition is similar to those used by Claudia Card,[18] with her emphasis on evil acts as involving "inexcusable, not just culpable, harms"; and Adam Morton's emphasis on evil actions being not merely wrong but going way beyond this, into a realm which causes revulsion, death, pain, and humiliation.[19]

---

[i] Buber makes the distinction between two fundamental attitudes of living with the use of two different pairs of words: I/Thou and I/It. The I of the I/Thou appears as a human subject in association with others; the I/It refers to how the human subject can become detached from being related. The realm of subjectivity contains both association and detachment.

Susan Neiman describes how evil is a phenomenon that shatters trust in the world. Evil acts destroy what is vital about being human, our feeling of being at home in the world.[20]

Evil doers are often seen as monsters; the connection between evil and outer monstrosity appears frequently in fiction,[21] such as with Frankenstein's monster, Dr Jekyll and Mr Hyde, and with Dorian Gray. Indeed, one significant theme of Romantic fiction was a fascination with dreams and nightmares and, through horror, with the dark side of human nature, and subsequently in early modernism with the grey zone between good and evil. This is evident in Baudelaire's poetry, such as in his book *The Flowers of Evil*, where in his poem *Le Voyage*, he promises the reader "an oasis of horror in a desert of tedium".[22]

But confining evil to "outliers" misses out the significant evidence that evil is not confined to the monstrous few.

The moral philosopher Stuart Hampshire wrote that it was during his work in the Second World War as an intelligence officer studying Himmler's central command activities and then interrogating some leading Nazis in captivity that he learned,

> how easy it had been to organise the vast enterprises of torture and of murder, and to enrol willing workers in this field, once all moral barriers had been removed by the authorities. Unmitigated evil and nastiness are as natural, it seemed, in educated human beings as generosity and sympathy; no more, and no less, natural, a fact that was obvious to Shakespeare but not previously evident to me.[23]

As a result of these experiences, Hampshire saw evil as a force or set of forces, "which are not merely contrary to all that is most praiseworthy and admirable in human life, but … actively working against all that is praiseworthy and admirable … If one is justified in speaking of a pure evil, then one is speaking of a great evil which brings with it no good thing and which destroys without benefit."[24] His work on procedural justice as a restraint against evil was a major theme of his philosophy. He proposed that one cannot fully understand the concept of justice without considering the forces of destruction obstructing the virtues of justice in private and public life. Evil in his view grows out of some basic failure to proceed with just arrangements.[25]

When one witnesses the remnants of overwhelming human destructiveness in the various terrains of evil, where such links are ruptured and the human world seems to have collapsed into meaninglessness, one has to face basic questions about our ability to value others. One is inevitably led up against fundamental questions about human nature, whether we are *disposed* to perpetrate evil acts, or do so as a result of being involved in particular *situations*, or both. One may wonder how much we are innately destructive, whether we are disposed by evolution to undertake excessively harmful acts and whether there is something inherently unstable about the human subject which puts us permanently at risk of being destructive. One can question how much environmental influences determine extremely destructive acts and what drives some people to participate in evil actions and others to resist them. One can ask then what makes us human, how much our "untamed" animal nature drives evil acts, or whether, as I shall maintain, the propensity for evil is a human issue, a consequence of a combination of our instinctual inheritance with the *human imagination*, hence the title of the book. To quote Philip Zimbardo, the originator of the Stanford Prison experiment I shall describe below,

> The same human mind that creates the most beautiful works of art and extraordinary marvels of technology is equally responsible for the perversion of its own perfection. This most dynamic organ in the universe has been a seemingly endless source for creating ever more vile torture chambers and instruments of horror in earlier centuries, the "bestial machinery" unleashed on Chinese citizens by Japanese soldiers in their rape of Nanking … and the recent demonstration of "creative evil" of the destruction of the World Trade Center by weaponizing commercial airlines. We continue to ask why? Why and how is it possible for such deeds to continue to occur? How can the unimaginable become so readily imagined? And these are the same questions that have been asked by generations before ours.[26]

As I shall discuss later, empirical evidence from primate research, such as that undertaken by Frans De Waal, shows that our nearest animal relatives are empathic, even though they can be aggressive on occasion. Bonobos for example strive to fit in with others, obey social rules, empathise with others, and try to mend broken relationships while objecting to unfair arrangements. Chimpanzees are more aggressive and can be killers. Humans share genes with bonobos that we do not share with chimps, but we also share genes with chimps that we do not share with bonobos. So, our species shares a mosaic of characteristics with both apes; we can be both empathic like bonobos and violent like chimps, giving us a disposition to both good and evil, not one or the other. But in both sets of apes, there is a considerable amount of cooperation and empathic concern for others from early on in their lives. Indeed, "Everything science has learned in the last few decades argues against the pessimistic view that morality is a thin veneer over a nasty human nature. On the contrary, our evolutionary background lends a massive helping hand, without which we would never have gotten this far."[27] Empathic maternal care for example is the prototypical form of altruism, the basic template for morality.

Evidence from child developmental research, mainly with securely attached babies, shows that before they can speak or walk, babies can judge the goodness and badness of other people's actions, feel empathy and compassion, and have a rudimentary sense of justice; they are natural moralists.[28]

Simon Baron-Cohen considers that evil acts are a consequence of a malfunctioning of the "empathy circuit", different elements of the nervous system involved with human emotion, acting together with various genetic and environmental factors.[29]

My reading of the scientific evidence, to which I shall return in the next chapter, is that human destructiveness is not a direct consequence of our animal nature, nor is it something we are usually born with (though there are some people genetically disposed to be callous and unemotional) but a consequence of being human, of the developed human imagination—hell is other people, to quote Sartre.[30] In his play *Huis Clos*, three characters are placed together in a room in hell; all three have annihilated the subjectivity of the other—one by murdering a baby, another by driving someone to kill themselves, and the third by destroying his wife's freedom by cheating on her and was then executed by firing squad for desertion.

If the human imagination accounts for our destructiveness, the implication is that whatever genetic predisposition to violence we may have individually or as a species, the role of the family and the social and political environment are crucial in triggering violence in individuals and groups. In addition, there are certain individuals such as violent criminals, who use extreme and malignant aggression, and from whom we can learn about some of the individual and environmental factors that predispose us to evil acts. The neuroscience of aggression has begun to give us some clues as to what brain areas contribute to the erosion of empathy in such acts, while evidence from social psychology, which I touch upon below, has contributed significantly to understanding the social forces that can turn ordinary people into killers.

Evolution is not the cause of evil, but it has given us the tools that our human imagination can use for evil purposes. One could indeed maintain that the evil impulse to kill and torture is biologically non-adaptive.[31] Our ability to resist violence is a matter of understanding what influences the human will and how human moral values can be transformed as a result of a wide variety of influences. Time and again one can see how ideologies mixed with certain social systems distort human relationships and moral thinking. As Hannah Arendt described,[32] ideologies are harmless, uncritical, and arbitrary opinions as long as they are not taken seriously, but once their claim to total validity is taken literally, they become the nuclei of paranoid logical systems; their logicality is the source of their insanity, creating a contempt for truth.

The sites of extreme destruction have witnessed not only brutal killings but also a disorienting change in the moral law, not just a moral void, when basic human values appear to be transformed and then eliminated or displaced in the name of some ideology or fantasied grievance. For example, Michael Burleigh in his book *Moral Combat*[33] shows how the Nazis and their partners in crime fundamentally altered the moral understanding of humanity, shifting the boundaries of morality so that evils acts became normalised. This was achieved not only by using the law to sanction lawlessness, but also by using a vision of apocalyptic violence as well as pseudo-religious images and rituals as the framework for a fantasied renewal or rebirth of an aggrieved nation. Instead of the Kantian ethical community uniting all humans through consensus, the Nazis propagated the concept of the *Volksgemeinschaft*, or "people's community" a racially unified and mystical concept uniting all Germans, but of course excluding all others, predominantly Jews.

> The myth of the *Volksgemeinschaft* derived from Germany's euphoric sense and collective memory of unity transcending class, party, and

confession, as proclaimed by the Kaiser in August 1914. With Germans traumatized by the defeat of 1918 and the Great Depression, the Nazis were able to appropriate the emotive power of the myth while transforming its essence from political, social, and religious inclusivity to racial exclusivity.[34]

One can see here a common theme of several evil acts—that destructiveness is wedded to some fantasy of renewal of the individual or of society, or both.

The danger is that there are and have been so many terrains of evil, and so many different versions of apocalyptic and related forms of violence, that one can become so deadened by the experience of examining these terrains that it is easier to pass them by without asking how they occurred; one then becomes yet another member of the large group of "bystanders" to human atrocity.

There are, however, some examples where people have been able to resist being caught up in the vicious cycle of violence and have provided a sanctuary for those in need, a true "home for otherness". One famous example is the village of Le Chambon-sur-Lignon in southern France, whose strong community links and sense of human value created an environment which provided aid and shelter to persecuted Jews in the Second World War. The villagers were morally decent but also backed by a strong underlying Christian commitment to the sanctity of human life, so that giving refuge, literally opening their homes to strangers, was natural to them. "The community of Le Chambon is an extremely moving example of the extraordinary good that can occur in response to evil in one of its most threatening forms, where the moral baseline of a community is very high."[35]

They could display what Jacques Derrida has called "absolute hospitality",[36] unconditional welcome to the stranger.

There is also evidence of assistance to Jews inside Nazi Germany: for example, a group of peaceable idealists, who came together in the early 1920s and who called themselves "the Bund", subsequently gave aid and support to Jews in camps, and sheltered dissidents and Jews on the run.[37]

It is also important to emphasise how much resistance has taken place within targeted and oppressed populations. For example, the history of

American slavery is rich with many examples of slave rebellions during their transport from West Africa, resistance from black field workers and from white Quaker and black preachers, fugitives, vigilantes, and a variety of activists. Slaves were not lacking agency, even when every attempt was made to eliminate it as much as possible by the slavery institution.[38] Similarly, during the Holocaust, Jewish partisan groups and underground resistance networks launched attacks, sabotage operations, and rescue missions, while resistance groups in ghettos organised social, religious, cultural, and educational activities and armed uprisings in defiance of their Nazi oppressors. In death camps, in the most extreme circumstances, resisters gathered evidence of Nazi atrocities and even mounted armed rebellions.[39]

Three levels of evil

In order to put some order into a very complex field of study, one can understand the terrains of evil at three basic levels, with some overlap. There is the *cosmic* level, where evil is seen as a condition of the world, the *situational* level, where evil can be considered a result of social and historical forces, and the *individual and group* level, where evil is mainly a function of personal and interpersonal or group factors.

Level 1

At the *cosmic* level, good and evil are seen a part of the world order, where evil is then something one just must accept as part of the fabric of our universe. In this view, evil is one of the basic aspects of our world, without which we would have no need to think of what is good. Dialectic between good and evil is seen as part of the structure of the world. In some theories good comes first, and then evil is introduced, for example by the serpent in the Christian view of the Adam and Eve story; or evil is always around but was brought into life as in the Hebrew version of Adam and Eve. In both versions, the serpent is an evil tempter, pretending to be good or offering various goodies; such an image was carried over into the later Christian notion of the Devil as tempter, against which one had to be perpetually on guard—evil or its rewards must then have been seen to be particularly tempting. In the various narratives involving the Devil or the equivalent, there is usually a moment of choice between "innocence" and "corruption", a crossroads when the person being tempted can refuse the Devil's offer or cross the line over to the "dark side". The crossing of a line beyond which lies evil, and where ordinary morality is discarded, is often to be seen in acts of atrocity, along with the idealisation of such transgression.

These images of good and evil also indicate how fragile is our ongoing commitment to being good and how vulnerable we are to the destruction or spoiling of good experiences.

Other religious thought may reveal a constant fight or cosmic battle between good and bad as in early Babylonian creation myths. Freud's view of the struggle between the life and death drives in determining the development of the human psyche could be seen as a transformation of this ancient view of evil. For Freud, the death drive is a primal urge to annihilate life, so as to return to a state of non-being. The life drive opposes this force, but in reality, most psychic phenomena consist of various combinations of the life and death drives.[40]

In Greek tragedy fate or chance can determine our destiny; in that sense cruelty and destructiveness are part of the order of things, one just has to take one's chances with life, but its outcome remains ultimately uncertain. Seeing the tragedy in the context of the Ancient Greek theatrical festival can have a "cleansing" effect, the so-called catharsis.

In somewhat similar terms, Robert Solomon shows[41] how Albert Camus's novel *The Plague* is a portrait of how we face death and the injustices of life. The true evils in life are often faceless, and they are inevitable; what the Greeks considered as our tragic fate, Camus described as the *absurd*. In his novel, the absurd confronts *all* of us, engendering a sense of solidarity. To deny these evils, or to attempt an escape from them, is what Camus (in *The Myth of Sisyphus*) condemns as "philosophical suicide".[42] Camus disagreed with his Marxist contemporaries, who defended Stalinist cruelties perpetrated for the so-called greater good of a future society.

As Bruno Bettelheim describes, in most fairy tales good and evil are "given body in the form of some figures and their actions, as good and evil are omnipresent in life and the propensities for both are present in every man. It is this duality which poses the moral problem, and requires the struggle to solve it."[43] He also points out that evil is not without its attractions—symbolised by mighty giants, powerful witches, and cunning figures such as the queen in *Snow White*. They are often in the ascendant for a while, until defeated, but only after a considerable struggle—that way the child can identify with the complexity of human actions and see that the human dark side is part of our inheritance, and that overcoming dark forces requires considerable effort and struggle.

In Shakespeare, the atmosphere of evil in, for example, *Macbeth* and *Julius Caesar*, is expressed poetically with external images of storms, the persistence of darkness, and the strange behaviour of beasts and unnatural phenomena such as the opening of graves or bleeding of statues. These external events match the inner turmoil of the protagonists as they contemplate their murderous acts.

Evil could be seen as an absence of the good, such as in Augustine's view that evil is essentially a privation of a fundamentally good reality and sin a perversion of our originally good nature with which we are endowed. This contrasts with Plato who saw evil as a matter of ignorance of the good, and hence as fundamentally irrational; evil is a failure of reason in some way. This view has some links with Hannah Arendt's notion that political evil involves the so-called "banality" of evil,[44] where far from being moral monsters, evil people, or ordinary people caught up in an evil institution or society, such as the totalitarian societies of Nazi Germany and Soviet Russia, go along with the regime's murderous and destructive processes without thinking of consequences, accepting as routine, that is, ordinary and banal, what in reality are horrendous acts. This represents some kind of failure of reason, or at least of a particular kind of "relational" reason, involved with recognising human otherness. The Jungian analyst Coline Covington uses this element of Arendt's thought to look at evil in a clinical and political context; for her "The most important distinguishing feature of evil is the absence of the capacity for thought, i.e. to imagine the experience of an other who is not an object but is a sentient thinking human."[45]

For Aristotle, evil is a natural phenomenon along with good; one must find some happy medium between good and evil in order to live a virtuous life. In that sense we all have a share of good and evil in various proportions. The predominantly evil person would have an excess of evil over good.

Evil as personified in the Devil has also been seen as the spirit of negation, the ultimate nihilist, his only belief in undermining human values, as Mephistopheles in Goethe's *Faust*. There is something similar in Shakespeare's portrayal of Iago in *Othello*. "Iago is a cynic and materialist who believes in nothing but will and appetite, and who regards all objective value as worthless."[46] Trying to make contracts or pacts with such figures can only lead to disaster as their whole intention is to undermine them.

Nietzsche challenges the cosmic tradition of seeing evil by maintaining that one must go "beyond" good and evil, leaving behind traditional morality which divides the world into good and bad and is linked to Judaeo-Christian thought as well as philosophy after Socrates. For him the language of good and evil constricts our natures and is a remnant of a "master/slave morality". Master morality is aristocratic and independent, the prototype of good, while slave morality, involving compassion and love of one's neighbour, is servile and full of resentment, seeing the master morality as evil. Instead, one needs to find new "positive" values and a new language for human motivations, detached or freed from the old good/evil dialectic and the old Judaeo-Christian moral values which for him were dead, along with their God. For him, this is provided by the "will to power" as involving the power of imagination and creativity. But a world without the usual good/evil dynamic is hard to imagine, and thought such as Nietzsche's has been open to misuse partly as a consequence. For example, it was expropriated by the Nazis in their racial world view of themselves as the master race exercising their will to power, which gave them licence to denigrate basic Judaeo-Christian values of human compassion and empathy for others and replace them with a new and destructive moral, or immoral, world order.

Level 2

The *situational* level of evil concerns the involvement of social and historical forces in understanding destructive acts.

There are for example certain social situations where ordinary morality breaks down. Thus, in times of war, ordinary character structure takes a hit as it were, leading sometimes to soldiers losing their ordinary moral compass. As Jonathan Shay describes in his study of Vietnam veterans, "moral" injury is often as common as physical injury, leading in a number of soldiers to lifelong psychological character changes associated with the more familiar post-traumatic symptoms.[47] Certain war conditions are more likely to have destructive effects on the personality, such as an excess of coercive control in authority structures leading to a soldier's loss of authority over his own mental functioning; and a sense of betrayal by the powers that be, such as being let down and blamed by those in charge, when it is clear, for example, that official policy is out of touch with the soldiers on the ground. The Vietnam experience had particular effects on the soldiers' mental states due to the skill of the North Vietnamese in undermining American soldiers' morale.

> In Vietnam the enemy struck not only at the body but also at the most basic functions of the soldier's mind, attacking his perceptions by concealment; his cognitions by camouflage and deception; his intentions by surprise, anticipation and ambush. These mind games have been part of war since time immemorial, but never in American military experience have they been directed so skilfully and with such thoroughness at the enlisted men as in Vietnam.[48]

Shay likens the soldier's state of mind under these extreme conditions, with psychic attacks both from the enemy and from within the unreliable military support network, to a form of captivity and enslavement, so that the institution of war itself becomes a perpetrator. Soldiers in Vietnam frequently experienced terror and helplessness, loss of communication with those outside the combat arena; they had a conviction that others had forgotten or had betrayed them; there was often inconsistent, unpredictable, and capricious and even violent enforcement of military rules, debilitation by sleep deprivation, starvation, drugs, and alcohol; and participation in sacrifice and victimisation of others, with sometimes participation in immoral, disgusting, or illegal practices, leading to a betrayal of basic human attachments.[49]

The Mỹ Lai massacre, the mass murder of at least 400 unarmed South Vietnamese civilians by US troops on 16 March 1968, including men, women, children, and babies, as well as the rape and mutilation of women and some children, can be seen in the context of war's stripping of the ordinary moral sense. This does not justify atrocities committed during war, but it goes some way to making sense of the propensity to commit them under war conditions. As Margaret MacMillan describes in her book about how the conflict of war has shaped us, war inverts what we think of as the natural order and morality in society. Destruction of basic infrastructure and murder and harm to others is acceptable under war conditions, and what in peacetime is grotesque or appalling, such as the smell of death and presence of corpses is just part of the fabric of war.[50] War also normalises unsociable behaviour such as constant swearing, or scrounging for supplies, which would ordinarily been seen as stealing; there can even be an exhilaration in the process of destruction, made more intense by the close comradeship of fellow soldiers, the band of brothers. Soldiers are also of course given licence to unleash primitive drives which are usually tamed or inhibited in times of peace. Jonathan Glover describes how in war the moral resources such as respect, sympathy, and the sense of a moral identity are often neutralised, but even when they still exist war often makes them ineffective.[51] Joanna Bourke has even argued that military violence and war-play have unfortunately become embedded in our lives, legitimating and facilitating violence in peacetime.[52] For Freud, war not only sanctions the removal of control over our drives but encourages those tendencies towards cruelty and destructiveness which the individual tries to restrain in peacetime, but barbarity remains present in the unconscious.[53] The primitive and evil impulses of mankind do not vanish in an individual, but continue their existence, though in a repressed state, but can display their activity, given certain conditions and opportunities such as during wars. Civil society requires these primitive drives to be repressed or sublimated, managed in some way, in order for ordinary life to proceed peacefully. However, it is clear from what happens in war but also in peacetime how these drives can be whipped up by populist leaders and intensified to the point of violence in group situations, such as when the Washington Capitol was stormed on 6 January 2021, following Donald Trump's incendiary speech.

The psychoanalyst Franco Fornari, in his study of the psychodynamics of war, makes the point that war has a paradoxical function, not to defend against an external enemy, which seems to be its obvious cause, but to find a way of deflecting, or defending against, the presence of internal persecutors, destructive enemies within.

> The fact that every man, while sleeping, may feel threatened by immanent destruction ... may be considered the emotional nucleus of an innate paranoia. Accordingly, war could be seen as an attempt at therapy, carried out by a social institution which, precisely by institutionalizing war, increases to gigantic proportions what is initially an elementary defensive mechanism of the ego.[54]

He is not providing a justification of war but warns that we cannot afford to ignore the complexity of the inner world if we are to more effectively manage society's destructive tendencies.

There is a price to be paid for war's reversal of ordinary morality, not just post-traumatic stress, but also the after-effects of the necessary numbing of ordinary empathy for fellow human beings—lasting and sometimes overwhelming guilt, or the opposite, a failure to mourn, as was evidenced on a large scale in Germany after the Second World War.[55]

There is a particular risk involved in modern warfare involving killing at a distance as with the use of drones or attacks through cyberspace, or through the use of artillery, bombing, and missiles as seen in Ukraine. Emotional distancing from the military target is far easier when the enemy are not within personal reach. This distancing process to become normalised began with the mass bombing of civilians in the Second World War. "In long-range war, distance virtually excludes human responses of any strength. It is possible for someone firing a missile to imagine the impact on people on the receiving end, but nothing has the immediacy of actually seeing a man holding up his trousers."[56]

Images and experiences of war have continued to have an impact on modern consciousness, affecting how we respond to the challenge of evil actions. Paul Fussell's book *The Great War and Modern Memory* charts with vivid literary examples, "... the way the dynamics and iconography of the Great War have proved crucial political, rhetorical, and artistic determinants on subsequent life. At the same time the war was relying on inherited myth, it was generating new myth, and that myth is part of the fibre of our own lives."[57] For example, poetry and prose at least on the British side were increasingly dominated by an acute sense of irony, beginning with the poems of Thomas Hardy's *Satires of Circumstances*, many of which were written before the war but published in November 2014. They often prefigured what would come to dominate the most significant poetry of the Great War. Typical was the poem "Ah, Are You Digging on My Grave?"

> Aware of a scratching sound above, the voice from the grave asks repeatedly who it is who digs at her grave. Is it her lover? No, a voice answers: he was married yesterday and is busy. Is it one of her kinfolk planting memorial flowers? No, they knew that planting flowers does no good. Is it then perhaps her "enemy" (a word which public events will soon weight uniquely) "prodding shy" in an easy revenge? No, her enemy, she is told, thinks her no longer worth hating "And cares not where you lie". Finally, "giving up", the speaker learns the identity of the digger from the digger himself, that he is her little dog.[58]

This news moves her to utter a stanza rich with "pre-war" complacency about the dog's fidelity. But the dog confesses he was just burying a bone to be available if he were hungry later and had quite forgotten that this was his mistress's resting place.

Other poems point to the contrast between a bright past and a gloomy present, anticipating the golden summer of 1914 and the appalling December of that year; there was even a poem about mass graves—"In the Cemetery", where a group of mothers quarrel over whose child lies in what grave.

While Fussell points out that every war is ironic because every war is worse than expected, the Great War was more ironic than any before or since as it reversed the very idea of progress, that things were getting better, that we were becoming an increasingly better civilisation. It was the end of "innocence", vividly portrayed in Siegfried Sassoon's Sherston novels, charting the idyllic world of rural foxhunting, whose illusions of tranquillity were soon to be shattered by the cruel realities of the trenches, bringing bitterness in place of the idealisation of military honour.

For the British, the battle of the Somme on 1 July 1916, where many thousands of troops were mowed down as they were ordered to advance towards the German lines, marked the time when "the innocent army fully attained the knowledge of good and evil ... That moment, one of the most interesting in the whole long history of human disillusion, can stand as the type of all the ironic actions of the war,"[59] and became the epitome of one dominating form of modern understanding that is essentially ironic.

Other powerful themes highlighted by Fussell that have continued to shape the modern sensibility include the notion of a seemingly endless war, the sense of "the other side", primitive binary thinking epitomised by a crude division into them and us, the sharp dividing of landscape into known and unknown with no-man's-land in between, trench warfare dividing the world of light and dark, day and night, with persistent images of the parapet, the wire, and endless mud, the sharp division between those at home who could not comprehend the war's horrors and the enclosed world of soldiers at the front, and the division between the demonic world of the front and the longing for an Arcadian innocence represented by the English countryside, an idealised home free from horror.

In addition, images of the war as theatre seemed particularly pertinent to the Great War experience. "The most obvious reason why 'theatre' and modern war seem so compatible is that modern wars are fought by conscripted armies, whose members know they are only temporarily playing their ill-learned parts."[60] The wearing of uniforms of course adds to the sense of make believe, while the soldiers learn to divide their psyches into actor and spectator, the one who shoots and the one who observes what is going on as if the whole thing were an illusion. This form of division of the psyche as a way of coping with unbearable experiences is not far from the descriptions made by Robert Jay Lifton in his study of Nazi doctors at Auschwitz. Lifton describes a psychology of "doubling", with the division of the psyche into two functioning wholes, so that a part self acts as an entire self. One part acts as a caring family father, while the Auschwitz self becomes psychically numb to the reality of death and destruction all around them. Doubling is,

> [T]he psychological means by which one invokes the evil potential of the self. That evil is neither inherent in the self nor foreign to it. To live out the doubling and call forth the evil is a moral choice for which one is responsible, whatever the level of consciousness

involved. By means of doubling, Nazi doctors made a Faustian choice for evil.[61]

One can see a more benign form of doubling in medical education, as doctors must learn to put up with unseemly sights and disgusting smells, as well as deal with ongoing human suffering without making too much of a fuss, thus in part deadening the immediate response to the human presence and becoming to some extent emotionally distant, in order to provide a medical function. The danger of course, as with the Nazi doctors, is when this deadening of the human response goes way beyond what is morally acceptable.

The after-effects of the Great War on the German psyche had a significant part to play in providing the substrate for the subsequent Nazi takeover. Many young Germans like their British counterparts went to the battlefield in 1914 with the idea that war was something great and glorious. The Germans "were filled with a feeling of certain victory, in which their dreams about the future Great Germany was reflected".[62]

But with defeat, "The dilemma of how to justify the sacrifices of sons, brothers and fathers after a lost war preoccupied (and divided) the German public for years to come."[63] The sense of betrayal, the so-called "stab in the back" by those in authority became a focal point for right wing anti-democratic movements.

> The absence of Allied soldiers on German soil before the official end of hostilities on 11 November gave rise to powerful conspiracy theories claiming that the Central Powers had not actually been defeated from outside but had only collapsed as a result of a "stab in the back" by subversive elements or "fifth columns" on the home front.[64]

From this fantasy arose the notion of a day of reckoning when the enemy within, increasingly associated with Jews and Bolsheviks, would be combated ruthlessly and mercilessly.

The legacy of the First World War consisted not only in images which became central to the human imagination in the twentieth century as outlined above, but also, as Ian Kershaw states, to continuing ethnic conflict and "(1) an explosion of ethnic-racist nationalism; (2) bitter and irreconcilable demands for territorial revisionism; (3) acute class conflict—now given concrete focus through the Bolshevik Revolution in

Russia; and (4) a protracted crisis of capitalism (which many observers thought was terminal)."[65]

In order to trigger the major crisis that brought Europe to the verge of self-destruction in the Second World War, these four components of the post First World War crisis intermeshed in various ways, affecting most European countries, but, especially in Germany, reinforced each other with explosive effect.[66]

German society following the First World War had to deal with a series of traumas—the humiliation of the loss, hyperinflation and economic chaos, the shock waves from the 1929 Wall Street crash and subsequent great depression, the increasing fragmentation of social relations heightened by racial conflict and increasing anti-Semitism, in the context of a lack of democratic resilience in German society. Though the Weimar Republic was founded in 1918 and existed as a democratic constitutional republic, it continued to remain unstable, though at the same time a brief source of an explosion of experimental modernist culture.

There are many factors accounting for the rise of Hitler and Nazism, but the following factors seem of particular relevance—the four critical components summarised above, the European and international setting, with the rise of nationalism, militarism, and civil unrest in much of central and Eastern Europe, the weakness of opposition to the rising dictatorships out of fear of a new world war, the fact that German unity was only relatively recent and was unstable, and the increasing power of a Nazi ideology as providing a narrative of revenge for the past supposed national humiliation together with the renewal and rebirth of German society and nationhood.

The concept of a nation is, as Eric Hobsbawm pointed out, a relatively new one.[67] The equation nation = state = sovereign people only arose during the latter part of the eighteenth century and early nineteenth century with the French Revolution and the Declaration of Rights of 1795. Most states of any size were not homogenous and were (as even now) made up of a variety of ethnic and linguistic groups, sometimes all vying for dominance. Indeed, as Benedict Anderson has shown, the nation is a compound of fact and fiction. Anderson defines the nation as a cultural phenomenon, an imagined political community, imagined as both inherently limited and sovereign. A sense of a unified home nation then owes as much to *imagination* as to any political realities. The nation had to be invented, "imagined, modelled, adapted and transformed".[68] This makes the idea of a nation or nation state susceptible to incorporating all kinds of conscious notions and unconscious fantasies into its final but unstable version. Hobsbawm described how the rise of the Nazi state, with the resurgence of militant nationalism, arose as a way of filling "the void left by failure, impotence, and the apparent inability of other ideologies, political projects and programmes to realize men's hopes".[69]

The trajectory from the rise of Hitler to the enacting of the attempt to destroy all European Jews has been well documented on many occasions, notably by Raul Hilberg.[70] The point to make at this stage in my argument is that in order to understand the nature of societies organised around hateful violence and genocide, only a multidisciplinary account of their origin and ongoing workings can hope to give some clue as to how to reduce the risk of a recurrence. To do so, one needs to examine societal weaknesses and fractures that can allow extreme violence to become established and then to escalate out of democratic oversight and control, as well as wider economic and political factors that make for a society vulnerable to violence. It also means examining some of the unconscious collective fantasies that helped create the imagined community that makes up the idea of a particular nation, my particular focus.

Zygmunt Bauman considers that it was the rational world of modern civilisation that made the Holocaust, the epitome of evil, thinkable. The Holocaust, with the reality of the mass killings of millions on an industrial scale, was an event

> which disclosed the weakness and fragility of human nature … when confronted with the matter-of-fact efficiency of the most cherished among the products of civilization; its technology, its rational criteria of choice, its tendency to subordinate thought and action to the pragmatics of economy and effectiveness.[71]

Thus, he argues that a major lesson of the Holocaust is that such destructiveness remains a permanent possibility of our modern civilisation, in view of the way that modern society tends, for example, to facilitate emotional distance between people, and to treat the human subject as a mere cog in a hierarchical structure dominated by technology. One can then see the dissociation of violence from moral oversight through the machinery of bureaucracy. Strong safeguards which recognise the susceptibility of modern society to become genocidal, particularly when a powerful monolithic ideology threatens to dominate political life, are then essential if we are to have a decent society with a reduced risk of unleashing unbridled destructiveness.

Paul Gilroy emphasises another aspect of modernity which is only now beginning to be faced, the role of slavery in forging modernity's institutions and practices. Gilroy proposes that the history of the African diaspora and a reassessment of the relationship between modernity and slavery require a complete revision of the terms in which modernity has been conceived.[72]

Looking at the influence of society on individuals, Ervin Staub argues that human beings come to experience the brutal killing of other humans through a series of steps.

> In essence, difficult life conditions and certain cultural characteristics may generate psychological processes and motives that lead a group to turn against another group. The perpetrators change, as individuals and as a group, as they progress along a continuum of destruction that ends in genocide. The behaviour of bystanders can inhibit or facilitate this evolution.[73]

James Waller charts how ordinary people commit genocide and mass killings as a result of a combination of a cultural construction or world view in a society that favours the collective rather than the individual and within an authority-based society, with particular constructions of others as, for example, dehumanised or a source of badness, together with group factors that enhance cruel behaviours and attitudes.[74]

In my book *Tolerating Strangers in Intolerant Times*,[75] I suggested that tolerating difference is essential to what I have called "subject tolerance", where one respects the other and others as subjects *of* their experience, with agency and capacity for independent judgment. This contrasts with "object tolerance", when the other and others are seen as mere objects to be treated as subject *to* those in power. Those that are merely tolerated as objects may be confined in a ghetto or walled off from society in less visible ways, but their object status remains—sometimes this is the prelude to physical violence towards those perceived in this way.

I argued that the fear of a *loss of home*, or more fundamentally a fear of the loss of a psychic structure which provides a central core of our identity—what I have called a *psychic home*—accounts for a considerable amount of prejudiced and intolerant attitudes to strangers; that basic fears about being displaced by strangers from our precious and precarious sense of a psychic home can tear communities apart, as well as lead to discrimination against those who appear to be different.[76] Demagogues can appeal to those who feel their psychic home is threatened by offering them a seductive haven for their prejudices, a perverse psychic home.

While on the positive side we all need to identify with various kinds of personal and professional groupings, indeed I would add that a psychic home consists of a number of these long-lasting different group identifications, loosely held together, irrational fears about the loss of coherence can lead to fearful and prejudiced reactions. Group dynamics in short-lasting groups of people coming together for an activity or in a mass rally can be dominated by powerful and destructive forces leading to evil acts, as I shall sketch below and describe in detail in Chapter 3.

I have also suggested that a decent society would be able to provide a *home for otherness*, where elemental fears about loss of identity can be managed effectively.[77] But for fears and conflicts to be managed in order to provide such a welcoming notion of home, I suggested that two basic limiting principles needed to be in place.[78] The first limiting principle is the *harm principle*, adapted from J. S. Mill, my version of which states that one needs to tolerate people's practices, beliefs, or values provided they do not significantly harm the current society and offend the basic rights of its citizens. The second principle limiting prejudice is the *respect principle*, that is, any action towards others starts with the assumption of the right for people to receive *mutual* respect for different ways of life, based upon a reasoned and empathic or at least sympathetic judgment of the other's behaviour, ideas, and values. Both principles are needed together in order to provide a framework for subject tolerance; the harm principle on its own could justify intolerance, for example, if some ideologue promoted the idea that one group is harmful to the nation and therefore should be persecuted. The respect principle is a counterbalance to such a possibility, as persecuting groups would involve a failure to respect them.

As a simple illustration of the two principles at work, it would be incorrect to tolerate someone who showed no mercy, who considered beheading hostages and displaying their images in the internet as acceptable, as it would be inconsistent with both the harm and respect principles. Such active intolerance in these and similar circumstances could be accorded the label "evil", as it goes way beyond what is generally accepted as human. A society where these two principles are weak may well be at an increased risk of significantly destructive acts towards its citizens, as in totalitarian societies. Evil doers cut through the delivery of these two principles and undermine the just human arrangements that make civil society work effectively.

Level 3

The *individual and group psychology* level of evil is influenced by the previous two levels, particularly by societal factors in a particular historical context.

Much has been researched and written concerning how ordinary men and women have become entangled in acts of extreme violence such as during the Holocaust, how a variety of factors can lead step by step to the transformation of a "normal" or "ordinary" person with no obvious psychopathology or history of past violent acts into a seasoned killer. While studies such as Christopher Browning's *Ordinary Men*[79] are brilliant when it comes to a detailed examination of the evidence that reveals the individual steps that lead to evil acts, there is a gap in a deep psychological understanding of how this could happen. Browning, like many other historians and commentators, cites the classic studies by Stanley Milgram on the role of obedience to authority shaping an individual's propensity for perpetrating harmful actions, and the Philip Zimbardo Stanford Prison experiment with groups of people randomly divided into guards and prisoners, in shaping perpetrator behaviour at the group level; but these studies, though alarming in their revelation of the ease with which ordinary people can become taken over by violence, do not provide much detailed understanding of underlying personal motives, or the complexities of group dynamics driving evil acts, which I shall discuss in Chapter 3.

The Milgram experiments were carried out soon after the trial of Adolf Eichmann in Israel and were designed to see how far ordinary people were just "following orders" when told to perpetrate genocidal acts, as so many Nazis had maintained at previous criminal trials, that is, how far an individual could resist non-coercive authority. The context was also fear about the Cold War situation, the anxiety about mind control and brainwashing common at the time.

An experimenter in a white coat would instruct an ordinary person to deliver increasingly strong painful electric shocks to another person in a separate room as a response to the incorrect answering of various questions. The apparent victim was actually an actor pretending to be suffering from the effects of the shocks. Despite showing signs of increasing distress and even suffering apparently fatal shocks on occasions, the majority of people continued to give shocks, despite themselves showing increasing distress over their actions, encouraged to do so in the name of science by the "experimenter" in charge of the proceedings; the latter's presence, assuring them that their actions were justified and were their duty, seemed to be a crucial factor. Only a minority refused to comply with the orders to give shocks, except when another apparent fellow participant was present; that seemed to greatly reduce the will to conform. The participants would also be less likely to produce increasing shocks in the absence of an authoritative experimenter, or if someone in the room other than the experimenter or participant contradicted the experimenter's authority—giving one a certain amount of hope that human beings are not destined to obey authority automatically. However, from work on the social psychology of prejudice and bystander psychology, which I shall cover in the next chapter, free thinking is less likely when there is a strong group ethos of conformity.

There have been various attempts to explain the disturbing results of these experiments, and their validity remains questionable, given the artificial nature of their setting. But they do reveal the human subjects' basic vulnerability to accepting hierarchical structures and a predisposition to conform when in a state of uncertainty and when being persuaded by an authority figure that they are making the correct decision. They also show how vulnerable people are to losing their sense of autonomy and the responsibility for their actions when there is a single-minded, unequivocal and manipulative source of authority influencing them, an unfortunate frequent accompaniment of those who rationalise their own participation in atrocities. One can also see such malignant influences present to a greater or lesser extent in institutions such as the army and prison and more obviously in totalitarian societies where there are no balancing forms of authority.

Milgram described how normal people can under certain circumstances enter an "agentic" state in which they become the instrument of another's will. In psychoanalytic terms this is basically a dependent transference towards a strong parental figure in the person of the experimenter, where the participant's adult ego capacity became weakened by the intense and unusual context of the experiment. The latter may have produced a feeling of near infantile helplessness in the participants, who were then susceptible to the suggestions of the parent-like experimenter. This reveals how vulnerable we are to the influence of authority figures if they appeal to basic infantile desires. A strong transference can at times lead to quite delusional feelings and a reduction of reality sense, akin to the power of hypnotic suggestion, making a person susceptible to undue influence.

While the participants in the Milgram experiments seemed not to be motivated by sadism when giving shocks, so much as obeying authority, the social psychological experiment undertaken by Zimbardo and associates, the Stanford Prison experiment in the early 1970s, examining the influence of external behaviours and roles on human interactions, revealed how sadism can be easily released in certain group situations. Twenty-one male undergraduates were paid 15 dollars a day for the experiment, where they were randomly assigned to one of two groups—prisoners and guards for a two-week study of prison life; the aim being to examine what made prisoners and often prison guards so disposed towards violence. The students were screened beforehand to be checked as mentally stable and with no obvious potential for violence.

In order to prime the participants, the student prisoners were arrested in their homes by real officers from the local police department and were then subjected to the usual stripping of personal belongings, etc. that prisoners have to undergo on their entry into prison. Student guards were given uniforms and dark glasses as well as clubs as potential weapons. The students were left to define the rules of engagement between prisoners and guards. Very soon several of the "prisoners" and "guards" began to act out like their counterparts in the real world, with the student guards becoming increasingly sadistic in their treatment of the student prisoners, and student prisoners becoming increasingly resigned, submissive, and depressed. When a third of the guards became brutally sadistic, the experiment had to be stopped after only six days. A few guards tried to help the prisoners and some guards were in the middle, doing nothing excessively good or bad.

The experiment revealed that ordinary people can become brutal as a result of being within the orbit of a legitimised social hierarchy committed to violence, revealing how roles, rules, and norms can transform people's character and make ordinary people sadistic towards others. When this transformation occurs, others are perceived as anonymous with no subjectivity, what Zimbardo calls "deindividuation". Others are also perceived as lacking ordinary humanity, becoming objectified or seen as less than human, by what he calls a process of "dehumanisation". He sees these two processes as the core of much evil.[80]

Christopher Browning notes that the spectrum of the guards' behaviours matched the groupings that emerged within the killing unit Reserve Police Battalion 101, who killed many thousands of Jews in central and Eastern Europe

> a nucleus of increasingly enthusiastic killers who volunteered for the firing squads and "Jew hunts"; a larger group of policemen who performed as shooters and ghetto clearers when assigned but who did not seek opportunities to kill (and in some cases refrained from killing, contrary to standing orders, when no one was monitoring their actions); and a small group (less than 20 per cent) of refusers and evaders.[81]

The experiment also reveals the power of group dynamics and what Freud had already described in *Group Psychology and the Analysis of the Ego*,[82] where in the group setting the individuals are brought under conditions which allows them to throw off the repressions of their unconscious instincts. Idealisation of a strong, often narcissistic, leader encourages the relinquishing of the individual's superego function, or conscience, by identification with the leader or the leader's ideology.

In fact, what wasn't emphasised enough about the Stanford Prison experiment was what an important leading role Zimbardo himself played in the setting itself; rather than being a detached observer, he served as the prison's "superintendent", setting the ground rules and regularly meeting with the guards. Thus, there was an obvious element of suggestion, with marked influence by a charismatic leader, to whom there was in all likelihood a strong dependent transference.

In addition, the Milgram and Stanford experiments have been criticised for ignoring data which showed how many participants actually resisted the pull of authority.[83] Nonetheless, The Milgram and Stanford experiments were revealing about the influence of external factors on the individual and group's behaviour, as was Solomon Asch's earlier conformity experiments, covered in the next chapter, which revealed how much social pressures influence what people are willing to believe,[84] even making people doubt their perceptions of simple facts, but were not that illuminating about the inner worlds of potential evil perpetrators. Of course, perpetrators are not necessarily forthcoming when it comes to revealing their inner motives. For example, the Nazi doctors interviewed at length by Lifton were often evasive in their answers and keen to justify their actions. However, attempts to find a form of typical genocidal Nazi psychopathology, or indeed a typical perpetrator in other genocides, has been fruitless. "The truth seems to be … that the most outstanding common characteristic of perpetrators of extraordinary evil is their normality, not their abnormality."[85]

However, there is a considerable literature on the psychology of cruelty, violence, and murder as well as the forensic psychology of serial killers, whose character is undoubtedly abnormal, and whose horrendous acts that go beyond the boundary of ordinary morality, mirror those involved in genocidal killing. So, while the study of abnormal states of mind may not tell us directly what sort of person becomes involved with extraordinary evil, it may well be enlightening about the states of mind that lead to and sustain acts of such evil, as well as helping us understand more ordinary aspects of the human mind.

Gwen Adshead, a forensic psychiatrist with extensive experience of assessing and providing therapy for criminals inside secure hospitals and prisons, tries to search for the meaning of the criminal act and how it fits in with the whole history of the offender's life, their self-narrative.

In her recent book, *The Devil You Know*, this narrative often turns around severe childhood adversity.[86]

C. Fred Alford[87] interviewed about sixty people, a group of various prisoners, working people, and students in order to discover how they experienced evil. This research indicated that evil was not just any expulsion of bad parts of the self, but a specific attempt to inflict an unbearable feeling of dread on others. The source of that dread, according to Alford, is very early experience at the level of what the psychoanalyst Thomas Ogden describes as the "autistic-contiguous position", prior to preverbal experience and symbol formation. This position is a source of both formless dread but also a source of vitality and meaning in life.[88] The evil doer cannot face the formless dread arising from such an early developmental level, so that the evil act is a way of managing the dread, trying to rid themselves of dread and remain alive in the act of inflicting it on others.

Roy Baumeister's study of perpetrator behaviour described four major root causes of evil. "Ordinary, well-intentioned people may perform evil acts when under the influence of these factors, singly or in combination. Combinations are harder to defeat."[89] These four factors are: the use of violence for material gain; threatened egotism, as when a person's favourable image of themselves is severely questioned; idealism or ideology; and finally, the pursuit of sadistic pleasure, as in serial killers, torturers, and rapists. Usually, violent impulses are restrained by inner inhibitions and conscience, but there are circumstances when such internal restraints break down, due for example to poor parenting, extreme stress, trauma, and group pressures. Then one or more of the root causes of evil comes into play.[90]

Baumeister focuses on trying to understand the actions and motives of those who intentionally harm others, using a broad, inclusive definition of human evil as "intentional interpersonal harm".[91] His aim is not only to explore what makes criminals commit major crimes, but how much this can enlighten us about how ordinary people can also commit evil acts. From his survey of depictions of evil, he suggests that the long-standing image of evil is a composite of several elements—the intentional infliction of harm, which is often done gratuitously and with the pleasure of inflicting pain, it involves attacking innocent and good victims, the victim or victims are seen as the enemy or outside the group, it represents the antithesis of order, peace and stability, and evil perpetrators are often highly egotistical and have poor self-control. Focusing mainly on the motivations of the perpetrator, he points out that they often do not regard their actions as evil, and they find rationalisations to explain their crimes, and so evil flourishes in the gap between the perspective of perpetrator and victim;[92] that is, there is no intersubjective relationship in evil actions.

In order to treat psychoanalytically those who have been subjected to major trauma such as severe abuse, it is necessary, or anyway inevitable, that the analyst becomes caught up directly or indirectly with the abusing experience. One has to "touch" evil before it can be neutralised, minimalised, or resisted, so as to help the patient extricate themselves from the power of the past. But this is not easy work and means that the analyst must bear difficult experiences when the analysis gets close to the traumatic core of the patient. One finds oneself then going in and out of being able to bear the emotions stirred up. In a similar way, when I was undertaking research for this book, there was only so much reading about evil and evil actions that I could manage at a time, an hour at most. I would then need to turn to other less horrendous reading as a counterbalance. In Chapter 3, I will investigate the psychoanalysis of evil from the point of view of survivors and perpetrators of evil as well as how psychoanalysis can illuminate the nature of evil acts. This will include looking at the nature of evil fantasies and evil states of mind, fears about doing evil, and the impact of witnessing and being subjected to evil.

The next chapter, the first involving a more detailed exploration of the various terrains of evil, concerns the science of evil; as it comes from a relatively objective position, it is perhaps easier to consider the nature of evil from this perspective without being too "contaminated" as a result.

CHAPTER 2

The science of evil

There is no purely scientific explanation accounting for acts of human atrocity, but findings from neuroscience, social psychology, developmental psychology and the study of animal behaviour, particularly of our closest animal relatives, bonobos and chimpanzees, gives us an insight into the states of mind and possible brain correlates of highly aggressive and dangerousness acts, as well as some insights into what makes for a moral or just society. Robert Sapolsky in his recent book *Behave*[1] has summarised a vast amount of scientific information about what makes us behave well and badly, moving from the immediate reactions of the brain and nervous system to hormonal influences, and then to the role of foetal, childhood, and adolescent experiences, the place of genetics, and then to the contributions of culture and evolution. The point he makes is that we need a multidisciplinary and multifactorial approach in trying to understand what makes us behave in good and bad ways, and that scientific understanding of human behaviour is intertwined with psychology, culture, and the understanding of human societies.[2]

There is now considerable information about the brain functioning of anti-social personalities, as well as those who have become anti-social in some way as a result of significant brain injury. While one must be cautious in applying such findings to understanding how ordinary people can become extremely anti-social, it would seem to be reasonable to assume that these findings as well as those from the neuroscience of aggression and the social psychology of prejudice, conformity and extreme behaviours, will give some insight into the factors that can trigger extreme violence, so long as one puts the findings into the wider perspective, as Sapolsky emphasises. I will also cover in this chapter some of the psychological factors involved in perpetrator behaviours, including how psychological trauma has a significant role in the development of violent behaviours, including its role in shaping brain development.

Neuroscience and dysregulated behaviour

The classic and oft-quoted case where brain damage altered behaviour was that of Phineas Gage, who in 1848 suffered extensive damage to his left frontal lobe after a mining accident, when blasting powder drove a three-foot tamping iron though his skull. Despite the injury he managed to survive, very likely thanks to the prompt actions of the physician who attended him and who subsequently wrote about him—John Harlow. Although a considerable amount of myth and distortion seems to have surrounded the facts of the case, it does seem that Gage's personality significantly changed after injury, becoming less reliable and more prone to emotional dysregulation. However, he did manage to improve to some extent, and within a few years of his injury was working as a stagecoach driver, perhaps because his remaining right frontal lobe took over some of the lost functions, revealing that the brain can be malleable up to a point.[3] Recent neuroimaging techniques used on Gage's preserved skull revealed that the rod damaged the prefrontal cortex, an area of the frontal lobes now recognised to be involved in emotional regulation.[4]

Other evidence linking the frontal lobes to disinhibited or inappropriate behaviour can be seen in some patients with frontotemporal dementia, where frontal lobe nerve cells are the first to be killed. Frontal lobe damage can also be seen in Huntington's Chorea, leading to behavioural disinhibition; the abnormal movements to be seen in this unfortunate disease are a result of damage to subcortical circuits.

There is also evidence that in criminal psychopaths there is decreased activity in the frontal lobes and less coupling of the prefrontal cortex to other brain regions.[5]

Alexander Luria, the Russian neuropsychologist, undertook extensive studies of soldiers who were brain damaged in the Second World War, a number of whom had received frontal lobe damage. Apart from problems in the area of constructive thinking, regulation of memory and the analysis of visual perception, some lesions produced "affective disorders in the form of lack of self-control, violent emotional outbursts and gross changes of character."[6] Intellectual operations remained potentially intact, while the patients were severely disturbed by the disinhibition of their mental processes, which led to uncontrollable impulsiveness and fragmentation, so that they could not carry out planned and organised intellectual activity. It is also worth pointing out that Luria also found from treating many injured soldiers that despite sometimes severe brain injury, uninjured parts of the brain could take over at least some of the damaged functions.[7] In addition, for Luria, while one can learn about the functioning of parts of the brain through study of damaged areas, the brain at work involves the constant *interaction* of three principal functional units[8]—the unit regulating tone, the unit receiving, analysing and storing information, and the unit for programming, regulation and verification of activity, the latter including the frontal lobes and other elements of the emotional circuit. These three units work together. The working of the brain as a whole system may also help to account for its relative flexibility when it comes to injuries.

One must be cautious, then, about interpreting data that looks at only one part of this whole system in isolation. Thus, scientific studies of parts of the brain involved in elements of behaviour can be illuminating, but there is a gap between such knowledge and how it translates into human interactions. For example, we know that prefrontal brain damage leads to disinhibited behaviour, but this does not easily correlate with a person with an intact brain losing their inhibitions and choosing to start killing people, or how criminals with intact brains are able to plan crimes with no evidence of any cognitive deficits such as seen in frontal lobe damage. However, there is evidence that a significant percentage of those in prison for violent crimes have a history of concussive trauma to the frontal cortex.[9]

A further complicating factor is that the left and right cerebral hemispheres appear to have different functions, with some overlap. According to Iain McGilchrist in his comprehensive interpretation of the neuroscience literature in his book *The Master and his Emissary*, the left hemisphere,

> yields narrow, focussed attention ... The right hemisphere yields a broad, vigilant attention ... and is involved in bonding in social animals ... This has the ... consequence that the right hemisphere sees the whole, and in their context, where the left hemisphere sees things abstracted from context, and broken into parts, from which it then reconstructs a "whole": something very different. [T]he capacities that help us, as humans, to form bonds with others—empathy, emotional understanding, and so on—which involve a quite different kind of attention paid to the world, are largely right-hemisphere functions.[10]

The right hemisphere is superior to the left in recognising faces and also plays a vital role in the expression of emotions, except in the case of anger, which is connected with left frontal activation.[11] The right hemisphere is open to the interconnectedness of things and is the mediator of empathic identification as well as playing an important role in the "theory of mind", the capacity to put oneself in another's position and to see what may be going on in that person's mind, a capacity which only comes together at about the age of four.[12]

Consistent with evidence from brain damaged studies, McGilchrist writes that patients with lesions in the ventromedial prefrontal cortex are

> impulsive, fail to foresee consequences and are emotionally disengaged from others; in particular the right ventromedial cortex, which has rich interconnections with limbic[i] [emotional circuit] structures, is critical to every aspect of moral and social behaviour. Moral judgment involves a complex right-hemisphere network ... Damage in the right prefrontal cortex may lead to frank psychopathic behaviour ... Our

---

[i] The limbic system is a part of the brain most notably involved in emotion; the main constituents are the hippocampus, amygdala, hypothalamus and septum. There are many connections between the frontal cortex and the limbic system and one of its functions is the regulation of the limbic system.

sense of justice is underwritten by the right hemisphere, particularly by the right dorsolateral prefrontal cortex.[13]

Allan Schore has argued persuasively that attachment theory provides a way of linking mental phenomena with brain processes. He describes how the emotional interactions of early life directly influence the organisation of the brain systems responsible for processing emotion and cognition. He proposes that the attachment experiences of early infancy are stored in implicit memory in the early maturing right hemisphere.[14] Indeed he emphasises how early relational trauma is particularly expressed in right hemisphere deficits. For example, children diagnosed with post-traumatic stress disorder manifest abnormalities in the right side of the limbic system, and that brain impairments are associated with severe anxiety disorders in children. Trauma leading to states of dissociation are also associated with right brain deficiencies.[15]

Schore essentially has a socio-biological model, emphasising the intimate relationship between the brain and social experiences. Thus, the emotion-processing limbic circuits of the infant's developing right brain hemisphere are influenced by implicit intersubjective interactions embedded in the attachment relationship between mother and child.[16] He proposes that the right prefrontal cortex is essential for self-regulation—indeed there is substantial evidence for this going back to Luria and others. As Antonio Damasio shows, the right brain has detailed maps of the body state,[17] which makes it suitable for regulating subjective emotional experiences. It is the right brain, for Schore, that plays a fundamental role in the maintenance of a coherent sense of self, which implies that right brain dysfunction will be associated with self-deficits. Recent research on the role of abuse and neglect confirms abnormalities in parts of the emotional circuits such as the amygdala[ii], hippocampus and cerebral cortex, showing how trauma can directly impact the development of the brain.[18]

It is worth adding here that the prefrontal cortex does not reach maturity until about the age of 25–26, only beginning to start maturing at late adolescence. As adolescence progresses, "activity in different parts

---

[ii] The amygdala, part of the limbic system, is a small almond-shaped cluster of nuclei embedded in the brain's temporal lobes. It is involved in emotional learning and regulation and is central to mediating aggression as well as recognising fear and managing anxiety.

of the frontal cortex becomes more correlated as the region operates as more of a functional unit ... there's steady improvement in working memory, flexible rule use, executive organization, and frontal inhibitory regulation."[19] The adolescent's brain gradually becomes more efficient and learns to inhibit behaviour more effectively. The typical risk-taking behaviour of adolescents is in part a consequence of the immaturity of their frontal cortex.

Late adolescence and early adulthood, when the prefrontal lobes are not yet mature, are when premeditated and impulsive violence peaks. Neuroimaging studies indicate that adolescent and adult criminal psychopaths both have less sensitivity of the prefrontal cortex and the reward system regulated by dopamine to negative feedback, less pain sensitivity, and less connectivity between the frontal cortex and the amygdala during tasks designed to test empathy and moral reasoning.[20]

This delay in the part of the brain most linked to moral thinking, for example, knowing when to hold back from acting rather than getting involved in violence, or "doing the right thing" as Sapolsky puts it, means that the experience of the child and adolescent's environment has a more fundamental part to play in shaping their lives than any genetic predisposition; or anyway that "by definition the frontal cortex is the brain region least constrained by genes and most sculpted by experience. This must be so, to be the supremely complex social species that we are. Ironically, it seems that the genetic program of human brain development has evolved to, as much as possible, free the frontal cortex from genes."[21]

In this context is noteworthy that a gene variant of Monoamine Oxidase (MAO), an enzyme involved in the breakdown of serotonin, is associated with anti-social and aggressive behaviour. When the variant is present, serotonin is not adequately broken down and higher levels lead to abnormal behaviours. However, even those with the gene variant do not become anti-social unless there is also the presence of severe childhood abuse.[22] If there is no such history, the variant is not predictive of any particular behaviour. These findings may partly explain why not all victims of maltreatment grow up to victimise others, and they provide epidemiological evidence that genotypes can moderate the sensitivity of children to environmental traumas.

There have been many neuroscientific studies of those with anti-social personalities, with investigations focused on the shallow emotions displayed particularly by the more violent criminals, so-called psychopaths, with their accompanying lack of fear, lack of empathy and remorse, as well as their tendency to be impulsive and use aggressive and predatory behaviour in a planned way to secure what they want, status or money, for example. Some of these studies may have some, though probably limited, relevance to how ordinary people can also lose their capacity for empathy in certain situations.

One kind of study shows reduced connectivity in psychopaths between the ventral prefrontal cortex (vmPFC) and parts of the limbic system such as the amygdala, as well as other reduced connections. For example, Motzkin and colleagues[23] showed that psychopathy is associated with reduced functional connectivity between vmPFC and the amygdala as well as between the vmPFC and the medial parietal cortex. The authors suggested that these data converged to implicate diminished vmPFC connectivity as a characteristic neurobiological feature of psychopathy. Reduced connectivity between the prefrontal cortex and the limbic system implies less inhibition of the limbic system in psychopaths, which one would assume correlates with less controlled and more impulsive behaviour.

Gregory and colleagues[24] undertook an investigation of anti-social male offenders, and those who were both anti-social and met criteria for psychopathy based upon a standard checklist of features. The researchers used magnetic resonance imaging (MRI) to scan the brains of 44 violent offenders diagnosed with Anti-Social Personality Disorder. Crimes committed included murder, rape, attempted murder, and grievous bodily harm.

The results showed reduced grey matter volumes in parts of the prefrontal cortex relative to those who were just anti-social and compared to non-offenders, again indicating the presence of structural brain abnormalities in the areas involved in empathic processing and moral reasoning. Damage to these areas is associated with impaired empathising with other people, a poor response to fear and distress, and a lack of self-conscious emotions such as guilt or embarrassment.

The authors of this study described those who were anti-social without psychopathy as hot-headed and those with psychopathy as cold-hearted. The cold-hearted psychopathic group begin offending earlier, engage in a broader range and greater density of offending behaviours, and respond less well to treatment programmes in adulthood, compared to the hot-headed group. This behavioural difference corresponds to very specific structural brain abnormalities which underpin psychopathic behaviour, such as profound deficits in empathising with the distress of others.

Another study[25] looked at psychological tests of executive function in violent offenders with and without psychopathy compared to non-offenders. Both groups of offenders failed to learn from punishment clues, to change their behavioural responses in the face of changing situations and made poor quality of decisions in the various tasks despite having longer to deliberate. These profiles indicate that offenders persist in anti-social behaviours despite knowing the negative consequences to themselves and/or others.

A recent meta-analysis of aberrant brain activity in psychopathy,[26] looking at functional magnetic resonance imaging studies, concluded that psychopathy is characterised by abnormal brain activity of bilateral prefrontal cortices and the right amygdala; hence, that aberrant neural activity can account for pertinent psychopathology in psychopathy.

The specific role of the amygdala in acts of aggressive behaviour is indicated by a few other findings. For example, in some rare conditions where damage is restricted to the amygdala, such as in some kinds of encephalitis, a congenital condition called Urbach-Wiethe disease, or where the amygdala has been ablated as part of the treatment of refractory epilepsy; such individuals are impaired in their ability to detect angry faces, though they can recognise other emotional states.[27]

Fear recognition is also linked to amygdala function. For example, Damasio and colleagues reported in 1994[28] on a patient SM with rare bilateral amygdala damage, showed an impairment in her ability to recognise fear from facial expressions. Ten years later, they showed[29] that her impairment stems from an inability to make normal use of information from the eye region to process the appearance of faces when judging emotions, a defect they traced to a lack of spontaneous fixations on the eyes during free viewing of faces. This finding provides a mechanism to explain the amygdala's role in fear recognition, and in addition, pointed to new approaches for the possible rehabilitation of patients with defective emotion perception.

A lack of fear response in psychopaths has been consistently found in many studies, and that this related to reduced amygdala responsiveness.[30] But, as the other studies I have mentioned show, this is part of a general issue about how the amygdala connects with other parts of the brain such as the prefrontal cortex. The reduced fear response, and the problem with recognition of fear in others, is likely to be part of the explanation for the difficulty that psychopaths have in being empathic and feeling remorse for their violent actions. "If psychopaths are unable to personally experience negative emotions such as fear, then there is little hope for them to understand the negative emotions of others, as these same emotional systems are responsible for affective empathy."[31]

There is increasing evidence that there is a small group of children who may be predisposed to becoming adult psychopaths. They have a conduct disorder and callous–unemotional traits with persistent and violent patterns of anti-social behaviour. They show limited empathy, little guilt and shallow affect. I have seen a few such children in my child psychiatry practice. One stands out as the most extreme. I was asked by the Family Court to assess him when he was thirteen as he had been admitted to a medium secure unit after a series of anti-social acts, including stealing, bullying and attempted knife crime. Ordinary measures had had no effect, and he was uncontainable at home, in foster care or in a children's home due to his level of aggression.

When I visited the unit to make my assessment, I first interviewed his parents, who had been continually threatened by their son with violence. He had always been difficult to manage and had never got on that well with other children. They had another son who was normal and doing well at school. Overall, I was struck by how caring the parents were. They had not rejected their violent son, though they could no longer manage him at home. Their family and background appeared otherwise without significant dysfunction.

When I interviewed the boy, who was large for his age, I was told I needed to have a male nurse in the room with me for my own protection. At first, I was rather puzzled by this as it would mean that I might not be able to elicit confidential or intimate information which could help with my understanding of his issues. In the event, the interview went along satisfactorily at first. He knew why he was in the unit, though he did not like being there, and I did not press him for details at that point and before I had tried to gain his confidence. I asked him about his school—he had been excluded for threatening other pupils with violence. He showed no empathy at all for anything he had done. "They deserved it" or "I don't see the problem" was his usual response. He had been finally admitted to this unit as he has taken a knife and had stabbed another boy in a children's home. When eventually I began to ask him about what happened, and if he felt any concern, the staff member immediately rushed the boy out of the examination room. When the nurse returned, he explained that I would have been attacked at that point, as it was clear to the nurse that talking about the stabbing was going to trigger his violence, and that he would probably have tried to strangle me—this had happened to a previous professional. If I had known that prior to the meeting, I would probably have opted out of that assessment. I was rather shocked that I had apparently been so near to being subjected to such explosive violence.

When I came to the writing of my court report, my conclusion was that he showed features of being callous and unemotional, unrelated to any obvious environmental abuse or neglect. I speculated that if he did not engage with some therapeutic work around his aggression and anger, then the future prognosis was poor. I thought that he would either kill himself or someone else at some time.

Indeed, about five years later, I was contacted by a solicitor at the urging of a Crown Court judge who had been shown my original report, as the boy, now about nineteen, had been charged with murdering another young man in an unprovoked attack. The judge had suggested I give an opinion as I had predicted what might happen. In fact, there was little I could add, and he was given a long custodial sentence. It was quite shocking to come across a person so young already on such a relentlessly violent path, with little sense of their ability to change.

Consistent with research on anti-social adults, children with a combination of conduct problems and callous–unemotional traits show low amygdala activity in response to seeing fearful faces.[32] Such children are also fearless and insensitive to other people's distress and can be difficult to treat. They not only display impulsive and reactive anti-social actions, but also commit calculated acts of aggression with little regard for other people's feelings. In contrast, children with conduct disorders and who are not callous and unemotional do not have pronounced deficits in empathy and remorse, and often commit acts of aggression that have clear environmental triggers, such as perceived threat or frustration, often in a social context. The callous–unemotional children however tend to be more self-focused and can be aggressive even when someone is showing distress, especially if they stand to gain something.

A recent study[33] suggests that boys with conduct and callous–unemotional traits can successfully represent mental states when doing so does not require processing of complex information or when there is some potential instrumental advantage. They may find it easier or be more motivated to mentalise about peers or people their own age, as mentalising about peers typically has instrumental value, they can manipulate them. Although the capacity to mentalise is intact, which is after all necessary to be able to manipulate others, the reduced propensity to empathise with the mind of the other may allow these boys to ignore the negative emotional consequences of their anti-social behaviour.

It is worth emphasising that it is only a small percentage of children who are callous and unemotional; the great majority of children with conduct problems show empathy. However, these latter children have a greater risk of physical and mental health problems, difficulties with personal relationships, as well as reduced employment and increased criminality in adulthood. This group merges with those studies by John Bowlby in the late 1940s and early 1950s of those who were classed as juvenile delinquents. Many of these children were physically and emotionally deprived, and it was based on this research that Bowlby wrote his classic book, *Child Care and the Growth of Love*,[34] in which he emphasised the ill effects on children of maternal deprivation, work which laid the foundation of his future theory of attachment and the importance of secure attachments for the health of the child. Subsequent research has shown how insecure attachments predispose to anti-social behaviour.[35]

Simon Baron-Cohen, in his book *Zero Degrees of Empathy*,[36] which interestingly was marketed in the US as *The Science of Evil*, puts forward a comprehensive theory of the origins of cruelty as a failure in one or more elements of what he calls the brain's "Empathy

Circuit". The latter consists of twelve factors[37] that can impact the empathy circuit—from the neurology of the brain, genetic makeup to early experience and culture and ideology, in a way that resembles to some extent the multi-dimensional model of behaviour proposed by Robert Sapolsky. Much of what I have already covered about the role of the frontal cortex and limbic system in regulating and modifying behaviour is described in the book but with even more technical detail. He examines "how some people become capable of cruelty and whether a loss of affective empathy inevitably has this consequence".[38] He looks at the brain basis of empathy as well as its social and biological determinants. Despite the book's American title, he aims to replace the unscientific term "evil" with the term "empathy erosion", yet he also retains the word evil in, for example, his first chapter—"Explaining 'Evil' and Human Cruelty", where he writes that his interest in the subject in part arose out of his own Jewish background and the awareness of the horrors of the Holocaust.

He argues that when someone treats another human as an object, which the Nazis repeatedly did, their empathy has been turned off. Thus, he aims to examine how empathy takes place normally and in pathology. His key idea is that we all lie somewhere on an *empathy spectrum*—from those with zero degrees of empathy at one end of the spectrum and who show underactivity in the empathy circuits of the brain (such as with the amygdala) and can thereby commit horrible and violent crimes, to those at the other end who are remarkably focused on other people's feelings.

Incidentally, Baron-Cohen is a well-known expert on those on the autistic spectrum and has designed screening tools such as the Empathy Quotient which can detect the likelihood of a child having autism. However, as he also shows in the book, though those with autism have difficulties in empathising, in understanding the other's state of mind, they are not zero-negative regarding empathy. Instead, he describes them as zero-positive, in that they develop a moral code through systemising, such as perceiving patterns in behaviour. Their brains do show underactivity in most areas of the empathy circuits, but they make up for this by systemising to an extraordinary degree.[39]

In his final chapter on reflections on human cruelty, he asks whether the zero-negative condition can explain human cruelty. There is no doubt that a lack of empathy accompanies acts of cruelty, so in that sense the empathy circuits switch off or are switched off in some way during violence. This may happen transiently in ordinary people, or for extended times in those who are labelled as psychopaths. But whether acts of cruelty occur *because* of the malfunctioning of the empathy circuit— Baron-Cohen's hypothesis—may be stretching the explanatory model too far. The empathy circuit may be malfunctioning as *result* of the cruel acts or in parallel with them, rather than as a cause of them. I am also not sure what value there is in exchanging the concept of evil with that of empathy erosion. Evil captures an extreme form of harm which empathy erosion or even the more scientific term zero degrees of empathy does not capture. However, his multi-system model, with many influences acting on a final common pathway in the brain is one worth studying as one element in understanding human evil and emphasises again that one needs to take some account of neuroscience in any explanation of human evil. But his model is thin on the details of the various influences on that final common pathway, including the detailed role of dynamics in individuals and groups and social and historical processes.

Child development and the origins of morality

The fact that is rare to find children who do not show empathy for others implies that for the majority a capacity for empathy and therefore for some form of moral thinking originates early in in childhood, that a rudimentary moral law is naturally present. Indeed, there is now research evidence to show that even babies from around three months onwards have a rudimentary sense of justice, as described in detail in Paul Bloom's book, *Just Babies. The Origins of Good and Evil*.[40]

Based upon developmental psychology, evolutionary biology and cultural anthropology, Bloom proposes that our natural endowments include a moral sense, with some capacity to distinguish between cruel and kind actions; empathy and compassion for others; and a rudimentary sense of fairness and justice.[41] Of course a baby has yet to develop the sophisticated nature of how to make impartial judgments in complex and conflicting situations. Bloom also cautions that innate goodness is limited, and that we are by nature indifferent or even hostile to strangers, and some of our instinctive emotional responses such as disgust can be the basis for cruel, even genocidal, acts. Thus, in order to resist evil, one needs to understand the basis of human propensities for both good and evil as well as the basis for irrational attitudes to strangers.

"Stranger anxiety" is a developmental phase, which usually shows itself fully around eight months, when the baby begins to have a sense of others as whole people. Infants are already learning to recognise their caretakers from early on, while also being interested in other figures, to whom they are less attached. But from around six months they begin to show unhappiness around strangers, and by eight months they may burst into tears if a stranger approaches or gets too close physically. This fear of strangers can last until around the age of two to a greater or lesser extent, but by then it also begins to reduce as children build up more of a sense of reality and learn to trust based on awareness of the other's trustworthiness. This kind of developmental picture assumes a normal attachment pattern, with the child making a primary and secure attachment to their caregivers. If they become secure with their parents, they feel during this period anxious when separated from them. In time, from about eighteen months, they learn to learn that the parent who goes will return; they symbolise presence and absence. However, children who have been traumatised or severely deprived may not develop secure attachments. Some of them, with attachment disorders, may show no fear of strangers and may go up to strangers, as if seeking some sort of lost primary parental object. A test for attachment difficulties is called the "Strange Situation", in which children are put in a room with their caretaker, the latter then suddenly leaves, and the child is then observed, both when the caretaker leaves and when they return. Secure infants are distressed when their caretaker leaves but are easily comforted when they return. Children with insecure attachments show a variety of abnormal responses, and may show various kinds of disorganised behaviours, which may lead on to attachment disorders and behavioural and emotional difficulties; as mentioned above, there is a strong association between disorganised attachments and anti-social behaviour.

It is difficult to know how much adult attitudes to strangers are affected by some of these early developmental considerations. But the latter do show that the fear of the stranger goes deep into our developmental histories, making it difficult to accept others who appear to be different; a "them" and "us" attitude runs deep in the human psyche. Stranger anxiety may have had an evolutionary protective factor; being wary of strangers would be appropriate in a potentially dangerous world. But we need to relearn how to trust the other if we are to have workable interpersonal relationships. As we learn to trust others outside our home circle, so we may also need to learn to trust the unfamiliar stranger by overcoming our elemental fears, but also having the possibility in mind that the stranger may be trustworthy, putting aside the tendency to view the stranger by nature as a suspicious figure.

Bloom described several research studies involving what I assume are securely attached babies, as they are not described as, for example, highly anxious or miserable or lacking in ordinary responsiveness. He and his colleagues wanted to test whether babies could accurately predict how individuals would respond to someone who was either kind or cruel to them. They created animations that babies could respond to, with, for example, a red ball trying to go up a hill, either being helped by a yellow square, or being pushed back by a green triangle.[42] They found that six- and ten-month-old babies prefer to look at helpful figures. And even three-month-olds show this tendency. Eight-month-olds will prefer a figure, such as a puppet, who is mean to a bad puppet over the one who is nice to it; so that there is already some sense of justice and the role of punishment.

With older children, three-year-olds are more likely to help someone who had previously helped someone else and less likely to help someone who had been cruel to another person, and this has been repeated with twenty-one-month-olds.[43] But before about the age of four, consistent with their earlier stranger anxiety, children show little spontaneous kindness towards strangers. However, again I presume with securely attached children, according to Bloom, children at all ages have an overall bias towards equality and fairness, for example in dividing various goods, though that must be weighed up against various tendencies to self-interest.

Babies make distinctions between those that are familiar and those that are strange to them from early on, even before structured stranger anxiety. Very early on they can detect their mother's smell and voice, preferring to look at their mother's face rather than at a stranger. The also like familiar faces. White babies prefer to look at white faces, and black babies prefer to look at black faces. But this is because babies are developing a preference based on people they know. Babies raised in ethnically diverse environments do not show preference for face colour. Hence, one could infer that racism develops out of racist environments. But one needs to understand the natural tendency for a baby to prefer what they know.[44]

Bloom's overall point[45] is that evidence from child development research indicates that our moral lives have two parts—what we are born with as beings with some basic moral equipment designed by evolution to relate to others, with some empathy, compassion, and capacity to judge others and even know when they should be punished; and then what subsequently emerges over the course of human history and individual development, and is a critical part of our morality, is when complex notions of justice and fairness come into play, something like Kant's notion of the moral law within us. But I would add that the evidence from history is that such moral thinking requires considerable individual and societal support to be maintained; without this there are only a few who have a strong sense of inner moral law, often buttressed by strong religious or political beliefs, that can resist attempts to be perverted or corrupted. These are the "resisters", as I shall describe below and in Chapter 7.

It would be interesting to compare the research on secure babies with those who are insecure and whether one can detect different ways of judging behaviour. Securely attached babies tend to be better adjusted as children; however, children with experience of abnormal parenting can show different kinds of insecure attachments. They can be anxious-avoidant or anxious-resistant or, in the more extreme cases, disorganised. If a child has continuously volatile or inconsistent parenting, they may develop an attachment disorder. This can be a disinhibited or a reactive attachment disorder, although there is some overlap between the two. Those with a disinhibited attachment disorder will show an indiscriminate sociability; those with a reactive attachment disorder tend to display fearfulness and hyper-vigilance in social interactions that is not responsive to reassurance. Contradictory or ambivalent social responses may also be present. Children with attachment disorders tend to have difficulty in regulating their emotions and may display outbursts of anger and frustration that are not easily soothed. Without help, such as compensatory parenting, such children are at great risk of developing a range of psychological problems, including conduct problems.

There has been much speculation in the past about how child rearing practices in a culture can affect subsequent adult behaviours, but little based upon scientific evidence. For example, the psychoanalyst Alice Miller, in her book *For Your Own Good*,[46] introduced the concept of "poisonous pedagogy" to describe the childrearing practices that were so prevalent in Europe, especially before the Second World War. She believed that the pain inflicted on children—"for their own good"— was unconsciously the parent re-enacting the trauma that had been inflicted on them when they were children, thus perpetuating the cycle of trauma continuing down the generations. Miller proposed here that German traumatic childrearing produced serial killer of children Jürgen Bartsch, and Adolf Hitler. Children learn to accept their parents' often abusive behaviour against themselves as being "for their own good". In the case of Hitler, it led to displacement against the Jews and other minority groups. For Miller, the traditional pedagogic process was manipulative, resulting in grown-up adults deferring excessively to authorities, even to tyrannical leaders or dictators like Hitler. "Good Germans", were compliant with Hitler's abusive regime, which Miller asserted was a direct result of how the society in general treated its children. Authoritarian child rearing was not restricted to Germany, but Miller asserted that it was extreme in Germany and declined more slowly than other European countries because of a cultural predisposition to militarism and obedience to authority.

Theodor Adorno and his colleagues[47] suggested that as a result of their upbringing certain types of people, with "authoritarian" personalities were likely to be prejudiced against groups of people different to themselves. Such people had always been brought up with extremely rigid discipline, which had produced strong feelings of aggression. But due to the rigid discipline they could not express the aggression, which was internalised and then turned against external targets, such as minority groups. This can certainly explain how some people become prejudiced but not how whole groups of people can do so.

Attachment research certainly shows how early life can impact on subsequent well-being and mental health; but it is big leap from such evidence to suggesting that whole nations can behave in certain fixed ways depending upon how they were raised as children. However, one can reasonably imagine that when the Nazi regime urged mothers to ignore their toddlers' emotional needs so they could raise hardened soldiers and followers,[48] such affects may well have had a significant impact on their children's subsequent emotional life. Similarly, the Soviet insistence that babies attend creches at a very early age in order to become more socially responsible may well have had lasting negative effects on these children's subsequent relationships. Authoritarian regimes are likely to foster authoritarian child rearing practices; whether authoritarian child rearing directly produce authoritarian regimes is doubtful.

If, as seems to be the case, human beings have some innate or anyway early sense of fair play and justice, what about the origin of destructiveness? Is destructiveness there from the beginning or do we become destructive as a natural developmental process, or as a result of distortions in development, or to we become so as a result of environmental impingements? Are humans inherently good but capable of evil, or inherently evil but capable of good? Certainly, we cannot confine destructiveness to those who become psychopaths; one merely has to look at human history to be aware of its ubiquity. One way to try to answer this issue is to look at evidence from primate research, to see if there is any evidence that destructiveness is part of our animal inheritance.

Peaceful or warlike apes

The primatologist Frans de Waal has written at length about the complex social life of primates, and how much one can apply findings from ape communal life to that of humans. In one recent book *The Bonobo and the Atheist*,[49] he specifically looks for evidence of empathic and moral thinking among groups of chimpanzees and bonobos, and how such findings may provide clues about the origins of our own sense of morality. Basically, he considers that the scientific evidence shows that the old view of humans as having a thin "veneer" of morality and concerns for others covering a basic selfish and brute animal nature is incorrect. Instead, there is overwhelming evidence for innate empathy, altruism, and cooperation in humans, apes, and indeed other animals.[50] The two main enforcers of the social code by which primates and children live are empathy and the desire for good relations and the threat and fear of physical consequences such as penalties from those higher up in the social chain. Generally, "primates strive for peaceful coexistence. Individuals unable or unwilling to abide by the social code become marginalised. The ultimate driver of the whole process, in an evolutionary sense, is the desire for integration, since its opposite—isolation and ostracism—drastically diminishes an individual's chances of survival."[51]

De Waal shows that our nearest animal relatives, chimpanzees and bonobos are empathic, even though they can be aggressive on occasion. Bonobos, for example, strive to fit in with others, obey social rules, empathise with others, and try to mend broken relationships while objecting to unfair arrangements. Chimpanzees are more aggressive and can be killers. They take their power games seriously and are ready to kill their rivals. There are examples of many cases seen in the wild of adult males killing other males, of males killing infants, and of females killing infants. De Waal has seen captive chimps brutally mutilating and castrating a political rival, which led to his death.[52] There is no such behaviour in bonobos, who are led by females and use sex or close contact between genitals very often as positive communication. Most observed chimp killings take place during territorial disputes, whereas bonobos engage in sex at their boundaries. They can be unfriendly to strangers and neighbours, but soon after a confrontation begins, female bonobos have been observed to go to the other side and copulate with males or mount other females, which rapidly changes the hostile dynamic into one more cooperative. Bonobos unlike chimps and like humans can have sex face to face. They also use sex for greeting, conflict resolution, and food sharing.

Humans shares genes with bonobos that we do not share with chimps, but we also share genes with chimps that we do not share with bonobos. So, our species shares a mosaic of characteristics with both apes; we can be both empathic like bonobos and violent like chimps, perhaps then giving us a disposition to both good and evil, not one or the other. But in both sets of apes, there is a considerable amount of cooperation and empathic concern for others from early on in their lives.

Neuroscientific studies of bonobo brains[53] show that areas involving the perception of distress in both themselves and others, such as the right amygdala and right anterior insula, are enlarged. Bonobos also have an enlarged pathway linking the amygdala with part of the cingulate cortex, a pathway implicated in top-down control of aggression as well as bottom-up restraints against harming others. Studies have thus suggested that their nervous systems not only support increased empathic sensitivity, but also behaviours like sex and play that serve to dissipate tension, thus limiting distress and anxiety to levels consistent with prosocial behaviour.

So, to answer to question as to whether humans are inherently good but capable of evil, or inherently evil but capable of good, evidence from primate research indicates an essential predisposition to both good and evil, or what de Waal calls mankind's essential "bipolarity".[54] We are, as it were, regarding our evolutionary history, some kind of hybrid between chimps and bonobos. In that case, the quality of upbringing, such as the quality of maternal care, and of the influence of society, will have a major impact on the ultimate mixture of good or evil dispositions.

The evidence from child development is that, given a secure attachment, infants and toddlers are not usually wilfully destructive, though they may enjoy throwing things away or pushing over a tower of bricks. A child from around the age of four or five may begin to have destructive tendencies, wilfully wanting to hurt others. And even younger children may wish to harm a newly arrived baby whom they may feel threatens their own place in their mother's affection. Children can generally become aggressive around the age of two, but not maliciously destructive. But evidence from psychoanalysis, which I will tackle in the next chapter, does reveal the presence of a rich vein of *aggressive and destructive fantasies and primitive ideas of retaliation* at some point in a child's early life, which may later become the basis for acting out of destructiveness. My own view from many years of seeing many mothers and babies and thousands of children in my clinics is that those children who show strong destructive tendencies with actual destructive actions when very young are usually very troubled and are likely to be in an insecure or very anxious home environment, that is when ordinary aggression can be turned into wilfully hateful action. Otherwise, when maternal care is good enough, the altruistic tendencies overwhelmingly predominate for the first two years or so; seeing young children as innately evil or with evil dispositions or full of hateful and aggressive impulses is by and large a projection onto the children from work with troubled adults.

This is confirmed by observations from Donald Winnicott who emphasised that the baby's loving relationship with the mother provides a framework for mitigating the baby's fears. Such fears are primitive in nature and

> are based on the infant's expectation of crude retaliations. The infant gets excited, with aggressive or destructive impulses or ideas, which he shows as screaming or wanting to bite, and immediately the world seems to be full of biting mouths and hostile teeth and claws and all kinds of threats. In this way the infant's world would be a terrifying place were it not for the mother's general protective role which hides these very great fears that belong to the infant's early experience of living. The mother (and I'm not forgetting the father) alters the quality of the small child's fears by being a human being.[55]

De Waal emphasises that the evidence from mammal studies is that the gladiatorial view of nature is wrong and that most social mammals strive for harmonious relationships. He gives examples from baboon society.[56] Two mature male baboons refused to touch a peanut thrown between them though they saw it land at their feet. In another observation in the wild two harem leaders, finding themselves in a fruit tree too small to feed both of their families broke off their inevitable confrontation by running away from one another, followed by their families, leaving the fruit unpicked. Such avoidance of open confrontation is also observed in chimp behaviour. There is also considerable evidence of reconciliating behaviour after open aggression, with a good deal of emotional control, including turn taking. In fact, adult male chimps need to be able to control their impulses as they are powerful enough to crush each other's bones. De Waal also notes that at an early age, "children show the same touching, embracing, and calming body contacts as apes, and girls do so more often than boys".[57]

Furthermore, "The child is a natural moralist, who gets a huge helping hand from its biological makeup. We humans automatically pay attention to others, are attracted to them, and make their situation our own. Like all primates, we are emotionally affected by others."[58]

Social psychology and evil

A constant theme of much social psychology research into human group behaviour tries to address the questions: *Why do people do things as a group that they would not do individually? How and to what extent do social forces constrain people's opinions and attitudes?* Much social psychology research in the 1950s and 1960s was not surprisingly driven by the horrors of the Holocaust, and some survivors were instrumental in conducting ground-breaking studies trying to answer how groups of people could appear to lose their ordinary sense of morality, become taken over by intimidating authorities or yield to peer pressure to undertake evil actions. There were also studies looking at how prejudice and discrimination shapes attitudes towards minorities from individuals and groups. More recent work on bystander behaviour, the tendency to remain silent or inactive in the face of bad behaviour, has added to our knowledge of the social psychology of evil.

Solomon Asch conducted one of the earliest post-war studies of the effects of group pressure on the ability to judge.[59] The immediate object was,

> to study the social and personal conditions that induce individuals to resist or to yield to group pressures when the later are perceived to be *contrary to fact*. The issues which this problem raises are of obvious consequence for society; it can be of decisive importance whether a group will, under certain conditions, submit to existing pressure. Equally direct are the consequences for individuals and our understanding of them, since it is a decisive fact about a person whether he possesses the freedom to act independently, or whether he characteristically submits to group pressures.[60]

In order to test group pressure, the experiment consisted of placing an individual in a relation of radical conflict with all the other members of the group and measuring what happens. A group of eight individuals was instructed over eighteen trials to judge a series of simple perceptual relations—to match a given line on the left of a card with one of three other lines; they had to decide which of the three lines on the right was equal in length to that on the left, and to give their answers out loud.

For the first couple of cards everyone agreed which line was the same. But then with the third trial one individual found themselves being suddenly contradicted by the rest of the group and this was repeated several times. In fact, the group, except for the one member, had previously met with the experimenter and received instructions to respond at certain points with wrong answers. Asch found that about 76% of the 123 men who were tested gave at least one incorrect response when it was their turn, and 37% of the responses, overall, were conforming. However, conformity was not absolute—in addition to the 24% of the men who never conformed, only 5% of the men conformed on all twelve of the critical trials.

Overall, Asch found that despite the stress of the situation a substantial proportion of individuals retained their independence throughout the experiment, while at the same time a substantial minority yielded, modifying their judgments in accordance with the majority. The responses varied if the stimulus was less clear and then the majority effect was greater. The majority effect was also a function of the size of group opposition, and there were striking differences among individuals, some always going with the majority, others completely independent, and a third who vacillated between the majority opinion and their own independent view. The hypothesis was that these differences were functionally dependent on relatively enduring character differences, in particular those pertaining to the individuals' social relations.

Serge Moscovici looked at the influence of minority opinion in groups. In his "blue-green" study of 1969, he placed two confederates together with four genuine participants, who had been tested to make sure they were not colour blind. The group were then shown 36 slides which were clearly of different shades of blue and asked to state the colour of the slide out loud. The two confederates had been instructed to give one of two patterns of answers that were different from the normal responses. In the *consistent minority* condition, the two confederates gave the unusual response (green) on every trial. In the *inconsistent minority* condition the confederates called the slides "green" on two thirds of their responses and called them "blue" on the other third. The minority of two was able to change the beliefs of the majority of four, but only when they were unanimous in their judgments. Moscovici found that the presence of a minority who gave consistently unusual responses influenced the judgments made by the experimental participants. When the minority was consistent, 32% of the majority group participants said green at least once and 18% of the responses of the majority group were green. However, the inconsistent minority had virtually no influence on the judgments of the majority.

Based on this research, Moscovici argued that minorities could have influence over majorities, provided they gave consistent, unanimous responses.

Subsequent research[61] has found that minorities are most effective when they express consistent opinions over time and with each other, when they show that they are invested in their position by making significant personal and material sacrifices, when they seem to be acting out of principle rather than from ulterior motives and consistently regarding their core arguments.

A study that influenced later experiments on group interaction was that of Muzafer Sherif's studies of young boys' behaviour at American summer camps in the early 1950s.[62] At Robbers Cave, Oklahoma, well-adjusted American boys aged eleven to twelve were divided into groups that were put in competition with each other. Hostility developed rapidly, followed by bitter conflict, resembling the events in William Golding's almost contemporaneous novel *Lord of the Flies*, where a group of boys stranded on an island become increasingly aggressive and destructive.

The boys at Robbers Cave arrived at camp in two separate groups: for the first part of the study, they spent time with members of their own group, without knowing that the other group existed. The groups chose names (the Eagles and the Rattlers), and each group developed their own group norms and group hierarchies. After a short period of time, the boys became aware that there was another group at camp and, upon learning of the other group, the campers group spoke negatively about the other group. Then the researchers began a competitive tournament between the groups, consisting of games such as baseball and tug-of-war, for which the winners would receive prizes and a trophy. After the Eagles and Rattlers began competing in the tournament, the relationship between the two groups quickly became tense, trading insults, and the conflict quickly escalated. The teams each burned the other group's team flag, and raided the other group's cabin, while within each group there developed more cohesion.

Attempts were made to reduce conflict by having some fun activities, which did not work well, but working towards a common task fared better in reducing the bitter conflict between the groups. One could say that this study is regularly replicated in countless sporting occasions between competing teams throughout the world.

Henri Tajfel demonstrated in various experiments that merely putting people into groups is sufficient for people to discriminate in favour of their own group and against members of another group.[63] The original experiments involved sixty-four boys, fourteen and fifteen years old from a comprehensive school in a suburb of Bristol. They came to the laboratory in separate groups of eight. They were given various tasks such as expressing a preference for paintings shown to them as slides, and they were then allowed to give monetary rewards for answers from their own and the other group. In making their intergroup choices a large majority of the subjects, in all groups in both conditions, gave more money to members of their own group than to members of the other group. Intergroup discrimination was the strategy used in making intergroup choices. In contrast the in-group and out-group choices were closely distributed around the point of fairness. Tajfel proposed that stereotyping (i.e. putting people into groups and categories) is based on a normal cognitive process: the tendency to group things together. In doing so we tend to exaggerate the differences between groups and the similarities of things in the same group. Of course, these experiments were undertaken with adolescent boys in an English setting. In cultures that emphasise cooperation more than competitiveness, the results may have been different.

Tajfel then went on to develop an influential *theory of social identity*, which argued that that the boys favoured their own group because it increased their self-esteem. Even though the boys were never giving points to themselves they knew that if they gave less to the other group and more to their own group that they would be in the group which gained most points, therefore improving their self-esteem because they belonged to the "best" group. From this follows that some people may be more prone to prejudice if they have an intense need for acceptance by others.

More startling in terms of their impact on society were the Milgram and Zimbardo experiments, I described in the opening chapter, looking at more extreme issues concerning conformity and group interaction. The Milgram or the so-called "obedience" experiments were designed to see if people would do horrendous things just because they were told to do so. While recent reviews of the experiments showed that they underplayed how many people resisted the instructions to administer severe shocks, they still revealed that a certain number of people would go the whole way with inflicting suffering on others. The findings are still disturbing, even if only a minority go all the way and give what appear to be fatal shocks.

A more recent study was undertaken to test out the validity of the Stanford Prison experiment and came out with somewhat different findings. The "BBC study"[64] involving fifteen "decent" men, was undertaken in 2001, and involved the documentary department of the BBC, which filmed the event.

In this case, with no overarching controller like Zimbardo influencing the guards, prisoners organised to resist the abuse from the guards, their morale increased while the guards' morale lowered. This resulted in a prisoner rebellion and a merging of roles with a cooperative sharing of power. However, this arrangement soon collapsed and a harsh authoritarian regime, led by four participants who had scored highest on scales of authoritarianism, and the study was ended two days early.

The findings from this study matched some of the Zimbardo findings in terms of how people can become cruel to one other in certain social roles, but it also showed that matters are more complex, and that resistance and rebellion are also within the human range. However, the fact that both the BBC and Stanford studies had to be terminated due to the outbreak of excessive authoritarianism is rather sobering and shows how ordinary people can get into abnormally violent states of mind in certain situations, where the now violent subject is enabled to annihilate the other's subjectivity. One can then see some of the features that characterise how violent regimes may exploit human vulnerabilities in order to perpetuate and practice violence on their population, when ordinary people can find themselves caught up in processes that ultimately lead to evil acts. Certain situations, what one might call "precursor situations", or "states", may be particularly favourable to the building up of malicious aggression. People, even morally decent people, seem particularly vulnerable to conformist behaviour when there is a combination of strong authority and homogenous group values. Group values that promote heterogeneity and plural viewpoints are less likely to promote aggression.

Zimbardo summarises the impact of these kinds of situational studies.

> First, we should be aware that a range of apparently simple situational factors can function to impact our behavior more compellingly than seems possible. The research ... points up the influential force of: role playing, rules, presence of others, emergent group norms, group identity, uniforms, anonymity, social modelling, authority presence, symbols of power, time pressures, semantic framing, stereotypical images and labels, among others. Second, the situationist approach redefines heroism. When the majority of ordinary people can be overcome by such pressures toward compliance and conformity, the minority who resist should be considered heroic. Acknowledging the special nature of this resistance means we should learn from their example by studying how they have been able to rise above such compelling pressures. That suggestion is coupled with another that encourages the development of an essential but ignored domain of psychology—heroes and heroism.[65]

Claudia Card as a philosopher comments about the Milgram and Stanford studies that what is particularly revealing about them is that is the

> lack of a morally defensible reason in those who kept pushing the lever and those who kept abusing prisoners that stands out ... In lesser wrongs, either there is no reasonably foreseeable intolerable harm, or the agent willing to inflict it has some good (morally defensible) reason ... The choices of the abusive guards and of the lever-pushers who did not quit were morally inexcusable.[66]

While lesser wrongs can also be inexcusable, they are not evil if they do no reasonably foreseeable intolerable harm. It is then not intolerable harm alone, but, "rather, that harm together with the lack of any moral excuse for it that distinguishes evil from lesser wrongs".[67]

One frequently discussed issue, as discussed by Thomas Blass,[68] is how far the Milgram experiments reveal what motivated the evils perpetrated during the Holocaust, how much blind obedience to strong authority seen in the laboratory matches what took place on the ground in Nazi Germany. There are certainly some parallels, though with some limitations. Many Germans, for whatever reason, did stand by while Jews were being rounded up, beaten, robbed of their livelihoods and then sent to their slaughter. This was evidence of blind obedience, of course made more effective by the widespread use of terror. Obedience to authority does not wholly explain why fully committed Nazis could be sadistic; other factors such as ambition, greed, and pleasure in violence, as well as virulent prejudice against Jews, also had a major contribution. However, the way that many Nazis, at least after the war and during the Nuremberg trials, tried to absolve themselves from personal responsibility for genocide, does have some similarity to the way that those who gave increasing shocks gave up their agency to the experimenter. That the shocks were given in an incremental way also parallels the evidence that a step-by-step process of destruction took place as the Nazi escalation of violence went from exclusion of Jews from jobs to exclusion of Jews from this world.[69] Finally, the world of the laboratory where the shocks took place, with the lack of ordinary emotions, does parallel the cold and heartless manner in which Jews were rounded up and shot, children and even babies were beaten to death, and how the harsh world of the concentration camp was pervaded by a pseudo-scientific veneer.

Regarding the relevance of the Stanford Prison experiment with regard to the evils of the Holocaust, I described in this and the previous chapter that Zimbardo emphasised how roles, rules, and norms can transform people's character and make ordinary people sadistic towards others. When this transformation occurs, others are perceived as anonymous with no subjectivity, what Zimbardo calls "Deindividuation". Others are also perceived as lacking ordinary humanity, becoming objectified or seen as less than human, by what he calls a process of "Dehumanisation". He sees these two processes as the core of much evil, and they can certainly be seen in many aspects of the way that Jews in particular were seen as less than human, and became objectified and dehumanised, with their subjectivity annihilated prior to being physically annihilated.

Central to many of the harmful attitudes to others is *prejudice*, the classic study of which was that of Gordon Allport, in his book *The Nature of Prejudice*, originally published in 1954.[70] As with the immediately post-war social psychologists, such as Asch and Tajfel, Allport was deeply affected by the persecution of the Jews in the war, but also by the prejudiced attitude to black citizens in the US, and how irrational notions of "race" came about to harm both sets of people.

He set out to study such prejudiced attitudes towards ethnic minorities as a psychologist, and includes considerable research data to back his arguments, while taking account of a range of factors including historical, socio-cultural, situational, and psychodynamic influences, and how they all interact. In a way still very relevant today, he defined ethnic prejudice as, "an antipathy based upon a faulty and inflexible generalisation. It may be felt or expressed. It may be directed to a group as a whole, or toward an individual because he is a member of that group".[71] He describes how when prejudice takes root in life, it can continue to grow, while its specific object is more or less immaterial. It can deeply affect the inner life as well as influence actions. It is a "complex subjective state in which *feelings* of difference play the leading part, even if the differences are imaginary".[72]

He describes how human beings slip into prejudiced attitudes easily through erroneous generalisations and hostility. Being part of an in-group opposed to an out-group, though natural to humans and integral to human survival, often lays the ground for prejudice, leading to denigration of others and gross overgeneralisation about supposed characteristics held by the other group.

As a way of ordering the massive amount of data he presents, Allport described an empirically based five-point scale of ethnic prejudice,[73] going from basic hostility at one end to extermination at the other. Violence is described as almost always an outgrowth of milder states of mind. Prejudice may begin with verbal insults, such as jokes about a minority group. Though often seen by the majority as merely harmless fun, it sets the stage for more severe outlets of prejudice. The next stage is avoidance, where people in a minority group are actively avoided by the majority group. Though no direct harm may be intended, harm is done through increasing isolation. This can be followed by active discrimination and harm to a minority, when equal opportunities for work and facilities are denied. This can be followed or accompanied by physical attacks, with property being vandalised, individuals attacked or killed, such as seen in lynchings of blacks, pogroms against Jews, and against other minorities. The final stage is mass extermination, with an attempt to liquidate an entire group of people, Native Americans, Jews, Muslims in Bosnia and in Myanmar, etc. Not all these steps will occur, but under certain circumstances, such as in Nazi Germany, there was a rapid "stepwise progression from verbal aggression to violence, from rumour to riot, from gossip to genocide".[74]

In terms of what causes prejudice, Allport cites several interlinking approaches.[75] A person acts with prejudice first of all when they perceive the object of their prejudice in a certain way, partly as a result of their own personality. The latter is formed as a result of how they were socialised in the family, school, and neighbourhood, and influenced by the existing social situation which may also be a determinant of their perceptions and misperceptions. Behind these forces lie other more remote causal influences, from the structure of their society, and long-standing economic and cultural traditions, as well as national and historical influences.

As a result of several surveys, Allport also distinguished prejudiced or intolerant from tolerant personalities.[76] The former tends to have a rigid monopolistic way of thinking, only seeing one side of a picture or an argument, with a tendency to stereotype people. While the latter tend to have more flexible, or what one could call dialogic, thinking, open to ambiguity, more able to accept ignorance and sceptical about single categories of explanation. Changing people's attitudes is of course far from easy, especially when they are embedded in long-standing historical prejudices. Allport, and subsequent research[77] has shown that increasing contact between groups suspicious of one another can help reduce prejudice, at least temporarily, but that more comprehensive educational programmes that address individual and group processes are necessary to elicit more substantial change.

Another way of understanding prejudice comes from Tajfel and Turner and their social identity theory.[78] They proposed that there are three mental processes involved in evaluating others as "us" or "them". These take place in a particular order. The *first* is categorisation. We categorise objects in order to understand them and identify them. In a similar way we categorise people in order to understand the social environment. We use social categories like German, Christian, Muslim, student, and postman because they are useful. In the *second* stage, social identification, we adopt the identity of the group we have categorised ourselves as belonging to. If, for example, you have categorised yourself as a student, you may adopt the identity of a student and begin to act in the ways you believe students act (and conform to the norms of the group). There will be an emotional significance to being identifies with a group, and self-esteem will become bound up with group membership. The *third* stage is social comparison. Once we have categorised ourselves as part of a group and have identified with that group, we then tend to compare that group with other groups. If our self-esteem is to be maintained our group needs to compare favourably with other groups.

Thus, to reduce prejudice one must understand issues of identity, both what brings people together, but also what makes them feel different from others. As I mentioned in the previous chapter, I have argued that the fear of a *loss of home*, or more fundamentally a fear of the loss of a psychic structure which provides a central core of our identity—what I have called a *psychic home*—accounts for a considerable amount of prejudiced and intolerant attitudes to strangers; that basic fears about being displaced by strangers from our precious and precarious sense of a psychic home can tear communities apart, as well as lead to discrimination against those who appear to be different.[79] Attention to such issues may be able to help to reduce tensions between different ethnic groups, but requires consistent and organised approaches, probably based upon multiple interventions.[80]

Another area of psychology research relevant to understanding the pervasiveness of extremely harmful acts concerns so-called "Bystander" behaviour, the fact that ordinary decent people may well stand by and fail to intervene when faced by obvious discrimination, abuse, and malicious action. Much of this work is well summarised by Catherine Sanderson in her recent book, *The Bystander Effect*.[81]

She covers much of the ground I have already about individual and situational factors that can lead people to conform to authority or lose their sense of personal responsibility, and thereby remain silent in the face of bad behaviour, including data from the Milgram and Stanford experiments. However, she adds a recent study looking at people's attitudes to the Milgram results.[82] Reicher and colleagues[83] found that identification with the aims of the experiment influenced attitudes to obedience, so that people may engage in or approve harmful behaviour not simply because they are absolved of responsibility, but also because they come to believe that their actions are serving a worthy purpose, such as enlarging human knowledge.

Sanderson then suggests that such an explanation can provide insight into some of the factors that led to the effectiveness of Nazi rule.

> People were not simply begrudgingly or numbly following orders; in many instances they embraced the broader social vision and mission of fascism. They identified with the dangers that Hitler was articulating, shared his muscular patriotism and nostalgia for a simpler past, embraced his hatred of outsiders, and bought into his vision of a racially pure society.[84]

Specific research on bystander inaction began in 1964 when a young woman Kitty Genovese was murdered outside her apartment building, while none of the many people who saw or heard the attack came to her assistance or called the police to help. Subsequent studies found that people are more likely to be helped in an emergency if it takes place in front of just one person; if it takes place in a larger group, each person may well wait to see if someone else will act. People's sense of control over their actions and their consequences tends to diminish the larger the group, where people can feel anonymous and hide behind their anonymity. The more ambiguous the situation, the less likely will people come to the rescue. However, in a clear emergency, people will step up and the group can be helpful.

The phenomenon when most group members privately hold one belief, but incorrectly assume that most others hold a different belief is called "*Pluralistic Ignorance*".[85] For example if a group of employees hear sexist, racist, or homophobic comments, they will tend to look to see how others respond to determine how they will react. If others appear not to be bothered, they will infer, even if wrongly, that such language is being supported or at least condoned. So, people stand by, silent, not just out of shyness or embarrassment, or fears about criticism, but because of misperception of other's motives. There also group dynamic issues, which Sanderson does not cover, with an inevitable increase of psychotic anxieties, such as a fear of fragmentation and loss of identity that often takes place in large groups, making it difficult to speak out, as I shall cover in the next chapter.

There has been some research on those who manage to *resist* bystander silence, such as during the Holocaust. One study[86] investigated the extent to which personality variables can be used to discriminate non-Jewish heroes of the Holocaust from bystanders and from a comparison group of pre-war European immigrants who left their countries of origin prior to the Second World War.

> People who risked their own lives to help Jews differed in several ways from those who did not. They scored higher on independence and perceived control, indicating that they were willing to stick with their own beliefs even if others disagreed ... They also scored higher on risk-taking ... This combination of attributes appears to have given them the confidence to show courage.[87]

Unsurprisingly, the group of helpers also showed more altruism, empathy, and social responsibility. This and other studies paint a picture of a moral rebel as, someone who is confident, independent, and altruistic, with high self-esteem and a strong sense of responsibility. One might add that if there is a community such as the French village of Le Chambon I mentioned in the previous chapter, which can promote and sustain such attributes, then there is more likelihood that individuals would be able to avoid bystander apathy and act to resist evil.

CHAPTER 3

Psychoanalysis and evil

There are three main and overlapping areas where psychoanalytic thinking has contributions to make towards understanding evil.

The *first area* concerns the nature of group processes, including how groups function and influence individual behaviour. This can help us to understand more about how individuals can lose their moral sense and their capacity to think, judge, and take personal responsibility, particularly when under the influence of a powerful ideology.

The *second area* concerns the specific nature of so-called evil characters such as psychopaths, and individual and serial murderers, and how this may also impact on our understanding of evil states of mind and evil acts.

The *third area* concerns psychoanalytic views about the nature of aggression and destructiveness and how much distorted development may influence what pushes people into violent acts; but also, what psychoanalysis has to say about the nature of evil and evil states of mind as a further contribution to making sense of genocidal acts.

The role of historical and social factors in the terrains of evil has been touched on in the introduction but will looked at in more detail in the chapter on genocide and slavery (Chapter 5), though these factors will also be touched on in this and the following chapter on philosophy and evil.

Evil and group processes

Previous chapters have examined some of the cognitive and social forces or situations which can impede individual autonomy and agency, leading to excessive conformism and sometimes violence. Psychoanalytic thinking with attention to unconscious factors offers a further and nuanced understanding of the dynamics of groups leading to a loss of the individual's sense of personal responsibility and the unleashing of powerful destructive forces. Large unstructured groups, that is, groups of more than about twenty people, tend to foster intense projective processes. Even smaller groups, and those groups with more organisation and hence more rational control, will at times unleash such projective processes. Already in 1921, in *Group Psychology and the Analysis of the Ego*,[i] Freud had grasped the kind of group forces which allow those in the group to throw off the repressions of their unconscious instincts. Freud points out that in the group setting there is a reduction of rational activity (*Denkhemmung*) and an intensification of affects, that is, of desire, and that, in a group,

> … the individual is brought under conditions which allow him to throw off the repressions of his unconscious instinctual impulses. The apparently new characteristics which he then displays are in fact the manifestations of this unconscious, in which all that is evil in the human mind is contained as a predisposition. We can find no difficulty in understanding the disappearance of conscience or of a sense of responsibility in these circumstances.[1]

Thus, the characteristic feature of a group is that once it meets, rational activity, or what Wilfred Bion called the "work group function",[2] soon dissolves; instead, the group is dominated by the activities of the unconscious, or what Freud called "primary process" activity as opposed to rational or "secondary process" activity. The former is similar to what

---

[i] The German is *Massenpsychologie*, which is more accurately crowd or mass psychology.

Bion described in a group's functioning when it gets taken over by "basic assumptions"—the feeling of timelessness, failure to recognise understanding, and absence of any process of development. Groups dominated by basic assumptions can be particularly vulnerable to being taken over by a dominating individual. Instead of there being "safety in numbers", in fact group processes can generate powerful feelings of vulnerability and dependency.

In order to understand what can happen in these situations, Freud describes how the main forces keeping the group together are the kinds of libidinal ties that exist in groups whose sexual drives are aim-inhibited, that is, identifications. He refers to identifications of the members of the group with each other and with the leader: "A group is clearly held together by a power of some kind: and to what power could this feat be better described than to Eros, which holds together everything in the world?"[3] He clarifies that he is referring to love instincts that are not directly pursuing sexual aims, but they are still powerful. He compares this process to that of hypnosis.

> Hypnosis resembles being in love in being limited to two persons, but it is based entirely on sexual impulsions that are inhibited in their aims and puts the object in the place of the ego ideal. The group multiplies this process; it agrees with hypnosis in the nature of the instincts which hold it together, and in the replacement of the ego ideal by the object; but to this it adds identification with other individuals, which was perhaps originally made possible by their having the same relation to the object.[4]

The group facilitates identification with the leader, an almost hypnotic submission to their words, and the projection of hopes and ideals onto them, with the loss of individual reality testing. The identification with a strong leader encourages the relinquishing of the individual's function, or conscience, or what Freud later called the superego. As Sandler has described, there are situations when the individual's ego (or sense of self)

> ... will totally disregard the standards and precepts of the superego, if it can gain a sufficient quantity of narcissistic support elsewhere. We see this impressive phenomenon in the striking changes of ideals, character and morality which may result from the donning

of a uniform and the feeling of identity with a group. If narcissistic support is available in sufficient quantity from an identification with the ideals of a group, or with the ideals of a leader, then the superego may be completely disregarded, and its functions taken over by the group ideals, precepts and behaviour. If these group ideals permit a direct gratification of instinctual wishes, then a complete character transformation may occur; and the extent to which the superego can be abandoned in this way is evident in the appalling atrocities committed by the Nazis before and during the last war.[5]

One can see this abandoning of conscience and ordinary decency in those groups of "ordinary men" described by Christopher Browning[6] when their ties to the group, their identification with the uniform, and loyalty to their fellows, pushed aside any misgivings about slaughtering men, women, and children in vast numbers. Stepping outside the group mores seemed beyond what was possible for the vast majority.

One can see how easy it seems to be for groups of people to perpetrate what they could not imagine was possible as individuals. Powerful feelings of supposed humiliation or injustice or hatred can be intensified and, with the addition of a charismatic leader or leadership group, can lead to atrocious acts of violence, at least by those ready to be influenced. But there must be some element of choice in those who go along with the group. It is too easy to explain away participation in group violence as the fault of the group and not that of the individuals in the group. But choice can be easily lost in the almost delusional states of mind stirred up in some groups. The distance from reality in those groups dominated by a powerful leader and/or by strong ties of group loyalty can magnify social anxiety that can reach such delusional forms. Personal identity is then "so greatly called into question that the casting of doubt on either it or its justification gives rise to manifestations of self-defensive aggression, as a result of opening of narcissistic wounds and the threat to self-image and everything invested in it. The outcome is extraordinary violence."[7]

Roger Money-Kyrle, writing about the psychology of propaganda,[8] describes attending one of Hitler's rallies, shortly after he had come to power, providing vivid detail about the various phenomena whereby a charismatic leader and their audience can become merged in a dangerous way, leading to the loss of individual identity and the emergence of violence.

Hitler was preceded by Goebbels, and both orators said the same things in the same order, but the repetitions did not bore the audience, "… but like the repetition in Ravel's *Bolero*, seemed only to increase the emotional effect".[9] He describes that the speeches themselves were not particularly impressive, but the crowd was unforgettable.

> The people seemed gradually to lose their individuality and to become fused into a not very intelligent but immensely powerful monster, which was not quite sane and therefore capable of anything … with no judgment and only a few, but very violent passions. Yet there was something mechanical about it too; for it was under the complete control of the figure on the rostrum.[10]

There was a very loud repetition of a few basic messages—about the sufferings of Germany since the previous war, rage against the Jews and Social Democrats as the sole authors of these sufferings, and then open hatred to the point of being homicidal. But then a turning towards the increasing growth and power of the Nazi party, and a passionate appeal to all Germans to unite, even if that meant dying for her.

Money-Kyrle describes how each of the elements in the speeches appealed to something already in the unconscious. For example, people are anyway ready to respond to a suggestion that they have been ill-treated; people carry an imaginary enemy within, and for that reason are often over-ready to believe in a grievance of external origin, and to overestimate any real grievances. Then, there is also a basic primitive current latent in the unconscious that believes in magical thinking, ready to project into others the cause of our sufferings. But where the Nazis were particularly effective was not to leave the crowd wallowing in self-pity and grievance but to offer them hope for an ideal future by supporting the Nazi party and—to adopt a contemporary slogan—"Make Germany great again". Hitler also stirred up the "unconscious longing for the ideal family, in which no one should be injured, and everyone should be at peace. This Paradise, however, was only for true Germans and true Nazis. Everyone outside remained a persecutor, and, therefore, an object of hate."[11] The Nazis were adept at mixing fear and hatred, creating a sort of group paranoia among many Germans.

Money-Kyrle suggests that propaganda of this sort often seems to be a method of inducing a series of temporary and induced psychoses, starting with depression, passing, via paranoia, to a state of manic bliss. The most effective propaganda appeals to fear, stirring up the sleeping bogeys of the unconscious.

> It first points out symbols of the bad parents and so raises the sleeping demons of unconscious fantasy; and then erects compensatory symbols of the good parents, heroes who are strong enough to defeat the demons, and who can restore the people's lost belief in their power to do creative work, and give them courage to face real dangers often in fact far greater than the more or less imaginary ones they were first made to fear.[12]

One can add that the Nazi rally, like other fascist and extremist large-scale meetings provides a theatrical scaffolding for merging individual identities into an idealised but unnatural unity. The military element of the Nazi rally, with the display of uniforms, flags, and salutes, adds to the pageant of sameness, and prepares the crowd to receive the message from the rostrum with a state of willing acceptance.

More recent studies of large group processes emphasise the role of intense projective processes such as projective identification, where, for example, an individual projects unwanted parts of themselves into the other person in order to get rid of uncomfortable feelings, but as a result tends to lose their sense of self or have an impoverished sense of their own identity. The receiver of such projections may experience the other's disowned feelings in a concrete way, feeling invaded or confused or stuck with unwanted anger or anxiety. Such primitive projective processes can help to account for phenomena, such as loss of identity and responsibility in group settings, as well as the way that people can end up taking roles for the group.

This is illustrated in the classic paper on the functioning of large groups by Tom Main, based upon his experience of therapeutic groups at the Cassel Hospital, a psychoanalytically based therapeutic community. He describes, for example, how certain members of a group can be unconsciously forced by the group to feel certain things and to take on specific roles. "This one may be unconsciously appointed and required as a sinner, to feel and act accordingly; that one as the giver of wisdom; others as saboteur of the work, buffoon, invalid, etc., with various degrees of personal discomfort."[13]

He also describes how in large unstructured groups, where individual boundaries are often blurred, projective processes may be widespread and can lead to baffling or chaotic situations, where people's capacity to think is paralysed, or projected into certain individuals; individuals may lose their sense of themselves, do not "feel themselves"; or when there are massive and malignant projective processes, "All may become so invaded by projections that reality testing and judgment become flawed and relations only fantastic."[14] The personality of the individual may feel invaded and full of psychotic anxiety, such as fears of fragmentation and madness. At such times there may be a strong desire to find relief by turning to a leader, who will magically ward off the dangers to the self. "This is the world of psychosis and of extreme industrial and civil strife,"[15] and one might add, of the Nazi rally described by Money-Kyrle, or indeed the more recent mob actions of those who attacked the Washington Capitol in January 2021. If one adds to group psychology the pervasive presence of a destructive ideology, such as extreme popularism or racism, one has a very toxic mixture.

Theodore Adorno in his 1951 paper *Freudian Theory and the Pattern of Fascist Propaganda* discusses how to understand the mass psychology of fascist propaganda in the light of Freud's analysis of groups. He writes that according to Freud, the problem of mass psychology is closely related to the "new type of psychological affliction so characteristic of the era which for socio-economic reasons witnesses the decline of the individual and his subsequent weaknesses",[16] resulting in the individual now yielding to powerful outside collective agencies.

Adorno comments that Freud asks what makes the masses into masses, what psychological forces result in the transformation of individuals into a mass. As outlined above, it is the bond that unites them. The fascist demagogue artificially creates the bond that Freud is looking for, that bond which integrates individuals into a mass and is of a libidinal or love nature. (One only has to look at Donald Trump's expert playing of his followers, where he appeals both to their baser instincts, but also fosters a strong bond of loyalty; his followers really do love him.)

Fascist ideology and agitation are focused on the idea of the leader, "apt to reanimate the idea of the all-powerful and threatening primal father. This is the ultimate root of the otherwise enigmatic *personalisation* of fascist propaganda, its incessant plugging of names and supposedly great men, instead of discussing objective causes."[17] The mechanism which transforms libido into the bond between leader and followers is identification, which is facilitated by the leader becoming idealised. Identification through idealisation facilitates a form of togetherness, but this is different from group solidarity based upon respect for otherness and individuality. Narcissistic identification with the leader is facilitated by the leader appearing themselves to be narcissistic, full of absolute self-confidence. There is also narcissistic gain for the followers because the fascist propaganda says that they are better than the out-group, the cause of their problems. Hatred of the other becomes a unifying factor; with Hitler the race notion acted as a negative integrating force, feeding what Freud called the instinct for destructiveness.

The French psychoanalyst Janine Chasseguet-Smirgel argues that the capability of groups of people performing atrocities is not only due to the adoption of the group's moral criteria taking over the individual's superego but is the necessary consequence of the group's *ideology*, as Sandler described when narcissistic support is available to a group in sufficient quantity from an identification with the ideals of a group, or with the ideals of a leader.[18] Nazism and other totalitarian ideologies aim at *narcissistic triumph* over supposed enemies, offering the *illusion* of some utopian idealised future for those who follow the leader, not of course to the hated outsiders who are to be ruthlessly eliminated. (One is reminded of the title of Leni Riefenstahl's propaganda film *Triumph of the Will*, which chronicled the 1934 Nazi Party Congress in Nuremberg.) The aim of the illusion "is the idealization of the Ego (the fusion of the Ideal into the Ego), and there is no idealization of the Ego without projection, so those upholding the projection have to be harassed and ruthlessly annihilated … [M]urder is … perpetrated, above all, in the name of the Ideal."[19]

Chasseguet-Smirgel has also written about the specifics of the Nazi racist ideology and its links with historical forces and primitive psychological processes.[20] She speculates that various historical forces, such as the recent unification of Germany, the consequence of the Treaty of Versailles, the fragility of the Weimar Republic, the 1929 worldwide depression, unemployment, inflation, the disunity of the social democrat and communist opposition to Nazism, all led to the actualisation of an increasingly powerful fantasy involving destruction and renewal. Hitler had already described in *Mein Kampf* a vision of a world turned arid if there were to be a victory of the Jews over other peoples of the world. She compares this to the fantasy of a "Wasteland" which T. S. Eliot described in his long poem written at about the same time.[21] From her work as an analyst with sexually perverse and borderline patients, she proposes that there is an archaic matrix of the Oedipus complex, with a primary wish,

> immediate and inborn, to strip the mother's body of its contents in order to regain possession of the place one occupied at birth. All obstacles, which after birth, make access to the mother's body impossible to achieve have to be removed. These obstacles are identified with reality and are represented by the father ... Ridding oneself of paternal obstacles by emptying the maternal body, fighting against reality and thought, form a single identical wish: that of returning to a world without organization, to primeval chaos.[22]

I would add that this would be a world where subjectivity is annihilated.

She applies this notion of an archaic matrix of the Oedipus complex to the Nazi racist doctrines. Rather than seeing those doctrines as a rationalisation of anti-Semitism, she suggests that "anti-Semitism follows in the wake of Hitler's promise that Aryans are to rule the world for a thousand years (a renewal of the promise made to God's chosen people in the Apocalypse). It is that promise which sets in motion the machine of destruction."[23] She suggests that the promise rests upon the fantasy of the archaic matrix, in that the subject's body (the body of the German people, Aryans) is to become one with the body of the mother (the German homeland, *Heimat*) once all obstacles have been swept away.

> Racist ideology is based upon a symbiosis between the subject and Mother Nature ... The body of the nation must be purified. The German people ... must become a *single body* in order to be able to unite with Mother Nature (Blood and Soil) ... But in order to form a single body, its constituent cells must be identical, purified of all foreign elements liable to impair its homogeneity.[24]

The translation of the German nation into a single body made of identical cells was adopted literally, in order to create a "community of blood" (*Blutgemeinschaft*). There was also a pseudo-scientific racial theory backing the ideology, a form of biomedical ideology or fantasy world of scientific racism, where the so-called German race was at risk of becoming weakened by contaminants. Those deemed unable to join the pure community were to be systematically and "scientifically" eliminated; it began with the euthanasia of the disabled and mentally ill and soon escalated to anyone thought unable to join this primitive blood community, or whose blood would contaminate the purity of the Aryan race, Jews predominantly.

The Nazi ideology, or what I will call the "Nazi Imaginary" in Chapter 5, not only contained archaic fantasies concerning blood and purity, but also held put the promise of an absolute bliss and hope of a fusion with the mother and a return to a primary narcissistic state of being, where the superego, or conscience, is eliminated, a form of idealism which became relentless in its practice.

In short, she proposes that the wish of the subject to merge with the mother and the eradication of all obstacles between them and her is central to the Nazi ideology of Blood and Soil. Historical and social factors alone do not capture the essence of the Nazi phenomenon and its elemental power over the ordinary German.

Werner Bohleber also examines how unconscious fantasies of purity, unity, and violence have a significant contribution to the presence of anti-Semitism. He points out that the propensity for unconscious desires to attach themselves with such ease to national and ethnic ideologies is notably facilitated by notions about home and the body as the containers of collective and individual identity.[25] Thus, the Third Reich used the notion of fatherland or mother country to appeal to Germans' wish for an irrational and exclusive racial identity. That regime also used, as Chasseguet-Smirgel described, archaic fantasies about the purity of German bodies and the German body politic, which was seen to be threatened with "contamination" and or "pollution" by "lower" races, such as Jews and Slavs.

In further studies, Bohleber describes how psychoanalysis has arrived at important insights into the links between unconscious fantasies, destructive ideology, and malignant narcissism. He has used such findings to look at the nature of terrorism and fundamentalism, where "evil is externalized through projection, as demonstrated most clearly in fundamentalism's xenophobia and anti-Semitism: the failure of one's own group and [irrationally] of Muslim societies as a whole is blamed on a plot of subversive foreigners, usually consisting of Westerners and Jews".[26] One can see here how extremist groups can appropriate evil thinking in order to guide their actions.

Robert Jay Lifton[27] has described how the Nazi excesses were indicative of a particular kind of "apocalyptic violence", now visible in terrorists and even at times in the West's reactions to terrorist risks. Apocalyptic violence, whatever its origins in feelings of past humiliation or social disadvantage, involves extreme fantasies of spiritual renewal through killing. Hitler's followers

> sought to destroy much of what they saw as a racially polluted world by means of a vast biological purification program. Despite being murderously anti-Jewish and significantly anti-Christian as well, the Nazis drew upon what was most apocalyptic in both of those traditions. The Nazis came to epitomize the apocalyptic principle of *killing to heal*, of destroying vast numbers of human beings as therapy for the world.[28]

The idea of apocalyptic martyrdom, now so visible in ISIS and other terrorist developments, "intensifies the ordeal of the killer as well as his claim to spiritual renewal, while dramatizing his death as transcending those of his victims. The martyr brings his own being—the sacrifice of his own life—into the dynamic of world destruction and recreation, thus exemplifying that death-and-rebirth process."[29]

Unfortunately, the West, at least in the years immediately following the 9/11 slaughter, also responded with apocalyptic logic, maintaining that the forces of evil, the so-called "axis of evil", would be wiped out by the forces of democracy, cleansing the world of the extremists. In the name of destroying evil, each side sought to destroy the other. This kind of potentially very dangerous thinking continues to be visible today, for example in current relations with the North Korean dictatorship.

Christopher Bollas[30] describes in detail what he calls the "fascist state of mind", visible not only in genocidal acts but potentially in all of us. Whatever the social factors that might lead to genocide, the core element in the fascist state of mind is "the presence of an ideology that maintains its certainty through the operation of specific mental mechanisms aimed at eliminating all opposition". In this frame of mind, doubt, uncertainty, and self-enquiry are weaknesses and must be expelled. Language also becomes distorted in its uses, in ways already described vividly by George Orwell, for example in his essay "Politics and the English Language", where he shows how language can corrupt thought by "making lies sound truthful and murder respectable, and to give an appearance of solidity to pure wind".[31]

Bollas gives a detailed picture of the dynamics of how the fascist ideology becomes so destructive, as the intolerance of uncertainty and destruction of opposition creates a moral void.

> At this point the subject must find a victim to contain that void, and now a state of mind becomes an act of violence. On the verge of its own moral vacuum, the mind splits off this dead core self and projects it into a victim henceforth identified with the moral void … As contact with the moral void is lost through projective identification into a victim, and the victim now exterminated, the profoundly destructive processes involved are further denied by a form of delusional narcissism … As the qualities of the other are destroyed via the annihilation of the other, a delusional grandiosity forms in the Fascistically stated mind.[32]

One can thus see in the accounts from Chasseguet-Smirgel, Lifton, and Bollas how apocalyptic thinking in its various guises creates extreme forms of intolerance, offering a perverse moral universe, where the awareness of difference and subjectivity is destroyed. While intolerance may not reach the extremes perpetrated by the Nazi and communist regimes, the way that intolerant states of mind can arise and be sustained in groups, particularly when encouraged by a populist leader, is similar.

In my own work on the nature of intolerance, I have suggested that intolerance and tolerance inevitably go together; there is a dynamic between them.[33] One needs to provide a framework and willing atmosphere in which the conflict between them can be examined, with no perfect resolution. The resolution in a sense is the *processing* of the dynamic. I have suggested that a fundamental distinction can be made between "*subject* and *object* tolerance". By subject tolerance, I mean that one respects the other and others as subjects *of* their experience, with agency and the capacity for independent judgment. Those groups or communities predominantly organised around subject tolerance can provide a home for otherness. This contrasts with object tolerance, when the other and others are seen as mere objects to be treated as subject *to* those in power or in authority. Those that are merely tolerated as objects may be confined to a ghetto or walled off from society in less visible ways, for example, by means of discriminating practices, but their object status remains. The degree to which others are treated as subjects will vary, providing a complex interplay between subject and object tolerance. I suspect that evil occurs or is more disposed to occur when there is an extreme breakdown of subject tolerance, for example when destructive forces are predominant in groups and the harm and respect principles are attacked.

Tolerance thus requires a movement from object to subject tolerance. This form of tolerance requires a tolerant, imaginative internal space, and it also implies that one respects the other and others as subjects of their experience, with agency and capacity for independent judgment. Seeing the other as a subject, being open to otherness, requires some self-reflection, where otherness in oneself is seen as part and parcel of being human. Tolerance also requires acts of reflective judgment, and a special kind of enlarged mentality, where one takes account of the views and judgment of others, putting oneself in the position of others in the hope of coming to an agreement. This is a form of common human understanding, requiring thought and imagination. There needs to be an obligation to protect free and open communication, both by enabling practices of tolerance, but also by paying attention to how intolerance can undermine free public communication. This involves a fundamental change in attitude of citizens towards their fellows, an act of positive imagination. One could characterise this shift as providing what I have described as a "home for otherness". Tolerance is not indifference; it is a much more active process involving the burden for those who hold different world views to make the effort to respect, if not fully understand, other world views.

Herbert Rosenfeld describes a form of fascist type organisation in the psychic structure of narcissistic patients which adds to understanding of intolerant and destructive group processes. Destructive narcissism occurs in those who have contempt for others, particularly when they encounter somebody loving, understanding, and kind; they put all their energies into remaining sadistically strong, regarding any love in themselves as weakness, and they often show prolonged resistance to treatment.[34] He describes a form of "gang" organisation in the narcissistic subject that can be seen in individuals, and I would suggest also in groups dominated by a narcissistic leader.

> The destructive narcissism of these patients appears often highly organized, as if one were dealing with a powerful gang dominated by a leader, who controls all the members of the gang to see that they support one another in making the criminal destructive work more effective and powerful. However, the narcissistic organization not only increases the strength of the destructive narcissism, but it has a defensive purpose to keep itself in power and so maintain the *status quo*. The main aim seems to be to prevent the weakening of the organization and to control the members of the gang so that they will not desert the destructive organization and join the positive parts of the self or betray the secrets of the gang to the police, the protecting superego … This narcissistic organization is in my experience not primarily directed against guilt and anxiety but seems to have the purpose of maintaining the idealization and superior power of the destructive narcissism. To change, to receive help, implies weakness and is experienced as wrong or as failure by the destructive narcissistic organization which provides the patient with his sense of superiority.[35]

One cannot of course underestimate the trauma of being on the receiving end of persistent intolerant regimes, where obedience to a destructively narcissistic leader or group dominates. The Czech psychoanalyst Michael Sebek, having experienced at first hand living through the traumas of a communist regime, has written about the nature of the psychological processes involved in totalitarian regimes, emphasising the place of what he calls the "totalitarian object" that can come to dominate individuals in a repressive society, but may also function in post-totalitarian regimes as well as at times in more democratic societies. This is a repressive and intrusive form of psychic structure that becomes internalised in a society that demands compliance and obedience, where there is low tolerance for the difference of others, stressing unity and sameness. In addition,

> Totalitarian objects (external and internal) may also bring some safety to immature persons who like to merge with a strong authority in order to get a feeling of importance and wholeness. The idealization of totalitarian objects may be an important device for saving objects from destruction and using the process of splitting to attain some psychic balance.[36]

There is always a risk that the totalitarian object may take over the individual and the group's functioning, creating a rigid intolerance towards anything outside the narrow functioning prescribed as acceptable. This is visible not only in a totalitarian society but also in pockets of other forms of society, such as with radicalised youth, or any extreme political organisation that demands compliance, obedience coupled with an identification with charismatic leadership. When the identity of the individual or the group is in jeopardy, the tendency is to close ranks against that which is perceived as a threat. It is at this point that the individual and the group become most vulnerable to the charismatic leader who promises an illusion of power and security.

Jonathan Sklar addresses some of the psychodynamic issues present in evil regimes in the past and present, looking at how the denial of past atrocities continues to be present with the return of extreme nationalism and totalitarian parties in Europe, as well as with the disturbing rise of white supremacists and conspiracy theorists in the US and elsewhere. Opposing totalitarian thinking with its language of control, inflexibility, and deceit, "Psychoanalysis offers a path towards truth and reconciliation, and away from paranoid discourses towards alterity. The ability to tolerate the other, without allowing domination and at the same time as recognizing complexity, is the modern heritage of psychoanalysis."[37]

Apocalyptic and racist ideologies are by their nature consumed with prejudice. I have already discussed Allport's general observations about prejudice. He also tackles the psychodynamics of racial or ethnic prejudice, involving several elements—frustration, aggression, and hatred, anxiety, sex, and guilt, and projection.[38] He points out that anti-Semitism and other forms of prejudice tend to arise in periods of widespread frustration and insecurity attendant upon major social change, leading to an increase in group hostility and aggression and with a tendency to try to find scapegoats to blame for difficulties. Accompanying such often unconscious processes, aggression can easily turn into hatred towards out-groups, those perceived as different. It is easier to hate groups of people than individuals, as one does not need to test our unfavourable stereotype against reality. Anxiety about economic security and loss of status and esteem as well as fear of humiliation may fuel prejudice. While deep and irrational sexual anxieties may also add fuel to the flames of prejudice. Thus, in Nazi Germany

> It was common to accuse the Jews of gross sexual immorality. They are said to be given to overindulgence, rape, perversion. Hitler, whose own sex life was far from normal, contrived repeatedly to accuse the Jews of perversion, of having syphilis, and of other disorders suspiciously akin to Hitler's own phobias.[39]

Some of the ways that people handle guilt feelings are benign, but some ways unavoidably lead to prejudice and all to some extent involve projective mechanisms. This happens with the denial of personal guilt, discrediting anyone with a conscience as a troublemaker, assigning a hated person or group as the source of all badness, and projection of guilt feelings into others in order to evade guilt in oneself.

Such processes alone cannot explain prejudice. Allport adds to the mix the influential roles of cultural tradition, social norms, childhood upbringing and the parental model, and sheer ignorance of group differences.

John Steiner defines the basic mechanism of prejudice as the splitting off and projecting of undesirable aspects of one's self and of one's objects.

> Free of flaws, the ideal couple can enjoy superiority and solidarity while the recipient of the projections becomes the flawed and unacceptable object, often treated as if he is not fully human. In this way, the prejudice can sustain an idealization, but if the idealized object fails to live up to expectations, the idealization may collapse and the now degraded, formerly ideal, object becomes unacceptable and is treated with prejudice. Indeed, the

mechanism underlying prejudice is fundamental to the need to sustain idealized objects and is fundamental to the hatred of the idealized objects when they disappoint.[40]

Referring to Rosenfeld's concept of destructive narcissism and the internal gang structure I have already outlined, he considers that most, if not all, instances of prejudice involve complex organisation of this type.

> Typically, a difference between individuals such as those based on race, gender, religion, or age, is used to characterize a group to label it as a suitable container for the projection of unwanted characteristics. Because the unwanted elements are hated, the group in turn is hated and attempts are made to exclude it, to humiliate it, and, eventually, to annihilate it. At the same time, the persecutors can gain an idealized identity by getting rid of unwanted elements, as if to say, "We are pure; we are not like them" and to maintain the system a narcissistic organisation creates a gang-like structure that ensures that the members conform. The slogan, "*Ein Volk, ein Reich, ein Führer*" illustrates the unifying function of the organisation.[41]

Henri Parens, in studies of child development and styles of parenting, distinguishes between benign and malignant prejudice,[42] based upon early childhood experiences. A certain amount of prejudice or fear and suspicion of strangers is part of normal development, as is a natural ambivalence towards loved objects, as well as a very early ability to distinguish between the familiar and unfamiliar, as I have already covered in the previous chapter. This is what Parens calls benign prejudice. But when there is trauma, when there is abuse or high levels of conflict, and this can include the influence of group and societal factors, benign prejudice may turn into hateful malignant prejudice, the sort one sees in ethnic conflicts.

Evil characters

As I mentioned in the introduction, Roy Baumeister focuses on trying to understand the actions and motives of those who intentionally harm others, using a broad, inclusive definition of human evil as "intentional interpersonal harm".[43] His aim is not only to explore what makes criminals commit major crimes, but how much this can enlighten us about how ordinary people can also commit evil acts. From his survey of depictions of evil, he suggests that the long-standing image of evil is a composite of a number of elements—the intentional infliction of harm, which is often done gratuitously and with the pleasure of inflicting pain; an attack on the innocent and good where the victim or victims are seen as the enemy or outside the group; it represents the antithesis of order, peace, and stability; and evil perpetrators, particularly criminal psychopaths with little empathy for others, are often highly egotistical and have poor self-control. Focusing mainly on the motivations of the perpetrator, he points out that they often do not regard their actions as evil, and they find rationalisations to explain their crimes, and so evil flourishes in the gap between the perspective of perpetrator and victim;[44] or one could say that there is no intersubjective relationship in evil actions.

Psychopaths cross a personal and moral boundary, and have great difficulty in grasping moral rules, those which are usually organised by about the age of three, though as I have discussed, there is evidence that even babies usually have a basic moral sense. There have been various psychoanalytically based attempts at understanding this and other aspects of the criminal mind. Arthur Hyatt-Williams notably brought a psychoanalytic approach into the understanding of the criminal mind through therapeutic work with murderers and other criminals at Wormwood Scrubs prison for some twenty years. He described a theory of the "death constellation" to account for murderous actions. In the group of prisoners he studied, he uncovered what he termed a kind of intrapsychic organisation involving a constellation of fantasies, dreams, thoughts, impulses, and ruminations to do with killing, annihilating, and obliterating. The factors that activated this configuration were varied but usually involved a connection to a situation to which the killer was especially sensitive, a sort of Achilles heel. For example,

> Many of the prisoners serving life sentences had experienced events ranging from severe exposure—to bombing and seeing dead, dying, and grossly mutilated people—to much cruelty. Also,

they tended to do actively what they had once been forced to suffer passively. In one instance the baby boy battered by his father grew into a father-killing man. His victim was not his own father.[45]

The latter prisoner acted in panic and fear of his own death, but his reaction was potentiated by anger and revenge displaced upon somebody standing in place of his cruel father. Such a situation seemed to Hyatt-Williams evidence that murderousness was an evacuation of an indigestible fear of death. That is, evil impulses and acts can be a means to get rid of unwanted or indigestible parts of the self.

From the psychoanalytic viewpoint, murderous thoughts and fantasies of various kinds are ubiquitous, but the transformation from a murderous thought to a murderous deed requires certain circumstances to be present. Hyatt-Williams describes how that transformation is complex and involves both intrapsychic and interpersonal factors, including the collapse of the capacity to symbolise, the persistence of frequent and intense murderous fantasies and dreams, an inability to sustain mourning for the victims of the murders committed in fantasy, the pervasiveness of arrogance and narcissism in the offender so that victims are seen as subhuman or in part object terms, avoidance of depressive position feelings, and rapid shifts towards paranoid-schizoid thinking, as well as social environmental factors such as availability of a murderous authority figure with whom to identify, credibility of the deed of murder, ready availability of a weapon, and witnessing of killings as a source of identification with the perpetrator.[46]

The therapeutic problem is to

> bring the life-death polarity back into balance after it had been tilted toward death by one or more traumatic experiences to do with death. The relish of death was found to be more difficult to treat than the fear of death. After a traumatic experience involving the sight or threat of death, the intrapsychic situation usually oscillates between a kind of excited preoccupation with the experience—and fears of becoming both the victim and the agent of death—and a wish to become that agent.[47]

One may wonder how much this dynamic of the fear of and attraction to death in a terrain of evil may be a factor in how people become caught up in killing, becoming agents of death and destruction, where the death constellation predominates.

Some of the murderers Hyatt-Willams treated were able to express remorse for their offence, if they were able to work thorough the murderous thoughts and feelings associated with the death constellation instead of evacuating the fear of death as something undigestible. But many killers with a death constellation are not able to mourn, however much they may wish that they had not killed. "Detoxification" of the death constellation does require some capacity to mourn. Those who developed psychosomatic symptoms during therapeutic work were more able to do so than those who developed hypochondriacal symptoms, as the former was evidence of some identification with the victim, while the latter response was more about just feeling persecuted by having to process their murderousness.

Sometimes, however, even the mourning process for a past murderous act can be life-threatening. This was revealed while I was undertaking family therapy some years ago under Hyatt-William's supervision.[48] The two children of the family had presented with challenging and sexualised behaviour as adolescents and were threatened with exclusion from school as a result. They had experienced a very traumatic early life, witnessing the murder of their mother by their father. They were then raised by relatives who found their behaviour increasingly difficult to manage, and hence came for help. Death still obsessed the children and became confused with sexuality. There was a preoccupation with sadist pornography and images of death and dying. The boy even had a box of objects kept under his bed which he called "the coffin".

As we worked with the children and their step-parents, the situation did begin to improve, but just as the point that we began to talk about the murder itself rather than current issues, the stepmother suddenly suffered an acute life-threatening illness, causing the family to opt out of treatment. It was as if the life-link, associated with the mother, had been attacked, or the stepmother was unconsciously put in the position of the murdered mother. The murderous anti-life dynamic of the original murder became repeated in the family relationships.

Reluctance to face past horrors can then be accounted for in part by a fear of breakdown and a repetition of some deathly occurrence, though such fears of course do not justify denial of the past.

Christopher Bollas has described a "structure of evil" from a psychoanalytical perspective, with a particular focus on the causative role of trauma, using the extreme disturbance of the serial killer in order to illuminate the nature of evil acts and what such knowledge reveals about the human mind in general. Many serial killers experienced traumatic histories, such as severe physical and/or sexual abuse or extreme parental rejection, though such trauma is of course not enough to explain how the killers then transform such traumatic experiences into acts of killing.

Bollas described how the serial killer has in some way killed off their own sense of self; underlying their lack of empathy for the humanity of their victims is a logic, whereby they "go on 'living' by transforming other selves into similarly killed ones, establishing a companionship of the dead, as Masters concluded in his biography of Nilsen. In place of a once-live self, a new being emerges, identified with the killing of what is good, the destruction of trust, love, and reparation."[49]

The passionless act of killing undertaken by many serial killers, unlike murders driven by rage, are more like acts of genocidal killing, with the lack of emotional links to the victims. The

> genocidal person identifies not with the passionate act of murder, but with the moral vacuum in which the killing occurs, a meaningless, horrifying wasteful act. Carrying within himself this sense of horrifying waste, the killer finds a victim who will die his death, someone who will receive senseless blows.[50]

For Bollas, "Evil, considered as a structure, points to a complex reorganization of trauma, in which the subject recollects the loss of love and the birth of hate by putting subsequent others through the unconscious terms of a malevolent extinction of the self,"[51] or what I have termed the annihilation of the human subject.

For Bollas, evil is a signifier which we attach to any intention or action that expresses a specific structure that, wittingly or not, is undertaken by at least two people, and is not just limited to the psychology of the serial killer. It involves a series of steps, from the evil one presenting themselves as good, a kind of reversal of ordinary values and expectations, the creation of a false potential space for the recipient to receive the "good" offer, the facilitation of a malignant dependence because of the victim taking up this offer, and then a shocking betrayal, usually with extreme violence, which produces a state of catastrophic shock in the victim. The consequence of the latter is a radical infantilisation when the victim's adult self is annihilated, and the victim then experiences a psychic death, with or without physical death.[52]

Perhaps these sorts of phenomena seen in serial killers have direct application to other terrains of evil, such as during genocide, when a reversal of values, catastrophic shock at the action of perpetrators who may well come from the victims' own culture or community, and of course the use of sudden and extreme violence which wipes out the victims' psychological defences and produces a radical sense of hopelessness and helplessness, which adds to the vicious cycle of violence.

Related to Bollas's analysis of evil, the psychoanalyst Sue Grand views the nucleus of evil as catastrophic loneliness linked to what she describes as "malignant trauma". As she describes,

> Most trauma survivors do not become perpetrators. But most perpetrators have a history of malignant trauma, that is, an experience of psychic or physical torture, or both, inflicted by another. I propose that this traumatic history finds a singular articulation in the interpersonal and intrapsychic operations of evil.[53]

At the heart of those subject to malignant trauma there is a deep and unspeakable inner emptiness, a void, or an area of subjective deadness linked to their experience of the annihilation of their subjectivity, what Grand calls the "no-self". This notion is somewhat like that of Alford's notion of the key role of the unbearable feeling of dread in understanding evil acts, mentioned in the introduction. Through perpetration of a violent act, "[T]he survivor who becomes a perpetrator attempts to share his no-self by evacuating it into his victim."[54] In the moment of torture or killing or abuse, the perpetrator is both evacuating nothingness while also looking for some way to come alive, or as a way of registering the fact of their non-existence, the absence of their human subjectivity. The perpetrator may become addicted to repeating evil acts in order to manage an inner void; indeed, there is often a strong pull towards experiencing the void for that reason.

At the same time, they may often try to escape from any feelings of accountability for their crimes and do everything in their power to forget their responsibility for them. "[T]he disavowal of evil and the perpetration of evil are not separate variables representing surface and depth. Rather they are a singular manifestation of traumatic memory; together they *are* the deep structure of evil."[55] I presume that a failure to take responsibility reflects a general tendency to evacuate rather than contain painful emotional states.

Understanding this kind of evil dynamic does not justify evil acts, nor does it imply that one can treat all perpetrators, but it helps to see the kind of complex dynamics involved in such acts; they are not as totally incomprehensible as they can appear on the surface.

This dynamic may also help us to understand at least part of what happened to the "ordinary men" of the killing unit Reserve Police Battalion 101, described by Christopher Browning, after their first experience of killing, which they often found deeply disturbing. That initiation into killing became a malignant trauma, which, for the majority who actively participated, then became a source of further killings. This dynamic can also be seen in other wartime contexts, as described in the introduction.

Grand also points out how within human culture, the truth of evil seems to be in a continuous state of appearance and disappearance; there is a constant oscillation between the discovery of evil and its disavowal or denial. There is a frequent tendency to act as if nothing has happened, a pretence that crimes have not been committed, or genocides remain covered up as if nothing ever really happened.[56] She considers that the interdependence of malevolence and obscurity is an inevitability wherever evil originates in trauma survival, and she names it as "malignant dissociative contagion".[57] This is more than just a collusive obliteration of evil's presence, with the use of emotional numbing, concealment, and denial, but it is also characterised by attempts to know and recognise and stand up for what happened; knowing and not-knowing are always present in these situations.

This sort of dynamic can be seen clearly with child abuse, either when trying to understand whether it occurred, or when treating those who have been abused. The act of abuse involves a breakdown in the safety net around a child, within or outside the home; there is a fundamental gap in the child's holding environment, leading to the child suffering mental as well as physical pain. Leonard Shengold has described this as a form of "soul murder",[58] or what I would describe as an attempt to annihilate human subjectivity, and with it the child's reality sense and ownership of their own history. The child, faced with the abuser's denials of what has happened, can be torn between knowledge of what has taken place and a wish to forget the pain involved, that is, they are in the middle of the dynamic of knowing and not-knowing which Grand has described as the mark of evil.

In my own work with the psychoanalysis of those who have been sexually abused, the issue of knowing and not-knowing can come into the analysis in an intense way at some point, when something unbearable, a terrible feeling or a very painful memory, has to be tolerated. Not infrequently, the issue of abuse arrives in the analysis when the patient makes a particular kind of emotional impact on the analyst, which requires the analyst to "bear the unbearable", and thus help the patient to also manage very painful experiences. It would be too simplistic to describe the situation as being one in which the analyst becomes like the abuser in the transference; though not untrue in some ways, it is too gross a description of what takes place. Rather, the analyst often proves to be a disappointment or even a failure; there is a breakdown of the usual trusting relationship; something important may be missed. The reasonably empathic atmosphere may suddenly deteriorate, with the ready creation of misunderstandings, which can leave the analyst feeling as if they had somehow mistreated the patient. The abused adult, once on the receiving end of a malevolent perpetrator, will recreate an absent parenting figure, the parent who could not tolerate the child's pain and vulnerability, and who has left the child with a sense that the early environment has fundamentally failed them, and that there was, and remains, a kind of breach, or gap, in the parenting experience. An unbridgeable gulf may suddenly appear in the present between analyst and patient, with either party tempted to deal with it by precipitate action, such as termination of the analysis; there is an oscillation between facing the abuse and not wanting to know about it. Tolerating these intense moments of being, when the sense of parental failure (real or fantasied) may become repeated in the transference, and then linking this experience to the patient's past traumatic experiences, is an important part of the working through of the past trauma, converting this from malignant trauma to one that can be thought about and metabolised.

Being in the analytic session with the traumatised patient involves both being a "witness" to past trauma and being available to help the patient make sense of their past. Witnessing as an analytic function, "refers to the analyst as beholder, grasping and respecting both the patient's meanings and the meaningfulness of those meanings from a position of separated otherness".[59] Witnessing trauma involves a particular kind of listening activity, which challenges the analyst as listener in various ways, such as I have described with abused patients. It is also important for the analyst to maintain an open position with respect to what they are hearing, trying to avoid the dangers of just accepting everything they hear as literal truth, while also respecting the reality of the trauma. Working with Holocaust survivors or their descendants involves similar dynamics.

A seminal psychoanalytic work on issues concerned with witnessing the Holocaust is that of Shoshana Felman and Dori Laub's book *Testimony*.[60] Laub describes how in massive trauma, the observing and recording mechanisms of the mind may be temporarily knocked out. While historical evidence for the reality of an extreme traumatic event such as experienced by Holocaust survivors may be abundant, the trauma as a known event to the survivor, rather than just an overwhelming shock, has not been truly witnessed, not yet metabolised. The emergence of a narrative with someone such as an analyst who can listen and hear the survivor's experiences provides the possibility of digesting them; until then, the trauma remains undigested and the loss of representation that constitutes the traumatic experience will remain, like a gap or a hole or an absence.

The Holocaust as an extreme event challenges our usual understanding of the past, how we remember it and keep it alive or not, and how we represent it and the victims' experiences. The challenge of such extreme events is to ask how it is possible to work through what happened, and to wonder whether it is ever possible, or even desirable, to come to terms with those events. The Holocaust, and indeed any of the genocidal events of our times, challenge our views about history, the past, and our capacity to remember.

The nature of evil

Freud's views about the nature of evil provide the essential core of the psychoanalytical approach to understanding terrains of evil. In his 1915 paper, "Thoughts for the Times on War and Death", Freud writes, in the opening section about the disillusionment of the war then underway, that there is no such thing as eradicating evil.[61] Psychoanalytical investigation shows that the deepest essence of human nature consists of elementary drives which are similar in everyone and aim at the satisfaction of certain primal needs. Freud does not have the simplistic notion that we are all born evil or bad, on the contrary there is a basic duality in his thinking.

> These impulses in themselves are neither good nor bad. We classify them and their expressions in that way, according to their relation to the needs and demands of the human community. It must be granted that all the impulses which society condemns as evil—let us take as representative the selfish and cruel ones—are of this primitive kind.[62]

He makes the point that these primitive impulses have to undergo a lengthy process of development before they are allowed to become active in the adult. They are inhibited, directed towards other aims and fields, become commingled with their objects, or change their content, such as egoism turning into altruism, or cruelty into pity. The latter process is facilitated by the fact that some drives occur from the beginning in pairs of opposites—accounting for "ambivalence of feeling".[63] The point is that we cannot eradicate this basic *ambivalence*. Affirmation and negation are inseparable in the mind.[64] We are not innately good or bad, but we have innate drives that can be called good or bad depending on the outcome of their subsequent development.

In his 1930 book *Civilization and Its Discontents*, Freud's thinking about the role and nature of drives changes, though his emphasis on the psyche's basic ambivalence does not. Two of the main threads in the book concern people's quest for happiness in society and in themselves, and how on the other hand civilised society is perpetually threatened with disintegration due to people's primary mutual hostility towards one another. There are forces uniting people but also driving them apart.

In his earlier paper, "'Civilized' Sexual Morality and Modern Nervous Illness",[65] he had argued that civilisation is built up on the suppression of instincts. The renunciation of the fulfilment of sexual instincts has been a progressive one, from the free exercise of sexuality to its more legitimate and ordered form. The price of having to renounce the sexual instincts in the name of civilisation can be considerable; suppression of the instincts is seen as a significant cause of mental illness and suffering; hence, of personal unhappiness. However, by the time of *Civilization and Its Discontents* Freud had a much more complex view of the causes of our unhappiness. Our inherent bisexuality, which can usually not be fulfilled and the innate presence of our aggressiveness, means that our sexual life is inevitably full of conflict and a sense of guilt; any search for human love and lasting human happiness must take account of these basic facts of our psychic life.

The original title for his book was *Das Ungluck in der Kultur*, or *Unhappiness in Civilization*, and indeed the text contains a subtle and extensive examination of the ways that mankind strives to gain happiness and keep suffering or misery away. Of course, Freud was something of a pessimist. Rather like Schopenhauer, he seemed to see the world as a source of suffering, with life inherently unhappy. Such happiness as was attainable was elusive or even an illusion. This vision is very much the inheritance of the Romantic movement, with its overturning of the Enlightenment's optimistic dominance of the life of reason in determining man's state of mind and place in society. Romanticism transformed the Enlightenment optimism about the power of human reason to achieve answers about life into something more like our own more tentative view of the limits of human reason. Indeed, one could say that the Romantics, such as the poets Keats and Shelley, created new forms of despair, linking happiness and misery inextricably. They, like Baudelaire, created pictures of the dark delights of suffering, which certainly has Christian echoes, but invokes a new form of feeling, one to which we are heirs.

Freud also famously stated in *Studies on Hysteria* that, "Much will be gained if we succeed in transforming your hysterical misery into common unhappiness. With a mental life that has been restored to health you will be better armed against that unhappiness."[66] One may wonder what exactly is hysterical as opposed to ordinary misery, but one can say in this view that the task of analysis is to help the patient to move from being stuck with abnormal amounts of misery into a position of being able to bear the essentially unhappy human condition.

Freud's arguments in *Civilization and Its Discontents* about the place of human happiness and misery depend upon certain complex assumptions about what makes us happy, which can provide the basis for such a deep psychoanalytic contribution to the understanding of the nature of happiness. In his paper "'Civilized' Sexual Morality and Modern Nervous Illness" he had an optimistic notion about the possibilities of achieving human happiness. He maintained that civilisation represses sexuality, and this makes us unhappy, leading to neurosis or perversion. Potentially healthy and socially viable sexual drives are transformed by civilised morality, such as the demands of a poor marriage, or of sexual abstinence, into culturally useless nervous illness. Sex here is seen as essentially beneficial and freeing it up would make us happier, a theme taken up later by Herbert Marcuse in his book *Eros and Civilization*.[67] Marcuse put forward the idea of a radical transformation of society where sexuality, or the pleasure principle, would be liberated from the dictatorship of the reality or performance principle, and offer people freedom. But in *Civilization and Its Discontents*, sexuality itself, which is now seen as necessarily incorporating aggression, is the cause of unhappiness.

After looking at the various ways that mankind tried to become happy, much of the rest of *Civilization and Its Discontents* examines the sources of suffering, in particular those caused by the demands of civilisation on the individual, who must give up a certain amount of individual freedom for the sake of the wider community. Civilised man (*Kulturmensch*) has exchanged a portion of his possibilities of happiness for a portion of security.[68] The need for such a "social contract" comes from the fact that man is inherently aggressive as part of his make-up, and that this aggression needs to be inhibited if people are to live with one another in a reasonable fashion. For Freud, in a list of mankind's frailties that was soon to be enacted in Germany and Freud's Austria, men are:

> ... not gentle creatures who want to be loved, and who at the most can defend themselves if they are attacked; they are, on the contrary, creatures among whose instinctual endowments is to be reckoned a

powerful share of aggressiveness. As a result, their neighbour is for them not only a potential helper or sexual object, but also someone who tempts them to satisfy their aggressiveness on him, to exploit his capacity for work without compensation, to use him sexually without his consent, to seize his possessions, to humiliate him, to cause him pain, to torture and to kill him.[69]

Neurosis is the price we pay for having to curb our drives in the service of cultural ideals. While sexuality must be curbed and hence its importance as a source of happiness reduced by the demands of civilisation, as indeed he argued in his earlier work on civilised sexual morality, what he adds here is that sexuality itself, with its innate bisexuality and the coexistence of aggression adds to the sources of frustration and suffering. Our innate bisexuality means that we cannot generally satisfy both male and female wishes, and our innate aggression affects the quality of our love relationships, introducing for example sadistic elements.

But it is also the quality of our object relationships that creates dilemmas, in that in the process of civilisation we internalise aggression. "Civilization, therefore, obtains mastery over the individual's dangerous desire for aggression by weakening and disarming it and by setting up an agency within him [the superego] to watch over it, like a garrison in a conquered city."[70] The sense of guilt produced once the superego has formed is what Freud calls the most important problem in the development of civilisation; it is the price we pay for our advance in culture and is responsible for a loss of happiness. Without conscience, there is no morality and no control over evil impulses as he described is possible in groups.

One could add that much psychoanalytic treatment is focused on dealing with the effects of an overly harsh superego, both by tackling its effects within the transference and on external relationships. In this sense, psychoanalysis aims to reduce suffering by tackling one of its most consistent sources.

Freud ends his account by pointing out the dilemmas produced by the inevitable tensions between the needs of the individual and those of the community. There is a struggle between two urges within each of us—the one towards the individual's personal happiness, and the other towards union with other human beings, which will involve a tension between good and bad dispositions and drives. The aim of happiness remains but is pushed into the background.

Freud unified his thoughts in the book theoretically by seeing the situation with humans as involving an elemental tension between the forces of destruction, deriving from his recent concept of the death drive or *Thanatos*, and the life-enhancing forces of *Eros*, the life drive. The death drives aim towards the reduction of instinctual tensions to zero; their aim is ultimately to bring the living being back to the inorganic state. They are initially directed inwards and tend towards self-destruction but are subsequently turned towards the outside world in the form of aggression and destructiveness.[71] The life drives in contrast include the sexual and self-preservative drives and aim to bring living beings into ever greater unities. A further complication of this speculative vision of mankind is that there is usually a complex mix or fusion of the life and death drives. There can be no *Eros* without *Thanatos*, or vice versa, though one may dominate at any time. Civilisation is therefore a never-ending struggle between the life and death drives and involves various combinations of both drives.

Richard Bernstein, in a classic account of the nature of evil, to which I shall return in the next chapter, captures in his book *Radical Evil* the essence of Freud's late and bleak but prescient vision of mankind:

> Freud teaches us that, "in reality, there is no eradication of evil." We must never underestimate the power and energy of our basic drives and instincts, and the depth of psychic ambivalence. We must never delude ourselves into thinking that our instinctual destructive capacity can be completely tamed or controlled. We must never forget that all sorts of unexpected contingencies can unleash "barbarous" outbursts of aggression and destruction. This is true for individuals, groups, and societies. Unfortunately, the evidence of the massacres and genocides of the twentieth century, which have occurred under the most diverse conditions, "confirms" Freud's warning ... The drama of our individual and collective lives is always being played out against a background of ineradicable psychic ambivalence, where "evil impulses" may temporarily be held in check, suppressed, and repressed, but never permanently eliminated.[72]

Following on from Freud, Erich Fromm pursued the problem of the nature of evil and the choice between good and evil in his 1964 book *The Heart of Man*. He saw three phenomena as the basis for the most vicious and dangerous human acts—the love of death, malignant narcissism, and symbiotic-incestuous fixation. These three orientations together form what he calls the "syndrome of decay" as opposed to their opposite—the "syndrome of growth".[73] Only in a minority of people is one of the two syndromes fully developed; there is a usually a mixture of the two.

Malignant narcissism, in both individuals and groups, is an extreme form of narcissism, akin to Rosenfeld's destructive narcissism, and occurs in those obsessed with power for its own sake, those indifferent to others, and with those whose judgments are biased in favour of themselves at the cost of others. In contrast with benign narcissism, the malignant form "lacks the corrective element … If I am 'great' because of some quality I *have*, and not because of something I *achieve*, I do not need to be related to anyone or anything … In maintaining the picture of my greatness I remove myself more and more from reality."[74]

Intense incestuous fixations refer to pathological difficulties in emerging from a primary dependence on early attachments. At the most archaic level, where there may be a deep regression, the dependence conflicts with ordinary living.[75]

Regarding the love of death, Fromm agreed with Freud that the contradiction between Eros and destruction, between the affinity of life and affinity to death is the most fundamental contradiction that exists in mankind. However, in his view this duality is not based on one of two biologically inherent drives, but

> between the primary and most fundamental tendency of life—to persevere in life—and its contradiction, which comes into being when man fails in this goal. In this view the "death instinct" is a *malignant* phenomenon which grows and takes over to the extent to which Eros does not unfold. The death instinct represents *psychopathology* and not, as in Freud's view, part of *normal biology*. The life instinct thus constitutes the primary potentiality in man; the death instinct a secondary potentiality.[76]

The primary potentiality develops where the conditions for psychic growth are favourable, but when they are unfavourable such as an upbringing lacking life, love, and affection, a lack of stimulation and mechanical parenting, what Fromm calls a "necrophilic" or death-loving character may develop.

A necrophilic character is a person who is:

> ... attracted to and fascinated by all that is not alive, all that is dead ... A clear example of the pure necrophilous type is Hitler. He was fascinated by destruction, and the smell of death was sweet to him. While in the years of his success it may have appeared that he wanted to destroy only those whom he considered his enemies, the days of the Götterdämmerung at the end showed that his deepest satisfaction lay in witnessing total and absolute *destruction*; that of the German people, of those around him, and of himself. A report from World War I, while not proved, makes good sense: a soldier saw Hitler standing in a trancelike mood, gazing at a decaying corpse and unwilling to move away.[77]

Overall, Fromm's reconfiguration of Freud's death drive concept into the necrophilous character has been described as "putting flesh onto a theoretical construction, breathing experiential life into a high abstraction."[78]

Melanie Klein saw the death drive as being at work from the beginning of life and giving rise to the fear of annihilation and that this is the cause of persecutory anxiety.[79] She also saw envy as operative from the beginning of life with a constitutional basis, and that excessive envy can be very destructive of good experiences. More recent thinkers basing themselves on Klein's ideas, such as Donald Meltzer[80] and Franco De Masi,[81] define evil as a state of mind, characterised by disregard for the human quality of the object and the destruction of meaning and meaningfulness of life in and for others. Evil drains, perverts, and strips symbols of intentions and goals, leaving them empty of emotional significance. Anna Migliozzi agrees with the work of Meltzer and De Masi and proposes that evil is a state of mind derived from the death drive characterised by envy of life and vitality, the absence of *joie de vivre* and the destruction of emotional meaning.

> Physical violence, sadistic humiliation, even murder may be the result of evil, but the quality that is the hallmark of the evil state of mind, and

what I wish to call attention to, is the unprovoked exercise of power and cruelty and a tendency to destroy meaning and the meaningfulness of life. This often includes and is connected to sadistic phantasies.[82]

This is, she points out, analogous to what Rosenfeld described in destructive narcissistic organisations—an idealisation of the attack upon one's own self, with death pursued in a state of exaltation. Evil may then exert a seductive power that feeds upon itself and becomes an idealised self-fulfilling and self-generating force, serving no purpose other than its own existence. When this occurs and evil progressively expands, colonises and conquers the patient's mind, it leaves the part of the patient that seeks help feeling increasingly weakened, isolated, and abandoned. As Meltzer points out, the evil state of mind destroys the apparatus for thinking—the place for the creation of meaning—a generative sense of emotional life disappears and is replaced "by excitement shadowed by nameless dread".[83] Presumably under certain social conditions, these states of mind may predominate in groups, leading to destructive mindlessness.

This latter approach has some links to the philosophical thought of Hannah Arendt covered in the next chapter. There, I will return to several theoretical constructions in a survey of some themes from the philosophy of evil, before returning directly to the terrains of evil and to examine how relevant the ideas covered from social psychology, psychoanalysis, and philosophy are to understanding them.

An *overall theme* underlying a number of these views about evil is that for a variety of reasons, including trauma, specific perverse fantasies, participation in groups and powerful social forces, evil acts to eliminate otherness; the bonds uniting people in a human, intimate relationship of the I/Thou form are broken. This creates a moral vacuum, where personal meaning and responsibility, human subjectivity, with the owning of agency and a capacity for self-reflectiveness and respect for others, is weakened and in extreme cases annihilated, accompanied by various degrees of triumph or pleasure in the acts of destructiveness.

Exploration of this theme continues in the next chapter when tackling some philosophical views about the nature of evil.

CHAPTER 4

The philosophy of evil

Writing comprehensively about the philosophy of evil would entail covering much of the history of philosophy, and so a selection of thinkers whose themes are most pertinent to actual social and political problems and the main issue concerning evil as an attack on subjectivity and otherness can provide some focus. I will not be covering issues concerning theodicy, that is, debates about reconciling religion with the existence of evil, nor the many debates about what evil means, nor whether evil is a valid concept; I take it as read now that evil is a valid description that covers exceptionally harmful actions, as discussed in the introduction.

Kant on radical evil

Most philosophical accounts of evil take Kant's thought as seminal as he provided much of the thinking apparatus around complex moral problems.

Several basic elements provide the background to his specific account of evil. First, Kant's revolution in philosophy was to shift the focus of philosophical attention from objects in the world to the *human subject* and how we can have knowledge of the world. For Kant, enlightenment was about the ability to use one's own understanding or reason; a revolution may put an end to despotism and oppression, but unless ways of thinking were changed, then there would not be true revolution, which requires new ways of thinking. Enlightenment of this kind requires freedom, and for Kant freedom, as described in his essay "What Is Enlightenment?", is the "public use of one's reason in all matters".[1] Though Kant appeared in this context to refer to a scholar's freedom to write for a reading public, his construction of freedom can be interpreted in a wider sense, offering a substantial and pluralistic view of tolerance as a bulwark against prejudice and intolerance.

In this essay, Kant makes a distinction between the private and public use of reason. Private for Kant did not refer to what was merely individual, personal, or interior, but to the nature of the communication used. A private communication was one addressed to a restricted audience, such as when a clergyman addresses a religious gathering, and one defined by some external authority. A public communication was free and unrestricted, addressed to a plurality of other free human beings. A clergyman could make public use of his reason if as a scholar he addresses the world, enjoying then an unrestricted freedom to make use of reason and to speak in his own person. To enjoy such freedom would require tolerance within the public arena.

Kant recognised that his notion of enlightenment is more an ideal than a current reality, that we have a long way to go before men can be able to use their understanding confidently and well in what one could call a tolerant space; enlightenment is a process.[2]

Another theme relates to his picture of the human subject and their relationship with others. In the *Groundwork of the Metaphysics of Morals*, he puts forward a maxim for what has been called the "Formula of Humanity", which states that: "*So act that you treat humanity, whether in your own person or in the person of any other, always at the same time as an end, never merely as a means.*"[3]

This means that the fact that we are human has value in itself. If a person is an end-in-themself it means their inherent value doesn't depend on anything else. We exist, so we have value. I think that this implies that treating people as an end signifies that they are to be treated as free subjects, respected as persons with autonomy and without manipulation and coercion. "Kant thinks of the moral community of others as a 'kingdom of ends', a mutual association of free beings, in which each individual seeks to realize freely chosen goals compatibly with the freedom of everyone to do likewise."[4] Treating others as merely a means would imply they are seen as objects to be used without respect and concern. Kant thus puts treating others with respect and *as other* at the centre of his moral thinking. Presumably a formula of inhumanity would involve treating people as a means never as an end.

Next, there is Kant's vision of communication between people, and his exploration of the notion of sociability and community. In his *Critique of Judgment*, particularly in the first part where he examined the phenomenon of aesthetic judgments, matters of taste about, for example, the beautiful and the sublime, Kant writes that judgments in matters of taste seem at first sight to be far from relevant to political life, yet he points out that the faculty of judging is a special kind of reflective activity inevitably involving relations between people, and hence is of wide relevance and significance. The interest in the beautiful exists only in society, not in isolation, and

> [I]f we admit that the impulse to society is natural to mankind, and that the suitability for and the propensity towards it, i.e. *sociability*, is a property essential to the requirements of human beings as creatures intended for society, and one, therefore, that belongs to *humanity*, it is inevitable that we should look upon taste in the light of the faculty for judging whatever enables us to communicate even our *feeling* to everyone else.[5]

This faculty of judging requires reflection, and a special kind of enlarged mentality, where one takes account of the views and judgment of others, putting oneself in the position of everyone else in the hope of coming to an agreement This is a form of common human understanding, not to be confused with the ordinary meaning of common sense, but a special kind of *sensus communis*, or "public sense".

Kant proposes three maxims to elucidate different aspects of this common human understanding—the need: 1. To think for oneself and avoid prejudiced thought, 2. To think from the standpoint of everyone else, and thus have a broadened way of thinking involving a plurality of people in one's horizon, and 3. Always to think consistently, what he recognises as the hardest maxim to achieve.

The Kant scholar Onora O'Neill provides a detailed account of tolerance based upon Kant's notion of the public use of reason. Tolerance is seen to have a fundamental role in providing convincing grounds for reason, for putting forward standards or norms for rational inquiry. This may seem of only abstract philosophical significance, and indeed Kant's writings can be difficult to penetrate because of their frequent preoccupation with universal maxims, with possibilities and principles. Nonetheless his thought often has important practical consequences; indeed, much of his focus in the area under consideration was on "practical" reason, which he saw as more fundamental than theoretical reason.

As O'Neill points out, as Kant depicts it, "We reason only if we act, think or communicate in ways that (we judge) make it possible for others to understand, to accept or to reject our claims or proposals. If we merely assert, or assume, or appeal to 'authorities' that others do not (sometimes even cannot) follow, we fail to offer them reasons."[6]

For Kant, there are deep connections between reasoning and politics because both are activities in which a plurality of participants needs to engage with one another's thought and action. But as there may well be disputes between participants, coordination and shared assumptions must be constructed rather than just assumed.[7] Kant likened that kind of construction to that of a building project, one which must be modest given our capacities. Rather than build a Babel-like tower of reason reaching the heavens, we only have enough stock of materials to build a house, and rather than having workers each speaking their own language and hence unable to work in coordination, we need to find a common plan, which can provide a stable platform for a secure home—thus following Kant's three maxims of the *sensus communis*.

The central thought of Kant's account of public reason is that it cannot be derivative, cannot lean on external authority; instead of being like a cyclist trying to ride by leaning on objects, a reasoner has to let go of such supports if they are to find their balance.[8] Of course, it remains most unlikely that in the reality of the messy public world of politics such unrestricted communication is possible; it is more an ideal to work towards, or a standard of possible enlightened thinking.

O'Neill points out that Kant's distinctiveness lies in the fact that his discursive grounding of reason presupposes plurality, and the possibility of community; it does not presuppose isolated, "atomistic" subjects, but actual communities or ideal communities, subjects in relation to other subjects.[9] Kant had maintained that it is wrong to conduct our communications on principles that cannot be universally shared, and it would thus be wrong to communicate in ways that destroy or threaten those who wish to communicate. Orwell's description in his novel *1984* of the language, Newspeak, used by the totalitarian state Oceania, where freedom of thought is limited, with a restricted grammar and limited ideologically based vocabulary, "is an image of vile intolerance because it destroys the very possibility of communication. It damages not merely particular communicators and communications but whole practices of communication. In the end it destroys not just freedom of public speech but freedom of thought."[10]

Kant places the problem of evil within the realm of the human subject in a community of other subjects and their life dilemmas. He was the first modern thinker to make a predominantly secular theory of evil, while also trying to incorporate religious thinking within the boundaries of reason. For him, the overwhelming evidence from observing human behaviour and from introspection is that all humans have an innate propensity for evil, rooted in human nature, or what he called "radical evil", and for which the human will is responsible. His term "radical evil" refers not to some special sort of evil, but a kind of evil *rooted* in human nature, evil that goes to the root of the human subject—the Latin for root is *radix*, from which the term radical is derived. The title of the first chapter of the book that discusses the nature of evil—"Religion within the Boundaries of Mere Reason"—is subtitled, "Concerning the Indwelling of the Evil Principle Alongside the Good or of the Radical Evil in Human Nature".[11]

Kant recognises that empirically humans are good in some parts of themselves and evil in others, and that experience confirms this middle position between the two extremes.[12] However, from the point of view of trying to look for universal ethical principles, Kant considers that anything intermediate runs the risk of creating too much ambiguity. He considers that for a human being to be morally good in some parts and at the same time evil in others is not possible, for if they are good in one part, they will have incorporated the moral law into themselves as a maxim, or universal principle, and such a principle will concern the whole human being, not a part. Though even Kant recognises that in practice one can see mixtures of good and evil, which is irrelevant from the point of view of seeking universal ethical principles that bind human actions. Being good or being evil is not an empirical condition but something deeper, at the root of the human subject, and which grounds actions in the world.

Radical evil for Kant is a propensity *not* to do what duty requires and *not* to follow the moral law, the kind of universal maxims as, for example, formulated by the principle of humanity outlined above. Treating people as means and not ends would then be an example of radical evil.

Kant gives examples of various kinds and degrees of evil and different grades in the propensity for doing evil, from human frailty, to impurity, to the worst kind—depravity. He calls the worst kind of evils "diabolical vices", such as envy, ingratitude, and joy in others' misfortune,[13] all examples of the predominance of self-interest, or of wrong-doing, not quite what we would now consider as extremely harmful and inexcusable actions.

Kant adds, in a way that has the ring of "original sin" though with qualifications, that there is a fundamental propensity, rooted in human nature, for the human subject's will not to follow the moral law but to privilege itself over the good; the human will is essentially corrupt. It is corrupt because of privileging mere self-interest over the good of others or the general good. But humans have the *choice*, the absolute freedom to choose whether or not to privilege self-interest over others. The Nazi soldier or functionary can choose either to follow or to disobey higher orders. Here, as Richard Bernstein points out, Kant seems to be offering conflicting views—we are by nature corrupt but at the same time we can choose not to be. The propensity for evil is innate or inborn and yet we are responsible for it. Bernstein argues that this contradiction is in fact the source of Kant's relevance today, as "His uncompromising insistence that personal responsibility is inescapable goes against the grain of prevailing tendencies to find all sorts of excuses for our moral failures."[14]

Thus, Kant proposed that we can overcome our propensity to evil by taking responsibility for our choices. To become a morally good person, however, "… it is not enough to let the germ of good which lies in our species develop unhindered; there is in us an active and opposing cause of evil which is also to be combatted".[15]

Kant describes how one has to constantly work against the assaults of evil and keep armed for the battle on behalf of human freedom.[16] In order to fight such evils as envy, addiction to power, avarice, and the malignant associations associated with these, which arise as soon as humans come together in groups, he proposes the setting up of an "ethical community", or a "people of God", united in accordance with the principles of virtue.[17] Such a community, which can only be realised for him within the framework of a Church, strives for a consensus of all human beings in order to establish an ethical whole. He opposes the notion of a people of God with those united together in a bond to propagate evil. Once again, Kant argues for the central importance of human relations with one another, this time with the support of religion, as the bulwark against evil. A shining example of such a community in reality was the village of Le Chambon, the Christian community that saved many Jews from Nazi persecution.

Whether or not one agrees with Kant's analysis of evil and its sources, he provides a rich and complex framework to think about evil's origins and how to combat it. There is a danger in focusing on Kant's universalising maxims; they can be taken literally, or their meaning perverted, unless one takes into account all his thinking and the context for the maxims. One infamous example of such a perversion was how in his trial Adolf Eichmann quoted a version of Kant's categorical imperative[i] as providing him with the justification for his actions, that he was acting out of moral duty to follow the principles of law without questioning. Hannah Arendt quotes Eichmann as saying that:

> "I meant by my remark about Kant that the principle of my will must always be such that it can become the principle of general laws." Upon further questioning, he added that he had read Kant's *Critique of Practical Reason*. He then proceeded to explain that from the moment he was charged with carrying out the Final Solution he had ceased to live according to Kantian principles, that he had known it, and that he had consoled himself with the thought that he no longer "was master of his own deeds".[18]

---

[i] Kant's categorical imperative states that one *act only in accordance with that maxim through which you can at the same time will that it become a universal law*. The law of humanity is a version of this imperative.

Arendt points out how Eichmann had distorted Kant's imperative for his own use, leaving out the fact that Kant's philosophy is closely bound up with man's capacity for judgment, which rules out blind obedience. And that if anything he followed the Nazi version of the categorical imperative described by Hans Frank, former Nazi governor general of occupied Poland during the war: "Act in such a way that the Führer, if he knew your action, would approve it."[19] I would add that it also leaves out the rest of Kant's thinking about the importance of human relations, and above all the principle of humanity.

Machiavelli—men not wholly good or wholly bad

While Kant was the first modern thinker to make a predominantly secular theory of evil, but incorporating a role for religion, Machiavelli "laid the basis for a secular study of society",[20] one where religion, in particular Christianity and Christian values and morality of charity, peacefulness, meekness, and turning the other cheek, is seen as incompatible with what leads to a stable and well-governed society. He distinguished politics from morality, much as Hannah Arendt was to do centuries later.[21] He argued that there are, for example, times when, reversing the law of humanity, the end justifies the means if doing so preserves the safety and stability of society. There are times when in the sphere of politics, a good end can justify what is morally wrong. Or what may be wrong by Christian standards can be right when it comes to secular standards. The most obvious example of this view is the argument for a just war against the Nazis. War often involves destructive and terrible actions, difficult to keep in check or limit, and yet few would say that the war against Hitler was evil. Without it, a greater evil of a Nazi superpower would have taken root. Here we are already in Machiavellian territory—how to think realistically about the difficult choices to be made in political and social life, based upon humans as they are, with all their frailties, and not as they would like to be in an ideal world. As he put it in *The Prince*:

> [T]he gulf between how one should live and how one does live is so wide that a man who neglects what is actually done for what should be done learns the way to self-destruction rather than self-preservation.

> The fact is that a man who wants to act virtuously in every way necessarily comes to grief among so many who are not virtuous. Therefore, if a prince wants to maintain his rule, he must learn how not to be good, and to make use of this or not, according to need.[22]

Machiavelli emphasises that ideals can be dangerous as they can never be attained; they can only lead to ruin. "The reason is that nature has so constituted man that, though all things are objects of desire, not all things are attainable; so that desire always exceeds the power of attainment, with the result that men are ill content with what they possess, and their present state brings them little satisfaction. Hence arises the vicissitudes of their fortune [*Fortuna*].[23]

Fortune governs the affairs of men, or at least "half of the affairs of the things we do, leaving the other half or so to be controlled by ourselves".[24] Fortune is compared to a powerful river in flood that cannot easily be resisted. Those totally dependent on it risk disaster when their fortune changes, hence the need to adapt to circumstances and the times in order to prosper. Fortune, as described by Bernard Crick is "the sudden, awful and challenging piling up of social factors and contingent political events in an unexpected way";[25] what Harold Macmillan is reported, in popular legend, as having answered to a journalist's question to him about a politician's greatest challenge, as "Events, dear boy, events."

Machiavelli has at times attracted a reputation as the master of the evil dark arts of politics, almost at times equated with the devil, for example when he avoided prioritising Christian values, or argued that

> There would unavoidably arise emergencies in the life span of any state or city in which extreme measures of cruelty and of violence would be required in defence of the security of the state. A man who was not at all times fully prepared for such measures would not in fact remain in power for long, and he would put his country at risk while he remained in power.[26]

He also balances this proposition with the need for princes to avoid contempt and hatred, to honour their word, and that a prince would do better to have a reputation for compassion (*Pietà*) than for cruelty. He provides an account of human predicaments still relevant today and which embrace the complexity of how to reconcile a necessary action with what may appear to be a morally dubious one, and a pluralistic model of thinking about social and political forces.

While *The Prince* was concerned with what it takes to be a successful leader, Machiavelli's *Discourses*, an extended reflection on what can be learned from the history of the Roman Republic, particularly that of the Roman historian Livy's account of that history, offers a more nuanced discussion of how a republic, as the best form of government, can be established and survive. Machiavelli offers a wealth of observations about civic life, at the core of which I would suggest can be detected a particular model of the human subject as easily corruptible, however initially good and well-taught,[27] and neither wholly good nor wholly bad.[28] The latter can be a problem if it means being unable to act to safeguard the community; sometimes being single-minded is the only way to achieve that goal, while steering a middle course can be disastrous.

Machiavelli also notes that conflict between people is both inevitable but also desirable. Thus,

> To me those who condemn the quarrels between the nobles and the plebs, [in the Roman Republic] seem to be cavilling at the very things that were the primary cause of Rome's retaining her freedom, and that they pay more attention to the noise and clamour resulting from such commotions than to what resulted from them, i.e., to the good effects which they produced. Nor do they realize that in every republic there are two different dispositions, that of the populace and that of the upper class and that all legislation favourable to liberty is brought about by the clash between them.[29]

This vision of the creative role for conflict resembles the thought of Stuart Hampshire's notion of justice (discussed below) being about managing conflict, and that the greatest evil in society comes about as a result of suppressing conflict.

Indeed, Hampshire considered that Machiavelli gave an unsurpassed account of the salient features of political action still relevant today. Though in principle tyranny is now more open to challenge, the "… central dilemmas of power remain: deceit and guile, unjust violence and sudden aggression, ingratitude in relations with allies and friends, are still everyday weapons of government in most parts of the world".[30]

Isaiah Berlin argued that Machiavelli's originality and contemporary relevance arises from several features.[31] He is not fooled by men's strengths and weaknesses, which he faces squarely; he prioritises the virtues of courage, bravery, inner moral strength, and loyal public spiritedness and dedication to the city or state, or *Patria*, while not flinching from seeing the capacity of men to be corrupted. Mere lust for power is destructive, but power needs to be managed. Overall, he has a positive vision of society in which "human talents can be made to contribute to a powerful and splendid whole".[32] His various maxims are designed "to create or resurrect or maintain an order which will satisfy what the author conceives as men's most permanent interests".[33]

What in part gave him the reputation for being evil in a predominantly Christian society was the fact that he maintained that public life has a morality of its own, to which Christian principles or indeed any absolute personal values tend to be an obstacle. "This life has its own standards; it does not require perpetual terror; but it approves, or at least permits, the use of force where it is needed to promote the ends of political society."[34]

But what makes Machiavelli most original, according to Berlin, is that he went against a long-standing notion in Western thought and society that there exists some single principle which regulates both nature and ourselves, and that the world and human society consist at root of a single intelligible structure. The latter viewpoint is at the heart of Western civilisation, the rock upon which Western beliefs and lives had been founded, but Machiavelli essentially blew this notion apart when he argued that Christian values and arguments are not the only way to promote the good of society.[35] Instead, he proposed that there was not one ultimate end for human action, that instead there exist more than one end, "that there might exist no single universal overarching standard that would enable a man to choose rationally between them … a profoundly upsetting conclusion".[36]

Berlin goes further when he suggests that Machiavelli's cardinal achievement was

> his uncovering of a permanent question mark in the path of posterity. It stems from his *de facto* recognition that ends equally ultimate, equally sacred, may contradict each other, that entire systems of value

may come into collision without possibility of rational arbitration, and that not merely in exceptional circumstances, as a result of abnormality or accident or error … but (this was surely new) as part of the normal human situation.[37]

Thus, Machiavelli was, whether he knew it or not, one of the makers of pluralism, and ironically for him, thereby a promotor of tolerance. His subtle thought reminds us that like it or not we have to make agonising choices between what may be incompatible alternatives in our lives; this is an uncomfortable truth, but we must learn to live with it.[38] It also provides a counterbalance to any thought which insists on unitary thinking. The once customary picture of Machiavelli as the devil incarnate, the promotor of the use of evil means to achieve a necessary outcome, thus ignores the subtlety of his thought and his facing the consequences of his view that humans are neither wholly good nor wholly bad.

Arendt's radical evil

Hannah Arendt's view of the nature of evil draws on Kant's philosophy but gives the notion of radical evil a different emphasis in the context of the horrors of the Holocaust and the vicious cruelty of Stalinist Russia. She also puts forward in her other works a positive view of what can counter evil.

To understand the context for her views on evil, her 1951 book *The Origins of Totalitarianism*[39] provides a detailed examination of the nature of intolerant totalitarian regimes, using Nazi Germany and Soviet Russia as exemplars, which provide uncomfortable parallels with the current rise of "populist" movements in the West. Arendt describes a form of social pathology developed in modern times, emphasising the way these totalitarian regimes were mass movements of a particular kind. They recruited their members in Europe after 1930,

> from the mass of apparently indifferent people whom all other parties had given as too apathetic or too stupid for their attention. The result was that the majority of their membership consisted of people who never before had appeared on the political scene. This permitted the introduction of entirely new methods into political propaganda, and indifference to the arguments of political opponents.[40]

The mass of generally dissatisfied and desperate people increased rapidly in Germany and Austria after the First World War, with inflation and unemployment adding to the disruptive effects of military defeat, and this mass also increased after the Second World War, supporting extremist movements in France and Italy, and one can now add that there has been another increase globally since recent worldwide economic crises.

Arendt describes how social atomisation or fragmentation had preceded the mass movements, creating many socially alienated, lonely individuals, ready to be organised into a movement. "The totalitarian movements depended less on the structurelessness of a mass society than on the specific conditions of an atomized and individualized mass."[41] These mass organisations demand total, unconditional, and unalterable loyalty of the individual member, essentially making individual human beings "superfluous", and thus expendable.

She describes how in totalitarian regimes law has a particular quality which distances it from human relations. One could say that such regimes rule by using or misusing the law, not with the rule of law. The Nazis' racist ideology talked of the law of nature as justifying the elimination of genetically undesirable elements and set up complex racial laws to put this into effect. The Bolsheviks backed up their terror with the law of history and class struggle. Both regimes used the law courts as instruments of terror rather than to administer justice. Indeed, it is notable how many high-up Nazi functionaries were legally trained. It would be interesting for their specific history to be undertaken, as has already been done for Nazi doctors. Just to cite one example, the leadership of the *Reichssicherheitshaptampt* (Imperial Department of Security), with a central role in the formation and execution of genocide in Germany and the occupied countries, was made up of many young lawyers.[42]

The terror enacted by totalitarian regimes abolishes the protective boundaries between people.

> It substitutes for the boundaries and channels of communication between individual men a band of iron which holds them so tightly together that it is as though their plurality had disappeared into One Man of gigantic proportions. To abolish the fences and laws between

men—as tyranny does—means to take away man's liberties and destroy freedom as a living political reality; for the space between men as it is hedged in by laws, is the living space of freedom.[43]

Among the first steps towards the Holocaust was killing the legal restrictions which stripped Jews and other targeted groups of their human rights.

Arendt also points out how ideologies such as racism, which aim to explain everything and every occurrence by deducing it from a single premise, have come to play a useful part in sustaining totalitarian regimes.[44] Such regimes attack pluralistic thinking.

As a counterbalance to her dissection of totalitarian thinking, Arendt collected a group of essays written over twelve years titled *Men in Dark Times*, referring both to the contemporary scene which had witnessed the horrors of the mid-twentieth century, but also any period where the public realm is obscured, and people no longer have a sense of sharing a common world. The opening and key text in this collection, "On Humanity in Dark Times, Thoughts about Lessing", is an address given in Hamburg when she received the Lessing prize in 1959. Gotthold Lessing the German Enlightenment philosopher and dramatist (1729–1781) was a firm believer in tolerance and religious pluralism. Thus, in his drama *Nathan the Wise* (1779), he proposed that each of the monotheistic religions had an equal claim to truth, "the precise extent of which can be determined only after an indefinite, and perhaps infinite, period of time".[45] He held it as valuable and indeed inevitable that there would be plurality not only of religions but also of views about truth in general.

Arendt's address consists of several themes, including the relation of truth to the kind of free thinking promoted by Lessing and the quality of relations between people that enables open and human communication. For her, "We humanize what is going on in the world and in ourselves only by speaking of it, and in the course of speaking of it we learn to be human."[46] But of course open and public discourse requires a tolerant public place and space in which to speak. Totalitarian regimes make this impossible. People may then withdraw into an interior realm, into what she called the "invisibility of thinking and feeling", but this is not a fully human world.

In order to avoid such impasses, Arendt proposes in the Lessing address that, like Lessing, one remains suspicious of the existence of a single compelling truth (though not evidenced facts), and that instead one rejoices in the unending discourse among people in search of the truth but never reaching a single source of truth; the notion of single truth only leads to inhumanity.

> Lessing's greatness does not merely consist in a theoretical insight that there cannot be one single truth within the human world but in his gladness that it does not exist and that, therefore, the unending discourse among men will never cease so long as there are men at all. A single absolute truth ... would have spelled the end of humanity.[47]

There is some resemblance here to the pluralistic thinking of Machiavelli, also thinking of the social and political forces of his time.

Arendt describes a special form of tolerance, involving the gift of friendship, openness to the world, and with the genuine love of mankind. The ideal of absolute truth that she describes in its extreme form in totalitarian regimes threatens in all societies the political public space between people, which she prioritises as the site of freedom.

Arendt thus proposes a powerful positive vision of a tolerant public space open to all but needing to be guarding against the forces of intolerance, those who aim to limit open and public discourse, often in the name of some single and abiding "truth".

In relation to her examination of totalitarian thinking, Arendt has two ways of understanding evil, an earlier and later view. Her earlier view of evil was put forward in *The Origins of Totalitarianism*, where she appropriates Kant's notion of radical evil but gives it a different meaning; it essentially refers to the annihilation of what is human. For Arendt it refers to the unforgivable and absolute evil displayed by totalitarian regimes, which

> can no longer be explained by the evil motives of self-interest, greed, covetousness, resentment, lust for power and cowardice; and which therefore anger could not revenge, love could not endure, friendship could not forgive. Just as the victims in death factories or the holes of oblivion are no longer "human" in the eyes of their executioners, so this newest species of criminals is beyond the pale even of solidarity in human sinfulness.[48]

Instead, she describes a radical evil which

> has emerged in connection with a system in which all men have become equally superfluous. The manipulators of this system believe in their own superfluousness as much as in that of all the

others, and the totalitarian murderers are all the more dangerous because they do not care if they themselves are alive or dead, if they ever lived or never were born.[49]

Radical evil is then about making people superfluous as alive human subjects. She describes three essential steps on the road to total domination and elimination of subjectivity. The first step is to "kill the juridical person in man".[50] This occurs when certain categories of people are put outside the protection of the law so that people's civil rights are eliminated. This was done when the concentration camps were put outside the normal judicial procedures, while even before that Jews and some other minority groups had been stripped of their legal rights. She added that the inclusion of criminals in the camps was necessary in order to make plausible the propagandistic Nazi claim that the institution existed for asocial elements.

The next "decisive step in the preparation of living corpses is the murder of the moral person in man. This is done in the main by making martyrdom for the first time in history impossible".[51] Thus, the SS were brilliant in corrupting the sense of human solidarity, making decisions of conscience absolutely questionable and equivocal. Hence,

> when a man is faced with the alternative of betraying and thus murdering his friends or of sending his wife and children, for whom he is in every sense responsible, to their death; when even suicide would mean the immediate murder of his own family—how is he to decide? The alternative is no longer between good and evil, but between murder and murder. Who could solve the moral dilemma of the Greek mother, who was allowed by the Nazis to choose which of her three children should be killed?[52]

Evil here involves the eradication of moral choice with the pretence of offering a choice. In the camps there were also times when inmates were faced by what Primo Levi called "grey zones", ill-defined situations where boundaries between victim and perpetrator were blurred, where collaboration was promoted, putting prisoner against prisoner, in a sense mimicking the logic of the totalitarian state.[53]

Once the moral person has been killed, Arendt points out that the one thing that still prevents men from being made into living corpses is the differentiation of the individual, their unique identity. Taking away their possessions and stripping them naked on arrival, the arbitrary selections of who is to die, and of course the prior cramming of people into cattle trucks before arriving, all add to the stripping of the individual's identity and sense of them themselves as free human subjects. Random killings, unnecessary routines, and drills, all destroyed human attachments. She points out that after the annihilation of legal protection and the destruction of the moral person, the loss of individuality, the final step in dehumanisation, usually follows. The individual's spontaneity and "soul" is destroyed, making them living corpses, what Levi called the "drowned".

That all these processes come within the range of evil hardly seems controversial, their harm going well beyond what is excusable, and Arendt's exposure of the logic of totalitarian practices was masterly and still relevant today.

However, she courted considerable controversy, after attending and reporting on the Eichmann trial in 1961, with her famous later concept of evil, that of its essential *banality*, making a link between the ability or inability to think and the problem of evil.

Based upon her observations of Eichmann's testimony and delivery, she called into question the traditional notion of the evil monster, that people who do evil deeds must be vicious, sadistic, and monstrously wicked. Faced by this seemingly banal bureaucrat whose language was full of clichés, she described him as terrifyingly normal. In fact, this was something already known during the Nuremberg trials, when the great majority of the defendants who were psychologically tested were found to be normal, neither criminal psychopaths nor abnormal characters, whatever the horrendous deeds with which they had been involved. And of course, since the Milgram and Stanford Prison experiments, it is known that evil deeds can be committed by the ordinary person, not some moral monster.

She wrote that it would be comforting to believe that Eichmann was a monster, but "The trouble with Eichmann was precisely that so many were like him, and that the many were neither perverted nor sadistic, that they were, and still are, terribly and terrifyingly normal."[54] As she later put it, "The sad truth of the matter is that most evil is done by people who never made up their minds to be or do either evil or good."[55]

Her notion of the banality of evil was not some theory or doctrine, but something quite factual, the phenomenon of evil deeds, committed on a gigantic scale, which could not be traced to any particularity of wickedness, pathology, or ideological conviction in the doer, whose only personal distinction was a perhaps extraordinary shallowness. She saw in Eichmann an entirely negative quality, not stupidity but the inability to think from the *other's standpoint*. He knew that what he had once considered his duty was now called a crime, but he accepted this new code as if it was just nothing but another language rule, and not one which had human consequences. He emphasised the importance in his work of organisation, a job well done, of objects of the work achieved rather than the effect of his decisions on human subjects; that's what made the evil he perpetrated appear to be banal, almost a part of everyday life, but of course with a viewpoint devoid of taking personal responsibility for the outcome. Instead of evaluating the goodness or badness of his actions, he assessed them in terms of how well or how poorly he functioned within the totalitarian system.

Arendt wondered then if a certain quality of thinking could enable people to *resist* evildoing. Her last and unfinished book *The Life of the Mind* attempts to define what kind of thinking this could be, and, based upon an examination of the Socratic dialogue, she describes it as thinking in the form of the "two-in-one",[56] a duality of myself with myself that makes thinking a true activity, a kind of internal dialogue, a thinking dialogue between me and myself, a particular kind of self-reflectiveness that enables a person to make judgments about what is the right thing to do. This emphasis on the importance of thinking as dialogue seems to be consistent with her earlier emphasis on the free thinking that comes from public dialogue. The two-in-one thinking would need to be tested in dialogue with others; indeed, it involves being able to see other positions, not just one fixed viewpoint as in totalitarian thinking.

Arendt has been criticised, probably with some justification, for underestimating the degree to which Eichmann was aware of the reality of the concentration camps and his active involvement in genocide; he was not just some efficient bureaucrat but an *ideologically* committed Nazi who *intended* to put into effect the Final Solution, to eliminate all Jews from the world. Her emphasis on his lack of thinking seemed to minimise his criminal intent.

Raul Hilberg's[57] research on the other hand does show how the Nazi's success in carrying out their genocidal plans on such a vast scale was made possible by the routine application of countless bureaucrats and agencies. More recent research by Wendy Lower also emphasises what a significant role was played by ordinary women in the carrying out of genocide, acting as administrators, secretaries, welfare workers, nurses, teachers, and wives, at times actively participating in atrocities.[58]

Lifton notes that the ordinariness of Nazi doctors would appear to confirm Arendt's thesis, but not quite. "Nazi doctors were banal, but what they did was not. I describe banal men performing demonic acts. In doing so—or *in order* to do so—the men themselves changed; and in carrying out their actions, they themselves were no longer banal."[59]

However, Arendt's notion of the banality of evil does bring a new dimension into understanding the nature of evil in the contemporary world, and how normal people can commit horrendous crimes, or can be sucked into a nightmare system where killing becomes routine and hence in that sense banal, not requiring some extraordinarily monstrous personality or demonic presence, and where individual moral values can easily become eliminated, where some evildoers are sober and obedient bureaucrats rather than malicious sadists.[60] Their devotion to the bureaucracy gives them a sense of order in a chaotic world, and apparent legitimacy; but an order cut adrift from the just rule of law and to human concerns becomes evil—as illustrated well in Kafka's novel *The Trial*, where Joseph K. becomes lost in endless corridors, accused of being guilty of some unknown crime, guilty just for existing. This new form of bureaucracy, unlike that of the bureaucracies of previous eras in history, attacks the very soul of the human subject.

She also was instrumental in defining a new form of evil (not the only form of evil) that arose in the twentieth century, where desk murderers—and now we can add the controllers of drone technology—can eliminate human beings with a signature or a text, or a button, as if they were mere images on a screen.

Stuart Hampshire and barriers against evil

I have already described in the introduction how the moral philosopher Stuart Hampshire was deeply affected by his work as an intelligence officer in the Second World War. After studying Himmler's central command activities and then interrogating some leading Nazis in captivity he learned how easy it had been to organise the vast Nazi destructive enterprise, and to enrol willing workers in this field, once all ordinary moral barriers had been removed. He was struck by how unmitigated evil and nastiness are as natural in educated human beings as generosity and sympathy. A significant proportion of his subsequent moral philosophy was preoccupied with how to make sense of this observation and how to not only understand the nature of evil but also how to erect barriers against it with a vision of justice as a bulwark against evil.

For Hampshire, influenced by Freud, the human subject is essentially divided within themselves, and that as a result we experience moral conflicts arising from these divisions.[61] Moral thinking involves some kind of balancing of conflicting moral claims, an application of the use of practical reason, or reason as deliberation, which originated with Aristotle. This entails the weighing up of arguments for and against a proposal as in a council chamber, "in which the agent's contrary interests are represented around the table, each speaking for itself".[62] However, the events of the last century have shown that

> [R]espect for justice and any morality founded on concern for human welfare, are fragile constructions, liable to be toppled at any time by cruelty and fanaticism, and by the will to power. Alongside the balancing of conflicting moral claims, thinking about morality also includes thinking how barriers against evil are most reliably maintained; for this standard is always under threat … As morality is inextricably involved with conflict, so also it is inextricably involved with the control of destructive impulses.[63]

In his books *Innocence and Experience* (1989) and *Justice is Conflict* (1999), Hampshire adds flesh to his vision of how a particular kind of justice, *procedural justice*, which essentially looks at, or listens to, the "other side" of every argument, is the means to give some protection against destructive evil. Humans are always ambivalent, and driven by numerous desires; they always find themselves choosing between incompatible and irreconcilable projects. We should not necessarily look for consensus among different viewpoints but for the management of acceptable conflicts, for rationally controlled hostilities as the normal condition of mankind. This is a negative vision of justice but for him that is far better than following the dangerous path of promoting some overall or unified good for mankind. Like Machiavelli and Isaiah Berlin, he adopts a pluralistic model, which recognises the diverse and irreconcilable notions of what is good for a society. It is both a negative vision of justice and yet at the same time a positive vision of how such justice can work in the real world.

He sees the recognition of justice as a primary principle in human societies, including obligations of love and friendship and of families and kinships, duties of benevolence or at least restraints against harm and destruction of life, all this as the basic minimum condition for a tolerable human life.[64] I would add that the notion of an intrinsic virtue of justice matches evidence from developmental research as covered in Chapter 2, which described how even babies usually have an innate sense of fairness and justice.

Conceptions of justice are constantly changing and being revised as practical reasoning enters new and unexpected domains of practice, for example, the institution of slavery in Ancient Athens, would now be considered unjust as it involved treating human beings as less than fully human, even though at the time it did not come into conflict with the then prevailing concept of justice.[65]

In his consideration of Nazism and evil, Hampshire considers that the intention of the Nazi movement was from the beginning primarily aimed at creating unjust conditions and worldwide domination—and almost succeeded. "The plan was pure evil and the realisation of pure evil, with scarcely any counterbalancing good … If one is justified in speaking of a pure evil, then one is speaking of a great evil which brings no good thing and destroys without benefit."[66] He calls the "great evils" tyranny's domination by killing, imprisonment, and enslavement; they undermine ways of life and make life scarcely bearable; the greatest source of evil being the unrestrained natural drive to domination. Evil is not some strange alien phenomenon but grows out of some basic failure to proceed with just arrangements, and flourishes as a result of the destruction of basic just procedures.

One can learn about how justice can fail from studying the Nazi regime as it was a revolution of destructiveness, or of moral destruction, whose aim was to eliminate all notions of fairness and of justice from practical politics and from people's minds, and to create a "bombed and flattened moral landscape, in which there are no boundaries and no limits, as in the remembered no-man's-land of the First World War ... One can say without exaggeration that the aim was to invert all the values contained in the concept of justice."[67]

Instead of just procedures, revenge determined treatment of "enemies", loyalty to party and to "race" replaced impartiality, and favour and maltreatment depended upon a person's origins rather than character. Justice was identified with the interests of the powerful and the exercise of power required no justification and no restraint.

> When the use of force proved successful, and all the conventions of negotiation had been swept away, morality itself had been destroyed in public affairs ... An abyss was opened. The only reality in public affairs was to be pure domination and pure subjection, with no outrage forbidden and no limit set.[68]

Annihilation of justice and of human subjectivity went hand in hand. One can see then how the effective functioning of procedural justice involves respect for individual life.

Hampshire makes the point that the abolition of justice in public life and therefore of morality itself very nearly succeeded in Europe but was only blocked by the defeat of the Nazis at the Battle of Stalingrad and by the American and British armies in France. But the real possibility of

> absolute evil now remains a challenge to moral philosophy which cannot be conjured away. Not only is any particular morality fragile and always dependent on its survival in practice on contingent historical circumstances, but morality itself, the whole range of practices and institutions classifiable as morality is fragile.[69]

Given the fragility of morality, or what Martha Nussbaum has called the "fragility of goodness",[70] Hampshire argues that no decent and tolerable life is possible without some protection against evil, and that "Protection needs to be supplied by the social and political order, as well as by the prudence and the moral judgment of individuals,"[71] and, I would add, their courage. Procedural justice is about limiting human destructiveness and putting a reasonable and appropriate restraint on extreme human desires; the effective functioning of justice requires the erection of some kind of barrier. When barriers go down, then destructiveness is released. The image of the Washington Capitol rioters pushing their way through ordinary barriers before wrecking life and property comes to mind as an image of the human potential for unbridled excess.

Hampshire asks whether his concept of justice only applies to liberal societies or whether it has universal application.[72] He claims universality for his view as the predicament that gives rise to the need for protection against evil is universal; the tendency to dominate and destroy human freedom remains a permanent risk in all societies.

Jonathan Glover and moral history

Jonathan Glover's book *Humanity: A Moral History of the Twentieth Century* (2001) examines history and morality following the large-scale cruelty and killing of the last century, where technology meant that horror and death on a hitherto unheard of and massive scale became possible, in order to shed light on the dark side of our psychology. As he notes, "We need to look hard and clearly at some monsters inside us. But this is part of the project of caging and taming them."[73]

As a focus for his examination of twentieth-century atrocities he uses some key terms, the most central being *humanity* as opposed to *inhumanity*. Humanity for him refers to deep-rooted human responses such as respect and concerns for others, and Kant's law of humanity, where humanity must always be treated as an end not a means, so that people are treated with dignity and those we do not know can be treated with sympathy and respect. These are what he calls our "*moral resources*, which help us to act towards others with more than mere self-interest".[74] Such a conception is consistent with Martin Buber's placing of the I/Thou relationship at the centre of moral life.[75] Moral resources are often linked to particular communities and may also be attached to specific groups within a community; there can be in-group and out-group moralities, as we have seen in social psychology studies.

In addition, we have available our *moral identity*, our character, what makes us who we are, and what we want to be. A sense of moral identity helps to restrain us from supporting atrocities, so that one can say to oneself that "I am not someone who would support mass murder."[76]

Glover uses two concepts of moral resources and moral identity to focus his examination of how the dark side of human nature can take over, undermining moral resources or creating new moral identities where destructiveness becomes acceptable to the human subject and humanity gets lost. Human responses are the core of our humanity which contrasts with inhumanity. However, there are times when humanity is more an aspiration than a reality, particularly as it is clear that there is something deep in human psychology that urges us in certain situations to humiliate, torment, wound, and kill people. At such times moral identity is eroded, a person may slide by degrees into doing something that they would not have originally chosen to do; moral lines are then crossed, weakening the human response. Glover is hopeful that though human cruelty is part of the human condition, there is less possibility of a repetition of the mass cruelty of the last century. I would suggest that the jury is still out on that issue, given the continuing reality of genocide and slavery in the modern era.

Glover applies his basic concepts to the moral psychology of waging war, tribalism, Stalinism, and Nazism. I have already covered in the introduction some of the main ways that war affects our morality and how normal moral restraints are inhibited by the combat mentality. Glover adds the following key features. The human response is inhibited by training for battle and the culture of combat, where the ordinary soldier almost becomes a robot, trained to be emotionally hard and to obey superior orders, and making them do things that they would not do in civilian life, as well as seeing opponents as humiliated or dehumanised. Being remote from civilian life helps to erode ordinary civilian moral identity. Diffusion of responsibility also makes it easier to avoid threats to moral identity, when, for example, implementation of policy is spread over many people and different departments, or when people can imagine they are merely cogs in a large machine or institution. Moral sliding can occur over time with gradual shifts in war practices, for example, mass bombing of civilians, may be preceeded by conventional bombing so that bit by bit policy makers and crews may become hardened in their responses and willing to stretch the boundaries of the acceptable.[77] Sometimes moral sliding occurs through a kind of war momentum of its own, carrying on in conditions in which it would not have been started; the mass bombing of Dresden, for example, took place even though by then accurate daytime bombing was possible and safe due to the Allied command of the skies.[78]

There are however occasions where robot psychology, defensive hardness and distancing, and the assault on moral identity, all have their limits. "Sometimes the old, more human psychology breaks through the new hard crust."[79] Sympathy may break through, or a sense of shared humanity. One is reminded of the Christmas truce in the First World War when English and German soldiers reportedly exchanged gifts in no-man's-land and played football. But one must also take account of the fact that group solidarity can increase the soldier's wish to kill, and there is also an excitement in killing and in being destructive which can take over the soldier's mind, even if later a substantial number of soldiers may feel regret and guilt and are haunted by what they did, however much they may try to deny what had taken place during their military service.

In war, moral resources and moral identity are often neutralised but even when they are present, the "trap of war" can make them largely ineffective.[80] Soldiers are trapped in a closed system where obeying orders is the norm and disobeying orders may incur severe penalties, even death. Public support at home may add to the pressure to conform; media manipulation and censorship may contribute to the war effort by framing the war's narrative in ways advantageous to the governing powers. Mobilisation for war and an arms race has its own momentum and creates a warlike psychology, precipitating hostilities with otherwise reluctant parties. National pride may add to the toxic mixture trapping nations into going to war. The outbreak of the First World War showed a number of these features.

> This was a crisis whose full dimensions were not seen by those caught up in it. They were entangled in a web of each other's ambiguities, misperceptions and confused intentions. They were also in a trap created by military planners who were not under proper control, by military alliances and by public opinion. At a deeper level they were psychologically trapped.[81]

They were trapped by the mutual fear caused by the escalating arms race, and by the interaction of several different strands of belief—in nationalism and the belief in a pseudo-Darwinian survival of the fittest, as well as an increasingly outmoded code of honour, with the honour of the "nation" at the summit. Things became out of control and events took their place while, as has been said, the parties sleepwalked into war.

Getting out of the trap of war requires a flexible mindset and the willingness of leaders to understand the other side as well as recognising their own fallibility.[82] Glover describes how during the Cuban missile crisis of 1962, both Kennedy and Khrushchev were ultimately able to use their imaginations to call a halt to hostilities, despite pressure from hawks on both sides. They were able to imagine what a nuclear war would mean for the world and drew back from the brink.

Tribalism, when group hostilities dominate in wartime or peacetime, as in Rwanda, Northern Ireland, the Middle East, and elsewhere, has its own traps, creating a "spiral of hatred".[83] With the use of media manipulation and propaganda information about the "other group" may become trapped in a system of false beliefs, exacerbating irrational fears and increasing aggressive hatred and tribal hostilities. As covered in Chapter 2, there is a human disposition to group conflict under the right conditions, with group thinking focused around "them and us". Narratives around interpretation about past traumas may shape current prejudices; for example, during the Serbian–Croatian civil war, the narrative of the Serbs emphasised Croatian fascism during the Second World War, and the role of the Serbs in defeating the Croats and their Nazi allies. While the narrative of the Croats emphasised the stifling nature of communism, which was seen as a system imposed by the Serbs.[84]

Glover suggests that tribal hostility can be transcended by a sense of moral identity rooted in commitments outside the range of these kinds of narrative, such as to a religion or a profession with its own values and standards of conduct, or by a humanism which sees through tribal membership to the human being behind it.[85]

Stalinism created a trap of terror and escalating paranoia; the whole leadership system became trapped by fear of Stalin, and even he was trapped by his fear of their desire to get rid of him. What distinguished the Soviet terror from that associated with past regimes was the fundamental role of ideology, or the belief system underpinned by Marxism and Lenin's ruthlessness in using any means to achieve power in the name of the people. Beliefs were used to deaden human responses; traditional moral thinking was labelled as bourgeois and counter revolutionary.[86] Fear and the Soviet belief system eroded respect, hardness replaced sympathy, faith in the party overrode faith in human beings, and the utopian Marxist vision of an idealised future helped to distort perceptions of contemporary atrocities.

In *Nazi Germany*, as Glover describes, several of the features already outlined in the way that moral resources and moral identity can be eroded were also present, combining tribalism with belief, with elements specific to the Nazi regime. The core of Nazism centred upon irrational racial theories, with the fantasy of the pure German Aryan race going back in time to ancient Germanic tribes inhabiting the German woods and forests. Such images of a pure German identity were also directly linked with extreme nationalistic feelings and long-standing anti-Semitic trends, so that the Jews became a major source of racial impurity and thereby needing to be excluded from civil society, then segregated and eliminated, as part of the fantasy of a new moral order, a "pure" world without Jews and some other "impure" minorities. "The Nazis systematically attacked human responses. They set out to erode the moral status of Jews, homosexuals and others, denying them the protection of respect for their dignity ... [T]hey worked to replace sympathy with hardness."[87] Hitler specifically rejected what he called the loathsome humanitarian morality in *Mein Kampf*.

As part of the attack on humanity, the Nazis stripped their victims of protective dignity, and were distanced emotionally so that they were pushed outside the boundaries of the moral community,[88] and so that Jews in particular had no human status and hence no subjectivity. Along with the erosion of accepted moral identity there was the creation of a new post Christian moral identity in a world free from Jews and anything associated with Jewish history and traditions, including the Hebrew Bible, fundamental to Christian thought in the New Testament. This new Nazi identity, with its fantasy of being the master race and the inferiority of other peoples, was shaped by hatred and facilitated by fear. Glover suggests that the

> central lesson Nazism holds for ethics is that a sense of moral identity is not enough. Moral identity needs to be rooted in the human responses, rather than, as with the Nazis, adversarial to

them. It matters that people keep their humanity alive, and retain their scepticism in the face of leaders or theories telling them otherwise.[89]

I would add that in order to resist evil, one also needs to face the dark forces of the unconscious, and the power of group processes in facilitating evil acts.

In the next chapter I will specifically examine how such a dark ideology came to dominate Nazi Germany and create the horrors of the Holocaust, as well as how slavery can be seen as a form of evil which attacks the human subject's core.

CHAPTER 5

Journeys to evil: the Holocaust and British-American slavery

The aim of this chapter is to focus on some of the many factors associated with the evils of the Holocaust and of British-American slavery. As I mentioned in the introduction, a main reason for focusing on both these areas is their continuing relevance for understanding contemporary society and issues. As the philosopher Laurence Mordekhai Thomas, who is both African American and Jewish, has written, in his classic book *Vessels of Evil*, even if the Holocaust and British-American slavery are evil in very different ways, this difference as well as some similarities are very illuminating about the nature of evil and how such atrocities could have occurred.[1]

There are significant differences in the origins and in the institutions of slavery and the Holocaust, and as Thomas emphasises, our understanding of evil is deepened by looking at both without slipping into invidious attempts to rate the severity of each in comparison to the other. The extermination of Jews took place in secrecy and was state mandated and no groups of people in Nazi Germany were excluded from endeavours to exterminate the Jews, but slavery was openly part of American life and was not a required practice for everyone; the Nazi ideology towards children and adults was the same, all were to be eliminated, whereas, despite prejudiced attitudes towards black children, they were often allowed to enjoy a certain amount of childhood freedom and even allowed to play with white children; the aim of the Holocaust was to exterminate the Jewish people, but that of slavery was to foster dependence of blacks on slave owners; a dead slave was uneconomic; slavery attacked and erased many aspects of the black slaves' identity; National Socialism aimed to erase Jews as an entity.

Despite these fundamental differences, in both arenas human beings were reduced in all aspects of their humanity, with an extreme loss of agency and subjectivity mixed with corrosive racism, all sustained by the creation of an "evil moral climate",[2] or an evil imagination. One could also argue that the Nazi ideology as one of its many elements used the images and experience of imperial exploitation of slave labour to justify its own master-slave creed.

We continue to learn more about the Nazi past and the horrors of the Holocaust, such as recent studies of the role of women in committing atrocities and the extent of Jewish resistance which had been downplayed in the past; and our growing knowledge continues to raise uncomfortable questions about how easy it has been to eliminate people on a large scale, despite our altruistic predispositions.

Heightened awareness of the role of slavery in past and current societies has only recently reached public notice. There has been a long-standing blindness to how the politics and social fabric of Western society has been reliant on slavery as an important foundation of its economic wealth; and we continue to be haunted by the inability to process the harsh reality of slavery and its continuing after-effects. Just as an inability to mourn for the past atrocities against the Jews persisted in German society for years after the Second World War, we have only begun to face the need to mourn for the crimes that the British and then the Americans perpetrated against those subjected to the transatlantic slave trade.

The Holocaust and the Nazi Imaginary

My interest in Holocaust studies is not only based upon clinical work with survivors and their families over the years, but from my own family's experiences. While both sets of Jewish grandparents came from different parts of Poland to London after the First World War, many of their relatives remained and were killed in extermination camps. As a young boy in the 1950s and living in a suburb of north London, the recent fate of European Jews was part of our consciousness, but we felt privileged to have been kept safe. I do recall that at the age of about seven, at one of the many family gatherings at my paternal grandfather's house in Golders Green, I asked one of the older cousins about his tattoo, having heard that a couple of family members had survived the camps and that they had retained these tattoos. I do rather cringe now when I recall my naivety and lack of tact, but the cousin, a quietly spoken and dignified man in his fifties, was happy to show me the numbers on his forearm without a trace of shame or embarrassment. It was only later that I discovered that having a tattoo meant that you were not sent immediately to the gas chamber but were assigned to work, which meant possible survival.

It is surprising how the past continues to provide new information about family members. It was only very recently that we discovered, thanks to records from Yad Vashem, the World Holocaust Remembrance Centre, what had happened to my paternal grandfather's brother, who had escaped with his wife and daughter to Belgium, then France but was betrayed and then killed in Auschwitz. What brings his presence to life is that his photo has an uncanny resemblance to one of my sons. I also found out recently that the wife and daughter survived in France and that the daughter had a son now living in Belgium.

Growing up in Arnos Grove in north London, an area with only a small number of Jewish families, meant being aware of a certain amount of what one could call low-grade anti-Semitism; it was not as virulent as in pre-war Germany, but was in the culture. For example, there were curbs on Jews joining golf clubs, certain Masonic lodges, and on career advancement in professions like medicine at a number of hospitals, just to cite what was probably the tip of the iceberg. At my primary school Jews were excluded from the weekly religious lesson—we had to go to the large school hall and entertain ourselves until the lesson was finished. I went on a state-funded scholarship to a day public school, University College School, which was one of a few known not to have a Jewish quota. It was probably then no coincidence that I ended up in a profession, psychoanalysis, where Jews have played a key role; it was a kind of home for me.

I had hoped that anti-Semitic practices were a thing of the past in the UK, but unfortunately as was evident in the recent outbreak of anti-Semitism in the Labour Party, where for many years Jews had felt welcomed and an integral part of its culture, as well as increasing amounts of anti-Semitism towards Jewish students at universities, there is a new tide of racial prejudice both here and in other countries, along with the increasing power of populist and narrow-minded nationalist movements.

When black immigrants from the West Indies started coming to the UK in numbers from the 1950s onwards, we felt in our close family a certain kinship, as they were being subjected to public discrimination. It felt briefly that for once the Jews were not the only ones being excluded from the privileges of Englishness. I should add that I had a moment of epiphany about racial discrimination some years ago, when I was going to a case conference in Croydon on a black family, who were patients at the Cassel Hospital Family Unit where I was the consultant in charge for nearly thirty years. I went by London Underground and when I came out of the station, I felt very uncomfortable as I walked along the street on my way to the social services office. All around me were black men and women, with no white face visible anywhere. I felt alarmed and threatened. But then I saw a couple of black mothers and their babies in buggies, and I suddenly realised that I was just seeing ordinary people going about their business, but that this feeling of being threatened must be what a black person could feel in an all-white environment. I had come face to face with my own prejudice, and then could see things from a different perspective. This experience has remained a key moment for me in understanding the way that prejudice and preconceptions can alter perceptions and the interpretation of experience.

The Holocaust as an extreme event challenges our usual understanding of the past, how we remember it and keep it alive or not, and how we represent it and the victims' experiences. The challenge of such extreme events is to ask how it is possible to work through what happened, and to wonder whether it is ever possible, or even desirable, to come to terms with those events. The Holocaust, and indeed any of the genocidal events of our times, challenge our views about history, the past, and our capacity to remember. The word Holocaust, deriving from the ancient Greek word *holocautos* referring to a city on fire, or *holokauteo*, to make a whole burnt offering, itself related to the Hebrew word *Olah* meaning a burnt sacrifice offered whole to God, obviously refers to the reality of the burning of bodies in the crematoria and bonfires of the extermination camps. It thus has resonances both with the horrors of the camps but has some religious overtones to which some people have raised objection. It came to prominence as a term applying specifically to the extermination of the Jews in the late 1950s and early 1960s in preference to the general term genocide. It was probably part of the general trend of that time to start facing the reality of Nazi evils rather than remaining silent about them or only raising a whisper as it were. Raul Hilberg's classic study, which originally appeared in 1961, of what happened to the Jews in Nazi Germany does not use the term, nor does he use it in later editions. Instead, he refers to the destruction of European Jews, or the overall Jewish catastrophe between 1933 and 1945. Others have also used the Hebrew word *Shoah*, meaning catastrophe rather than Holocaust as referring to the annihilation of the Jews, as it has less of a religious and more of an historical emphasis, linking it to past Jewish catastrophes, and therefore has specific Jewish relevance. The problem in this area is that no word is ever going to capture the horrors of what happened to the Jews in Nazi Germany and the occupied countries, nor indeed what happened to the millions of other victims of Nazi persecution, including Russian prisoners of war, non-Jewish civilians, homosexuals, the Roma population, and many thousands of political prisoners.

Despite all these problems of definition I will continue to use the term Holocaust to refer to the planned total annihilation of the Jewish people in order to create a world without Jews.

The uniqueness of the Holocaust is that it was a genocide planned and organised in such a way as to leave no space for the survival of any otherness, making us feel the inadequacy of trying to present the suffering caused to so many people.[3] For a while, and still now to some extent, the phrase "after Auschwitz" has come to mean a break in human history, a discontinuity in the fabric of representation; meaning that life and thinking can never be the same after Auschwitz, that it represents a shift in our notion of human subjectivity. But it doesn't follow that we cannot attempt to trace what happened at Auschwitz to developments in German society, so that we can learn what factors make evil actions more likely in certain social situations, even if we still are often overwhelmed by the sheer scale of human destructiveness unleashed by National Socialism.

The evidence from previous chapters is that people can become caught up in evil for a variety of reasons, including for personal political and power reasons, or pushed on by fear and terror of the powers of a totalitarian regime, because it is easier to follow the crowd than take individual action, because of belief in a charismatic leader and driven on by large group processes, and for individual and more obviously criminal motives, with the quite frequent presence in their background of past trauma, or actions such as greed and ambition, sadism and psychopathy. The evidence from social psychology is that much blind obedience to strong authority seen in the laboratory matches to some extent what took place on the ground in Nazi Germany. The Stanford Prison and the BBC experiment indicate how roles, rules, and norms can transform people's character and make ordinary people sadistic towards others. When this transformation occurs, others are perceived as anonymous with no subjectivity. Others are also perceived as lacking ordinary humanity, becoming objectified or seen as less than human. These two processes can be seen as the core of much evil, and they can certainly be seen in many aspects of the way that Jews in the Holocaust were seen as less than human, and became objectified and dehumanised, with their subjectivity annihilated prior to being physically annihilated.

As described in Chapter 2, the BBC researchers found that identification with the aims of the experiment influenced attitudes to obedience, so that people may engage in or approve harmful behaviour not simply because they are absolved of responsibility, but also because they come to believe that their actions are serving a worthy purpose, such as enlarging human knowledge. Such an explanation can provide insight into some of the factors that led to the effectiveness of Nazi rule. People were not simply begrudgingly or numbly following orders; in many instances they embraced the broader social vision and mission of fascism.

The ease with which excessive authoritarianism can break out in social situations is rather sobering and shows how ordinary people can get into abnormally violent states of mind in certain situations, where the now violent subject is enabled to annihilate the other's subjectivity. One can then see some of the features that characterise how violent regimes may exploit human vulnerabilities in order to perpetuate and practise violence on their population, when ordinary people can find themselves caught up in processes that ultimately lead to evil acts. Certain situations, what one might call "precursor situations", or "states", may be particularly favourable to the building up of malicious aggression. People, even morally decent people, seem particularly vulnerable to conformist behaviour when there is a combination of strong authority and homogenous group values. Group values that promote heterogeneity and plural viewpoints are less likely to promote aggression.

As I have described, evil acts eliminate otherness; the bonds uniting people in a human, intimate relationship of the I/Thou form are broken. This creates a moral vacuum, where personal meaning and responsibility, human subjectivity, with the owning of agency and a capacity for self-reflectiveness and respect for others, is weakened and in extreme cases annihilated, accompanied by various degrees of triumph or pleasure in the acts of destructiveness. Sometimes the annihilation of the subject is accompanied by or motivated by the fantasy of psychic rebirth following death, as can be seen in some serial killers, terrorists, and as part of the Nazi ideology of creating a new society cleansed of non-Aryans. In the Nazi ideology history was also erased and then reconfigured; exterminating the Jews would bring apocalyptic deliverance, eliminating any debt to the Jews as the people of the Bible and building a society that owed no historical or moral debts to the Jews, whom they saw at the same time as immensely powerful, the source of all evil, of both capitalism and bolshevism, of those for *and* against the accumulation of capital. In the previous chapter I have also outlined the processes in the Holocaust by which people were stripped of their identity and in Arendt's terms became superfluous as human subjects.

One of the main themes I have emphasised is how the human imagination is at the root of much human evil, that evil is the product of the human imagination stirred up at a group and societal level and penetrating the individual psyche of individuals. And so, one way of trying to organise the vast field of information about the Holocaust is to look at what one might call the "Nazi Imaginary", the way that German society created an imaginary political community with which millions of ordinary Germans identified. As I described in the introduction, the concept of a nation is, as Benedict Anderson has shown, a compound of fact and fiction. Anderson defines the nation as a cultural phenomenon, an imagined political community, imagined as both inherently limited and sovereign, with its sense of a unity owing as much to *imagination* as to any political realities. The nation had to be invented, "imagined, modelled, adapted and transformed".[4] This makes the idea of a nation or nation state susceptible to incorporating all kinds of conscious notions and unconscious fantasies into its final but unstable version. Hobsbawm described how the rise of the Nazi state, with the resurgence of militant nationalism, arose as a way of "filling the void left by failure, impotence, and the apparent inability of other ideologies or political projects and programmes to realize men's hopes".[5] But more than filling a void, the Nazi imagined community pushed forward an elaborate mosaic of ideas, myths, conscious and unconscious fantasies, and slogans, bound together by a powerful but pernicious racial ideology of the superiority of the so-called Aryan race over other "inferior" races, which took over as the dominant element of ordinary German consciousness, and was a major driving force of Nazi atrocities and the behaviour of ordinary people towards Jews both in Germany and in the occupied countries. The Nazi Imaginary gave permission for the killing of "inferior" races; it became morally acceptable. The totalitarian Nazi regime with its use of fear and violence was able to put into practice what the Nazi Imaginary put forward as justification for the regime's genocidal acts, while language was constantly used to camouflage evil, with the use of euphemisms to cover up atrocities. Meanwhile, the image that the Nazi party aimed to portray was that of a youthful, forward thinking, and radical movement, which would appeal to those who had had enough of the "old" politics. Hitler and his propaganda machine were adept at conveying their image, for example Hitler pioneered the use of an aerial campaign during the 1932 elections, visiting several sites in one day, which might then culminate in a mass rally.

At such rallies, as I mentioned in Chapter 3, Nazism like other totalitarian ideologies aimed at narcissistic triumph over supposed enemies, offering the illusion of some utopian idealised future for those who followed the leader, not of course to the hated outsiders who were to be ruthlessly eliminated. It also provided a narrative of revenge for the past supposed national humiliation and wounded narcissism that followed from defeat in the First World War, together with the renewal and rebirth of German society and nationhood. The Nazi Imaginary, including some of its key images such as the swastika, continues to provide a model for some extreme nationalist movements; it provides them with a ready-made model of a revenge narrative with which they can identify.

Renée Danziger has written in depth about different kinds of revenge, from ordinary and proportionate revenge when one seeks justice for some intended harm, a crime or hurtful act, to radical revenge which takes no account of proportionality, intention, or culpability.[6] The Nazi Imaginary provided a model of radical revenge, in that its extreme incitement to hatred as a way of righting so-called wrongs lacked any sense of proportionality; there is of course no actual evidence that the Jews in Germany intended to defeat their own country, nor were they culpable of what Hitler and the Nazis accused them of, such as being part of an international conspiracy to do harm to the German nation.

Radical revenge, with decreasing concern for proportionality, intention, and culpability, unfortunately remains a powerful way of managing group and social narcissistically based grievances. One merely has to witness a Donald Trump rally, as indeed Danziger herself did from the inside, to witness radical revenge's power; the "lock her up" motive in the 2016 US election campaign targeting Hillary Clinton showed how important revenge was for many of Trump's followers.[7]

Chapter 3 has charted how easy it seems to be for groups of people to perpetrate what they could not imagine was possible as individuals. Powerful feelings of supposed humiliation or injustice or hatred and the wish for revenge on supposed injustices can be intensified and, with the addition of a charismatic leader or leadership group, can lead to atrocious acts of violence, at least by those ready to be influenced. But there must be some element of choice in those who go along with the group. It is too easy to explain away participation in group violence as the fault of the group and not that of the individuals in the group. But choice can be easily lost in the almost delusional states of mind stirred up in some groups. The distance from reality in those groups dominated by a powerful leader and/or by strong ties of group loyalty can stir up social anxiety that can reach such delusional forms, where the outcome may be extraordinary violence

Much time and effort has apparently gone into discussions about whether the course of the Third Reich was primarily determined by the decisions of Adolf Hitler, which were "intended" to realise the goals of an ideologically derived programme to which he had clung with fanatical consistency since the 1920s and described in *Mein Kampf*, or whether the structures and institutions of the Third Reich, including the Holocaust, were produced by the chaotic decision-making process of the regime, with an unsystematised and improvised shaping of bureaucratic policies to deal with the Jews, which then had a life of its own with increasingly extreme results. Such debates may be useful as a way of motivating researchers, but I am not sure that they are resolvable into single causes; most human situations involve many causes, and quite often there is just a mess, which one does one's best to put into order, however unsatisfactory. Different narratives may claim prominence for a while and then are superseded by new ones, as new evidence and new ways of thinking come to light. It doesn't make sense to pinpoint one person alone as responsible for the Nazi Imaginary, nor to ignore the role of groups of people in sustaining and elaborating the Nazi creed, nor to ignore the role of technology and bureaucracy in helping to put into practice the vilest elements of that creed, nor the political, social, and historical forces that allowed that creed to flourish.

Thus, if one asks who was responsible for the Nazi Imaginary, one can certainly cite as pivotal to the whole enterprise Hitler and those closest to him, such as Goebbels, Himmler, Göring, Hess, etc. But the elaboration of the creed and its application required many other participants at various levels and included the willingness of many ordinary Germans to go along with the regime's primary objectives. It is worth adding the obvious, that whoever were involved in acts of atrocity at whatever level were still personally responsible for those actions, even if the Nazi Imaginary was cobbled together as a result of many different individual, group, and social influences.

As a crucial element of the Nazi Imaginary, instead of the Kantian ethical community uniting all humans through consensus, the Nazis propagated the concept of the *Volksgemeinschaft*, or "people's community", a racially unified and mystical concept uniting all Germans, but of course excluding all others, predominantly Jews. With Germans traumatised by the defeat of 1918 and the Great Depression, the Nazis were able to appropriate the emotive power of this myth while transforming its essence from political, social, and religious inclusivity to racial exclusivity.[8]

The translation of the German nation into a single body made of identical cells was adopted literally, in order to create a "community of blood" (*Blutgemeinschaft*). There was also a pseudo-scientific racial theory backing the ideology, a form of biomedical ideology or fantasy world of scientific racism, where the so-called German race was at risk of becoming weakened by contaminants. Those deemed unable to join the pure community were to be systematically and "scientifically" eliminated; it began with the euthanasia of the disabled and mentally ill and soon escalated to anyone thought unable to join this primitive blood community, or whose blood would contaminate the purity of the Aryan race, Jews predominantly.

The core of Nazism centred upon irrational racial theories, with the fantasy of the pure German Aryan race going back in time to ancient Germanic tribes inhabiting the German woods and forests, a fantasy which seems to have even inspired the German philosopher and Nazi supporter Martin Heidegger, who built a hut in the middle of the Black Forest from which he composed much of his work.[9] Such images of a pure German identity were also directly linked with extreme nationalistic feelings and long-standing anti-Semitic trends, so that the Jews became a major source of racial impurity and thereby needing to be excluded from civil society, then segregated and eliminated, as part of the fantasy of a new moral order, a "pure" world without Jews and some other "impure" minorities.

> The Nazis systematically attacked human responses. They set out to erode the moral status of Jews, homosexuals and others, denying them the protection of respect for their dignity ... [T]hey worked to replace sympathy with hardness.[10]

As part of the attack on humanity, the Nazis stripped their victims of protective dignity, and distanced them emotionally so that they were pushed outside the boundaries of the moral community;[11] thereby Jews had no human status and hence no subjectivity. Along with the erosion of accepted moral identity there was the creation of a new post-Christian moral identity in a world free from Jews and anything associated with Jewish history and traditions, including the Hebrew Bible, fundamental to Christian thought in the New Testament. This new Nazi identity, with its fantasy of being the master race and the inferiority of other peoples, was shaped by hatred and facilitated by fear.

Alan Confino charts in detail how the Nazi attacks on Jews cannot be understood as merely a consequence of their perverse racial theories but was specifically a *religious* attack on Jewish history and identity. He asks why the burning of the Bible became an integral part of anti-Jewish actions. He proposes that it was because the Jews

> needed to be extirpated in order for a new Germany to arise. To create a Nazi civilization, a new European order and form of Christianity, Jewish civilization had to be removed. Germany's historical origins needed to be purified down to the Jews' shared past with Christianity via the canonical text.[12]

Confino seeks to add to the understanding of the Holocaust by focusing on what the Nazis thought was happening and how they imagined their world, and therefore what made the persecution and extermination of the Jews justifiable, conceivable, and imaginable. While study of the regime's racial ideology and pseudo-scientific world view adds to our understanding of the Holocaust, Confino argues that it leaves out a set of identities, beliefs, and memories that made Nazi Germany, in particular the way that the Germans imagined a world without Jews.[13] The Nazis used the presence of the anti-Semitic ideas prevalent in German society at the time, but gave them a new construction, reinterpreting the past of Jewish, German, and Christian relations to fit their vision of creating a new world. He does see that the history of European colonialism and exploitation and enslavement of indigenous populations is relevant in understanding this development, in that the Nazi notions of race and inferior peoples belonged to that tradition and set the stage for the Nazi genocide.

But the elimination of the Jews had specific meanings in the Nazi Imaginary. The Jews stood for the origins of the Bible and Christianity, and therefore in the Nazis' wish to recreate a new mythic origin for their homeland or *Heimat*, they had to be removed and eliminated from history so that there would be no reminders of their foundational role. The Nazis wished to wipe the slate clean, as it were; extermination of the Jews would then eradicate the debt to them and create a purified nation, a home for Aryans.

The Jews also represented for the Nazi regime the reality of emancipation and modernism, liberalism, and rootlessness as Jews were scattered throughout the world with at that time no specific homeland.

> Rootlessness and specific roots commingled in crafting the Nazi idea of origins. The Nazis persecuted Jews because as rootless cosmopolitans they did not belong with German identity and they also persecuted them because as the people of the Book they did not belong in German, Christian identity.[14]

Confino gives many examples, with visual evidence, of acts of violence against Jews early in the Nazi regime, with local parades, carnivals, and processions displaying vile anti-Semitic placards, the burning of books including the Bible, and marking out Jews for persecution. The visual evidence reveals a forest of anti-Jewish signs covering Germany, in hotels, restaurants, train stations, spas, at the beach, in local and provincial roads, ranging from "Jews are not welcome", to "Jews enter here at their peril".

> The forest of signs added to the story that the Nazis had already been telling about Jews and Germany. By burning books, Nazis excluded Jews from national culture; by having faith in the notion of race, they excised them from national history; by using public violence, they excused them from local life; and by seeing Jews everywhere, they excised them from the national space. The anti-Jewish signs marked every space in Germany, every locality, every site, every landscape, as a place that Jews could not trespass.[15]

Imagining a Germany without Jews had thus become a central part of the Nazi Imaginary, created in the years between 1933 and 1938. While the Final Solution had yet to be created, it was already possible to *imagine* Germany "cleansed" of its Jewish influence.

Anti-Semitism also had various other functions within the Nazi Imaginary, such as a means to deflect examination of the regime's own deficiencies as all failures could be put down to Jewish influence; as a motivating element in various competing departments, to see who could be the most efficient and energetic in their anti-Jewish practices; as a way of maintaining a unified party; as a means of plundering Jewish businesses and resources; as a way of finding scapegoats for the traumas of the last war and for defeats in the Second World War; as well as for satisfying sadistic and criminal needs of some of the Nazi elite.

There are also some general features of anti-Semitism relevant for understanding the Nazi variety. These are well described in the psychoanalyst Otto Fenichel's 1940 paper on anti-Semitism. Of course, Fenichel had mostly in mind the East European Jews in Czarist Russia or the Jews in the Middle Ages, while he was battling to understand the prejudice against Jews in a Germany where they were much more integrated. Yet his notions still have a contemporary resonance in trying to look at issues of projection and displacement, as well as paying attention to how psychoanalysis and social theory can enrich one another.

For Fenichel, the anti-Semite arrives at his hatred of the Jews by a process of displacement or projection, seeing the Jew as everything that brings him misery, not only from his external oppressor but also misery from his internal world, his unconscious instincts.[16] The Jew, as with other persecuted groups, can be a vehicle for such projections because of the difference in Jewish life and practices, their apparent difference in appearance, their "foreignness", and their long history of retaining their identity. There are of course also social factors, such as their role as moneylenders at a time when usury was a sin for Christians, which perpetuated their long-standing outsider role, and the historical fact that the Jews rejected Christ's message. A racial minority can become suitable as a carrier of projections because "One's own unconscious is also foreign. Foreignness is that which the Jews and one's own instincts have in common."[17] The foreigner can become "uncanny", a reminder of archaic and repressed desires. Thus,

> The Jew with his unintelligible language and ununderstandable God appears uncanny to the non-Jews, not only because they cannot understand him and therefore can imagine all sorts of sins in him, but

still more so because they can understand him very well somewhere in the depths, because his customs are archaic, that is contain elements which they once had themselves, but later lost.[18]

Perhaps the archaic history of the Jews, who were enslaved, gained their freedom from servitude, and then found their homeland, only to be expelled from it and forced to wander into foreign lands in order to settle, has a particular resonance, stirring up primitive fears about the loss of home and a threat to identity. It may also be possible to extend Fenichel's explanations about attitudes to Jews to prejudiced attitudes towards refugees from Afghanistan and other parts of the world, many of whom are also fleeing from a form of servitude.

I have already described in Chapter 3 how Werner Bohleber showed that unconscious fantasies of purity, unity, and violence have made a significant contribution to the presence of anti-Semitism. He points out that the propensity for unconscious desires to attach themselves with such ease to national and ethnic ideologies is notably facilitated by notions about home and the body as the containers of collective and individual identity. Thus, the Third Reich used the notion of fatherland or mother country to appeal to Germans' wish for an irrational and exclusive racial identity. That regime also used archaic fantasies about the purity of German bodies and the German body politic, which was seen to be threatened with "contamination" and or "pollution" by "lower" races, such as Jews and Slavs.

Kathy Phillips has pointed out how much mass nakedness was an element of the Nazi imagination, used in various contexts to assert control over victims' existence.[19] The Nazi policy of mass strippings had its aim to erase identity, humiliate, make victims feel weak and defenceless, and provide the perpetrators with both feelings of disgust and sexual titillation. There is also a link with images of Dante's *Inferno* and Last Judgment paintings, mentioned both by survivors, such as Primo Levi, and by Nazi planners of the camp system, where nakedness is a code for evil; inmates became the naked damned. "In Last Judgment paintings, everyone emerges naked from the tombs, but angels quickly robe the 'good', whereas the damned stay bare."[20] Phillips adds at the end of her paper that there is an unwelcome similarity between the posturing and gleeful degrading of Nazi camp guards of their victims' bodies to the attitude to the bodies of prisoners at Abu Ghraib prison, where "proudly self-photographed American guards rely on spiffy blue gloves and prestigious camouflage or khaki to distinguish themselves from the naked, fit for torment".[21]

Accounting for one of the more bizarre elements of the Nazi Imaginary, Eric Kurlander in his 2017 book *Hitler's Monsters* describes how some Nazi scientists were obsessed with death rays and supernatural phenomena, and that a belief in the occult was not uncommon among the Nazi elite. Kurlander argues that such dabbling was more than a quirky sideshow, but as with several extremist political groups part and parcel of their tenuous attitude to reality and truth.

What was also notable in the Nazi Imaginary was an obsession with recording in documents, photos, and film all the activities of the regime, however horrific. As George Steiner, described:

> It was one of the peculiar horrors of the Nazi era that all that had happened was recorded, catalogued, chronicled, set down; that words were committed to saying things no human mouth should ever have said and no paper made by man should ever have been inscribed with. It is nauseating and nearly unbearable to recall what was wrought and spoken, but one must. In the Gestapo cellars, stenographers (usually women) took down carefully the noises of fear and agony wrenched, burned or beaten out of the human voice. The tortures and experiments carried out on live beings at Belsen and Matthausen were exactly recorded. The regulations governing the number of blows to be meted out on the flogging blocks at Dachau were set down in writing. When Polish rabbis were compelled to shovel out open latrines with their hands and mouths, there were German officers there to record the fact, to photograph it, and to label the photographs … The unspeakable being said, over and over, for twelve years. The unthinkable being written down, indexed, filed for reference … The language was infected not only with … great bestialities. It was called upon to enforce innumerable falsehoods, to persuade the Germans that the war was just and everywhere victorious. As defeat began closing in on the thousand-year Reich, the lies thickened to a constant snowdrift.[22]

Perhaps it is then no wonder that it took the Germans years after the war to recover the ordinary decency of language, as it had become so infected with lies and distortions, so corrupted by the obsession with cataloguing and rejoicing in horror.

Anti-Semitism of course has a long history, and there has apparently been much debate about how much the Nazi variety was a continuation of that history and how much it marked a completely new phase, issues discussed in detail by Shulamit Volkov in her paper "Anti-Semitism as a Cultural Code". She cites Hannah Arendt's analysis of anti-Semitism as different from the age-old prejudice against Jews and as linked to the birth of the modern nation-state, and their role within it. Of all the peoples of Europe, the Jews appeared to be the only one without a state of their own, and in that sense, they represented an inter-European, non-national element in a world of growing or existing nations.[23] Both their recent emancipation and their separateness, however in reality assimilated, became a source of intense prejudice against them.

Other studies showed that while anti-Semitic political parties were relatively weak in Imperial Germany and elsewhere in Europe, anti-Semitism became endemic in many walks of life. Nazi anti-Semitism certainly took on new forms, but it grew upon institutional racism, as we would now call it.

In Germany Jews came to be seen as symbols of the modern world, "and antisemitism an immediate companion to a variety of anti-modern attitudes and a nostalgia for a pre-industrial past".[24] This nostalgia became linked to aggressive nationalism and the nationalist notion of the *Völk*, or people. By about the 1890s anti-Semitism was professed by all associations that propagated militant nationalism, imperial expansion, racism, militarism, anti-socialism, and support for a strong authoritarian government. By the end of the nineteenth century, Volkov describes how anti-Semitism had become a "cultural code" for the latter issues. Professing anti-Semitism became a sign of cultural identity.

There were certainly many examples prior to this period, as at the time of Jewish emancipation, when Jews were seen as threats to German identity, and some of the prejudice must have been based upon the age-old hatred of Jews as different, as moneylenders, as refusing Christ's message, etc., but its modern version became intimately linked to the rise of pseudo-scientific racial theories, taken on by the followers of German nationalism. Anti-Semitism became an emotional driving force for such movements. Unfortunately, many assimilated Jews in

Germany subsequently underestimated the new and deadly force of anti-Semitism as promoted by the Nazis, assuming it was just a variant of the age-old prejudices rather than a virulent new form mixed with violence, terror, and extermination.

It is worth pointing out that anti-Semitism usually blurs the complex relationship between Judaism and Christianity. There have been cycles of good and bad relations between Jews and Christians and also Muslims over the ages, which in this era of intolerance towards faiths is worth being reminded of. The question of the peaceful coexistence of different monotheistic faiths was a focus of attention in the Middle Ages. The Islamic world of the Middle Ages, such as during the period when the Iberian Peninsula was under Muslim rule, was a period of considerable tolerance towards other faiths, albeit with some restrictions. Both the major philosophers of Judaism and Islam of that time (who also both grew up in Muslim Cordoba)—Maimonides and Ibn Rushd (Averroes) produced arguments for a certain amount of tolerance towards other faiths. They both defended the search for philosophical truth against religious dogma.

Ibn Rushd had the more compelling argument for toleration, asserting that Christianity, Judaism, and Islam had several equivalent ethical positions; that there was much in common at a high level of thinking, with the common search for a form of faith, of reasoned arguments, and morality.

However, subsequent history of relations between the faiths consisted more frequently of ongoing clashes between doctrines. One may focus on relations between Jews and Christians from the Middle Ages as an illustration.

Jacob Katz in his book *Exclusiveness and Tolerance*[25] charts these relations in exemplary fashion, from the viewpoint of the Jews towards their non-Jewish environment from the Middle Ages to the Enlightenment era. What is both significant and helpful in this study is how he looks at the way that *both* faiths frequently maintained stereotyped attitudes to one another, preventing *mutual* understanding when such attitudes predominated. Indeed, there were clearly reciprocal relationships between Jews and Christians, each conditioned in their behaviour by the other, though with different emphases on each side.

On the one hand, Jew and Christian share a common Bible tradition with considerable overlap in values and even moral commandments. However, they have different attitudes to religious truth. On the other hand, the Jews believed that they had a special covenant with God, while for the Christians that covenant no longer stood with the appearance of Jesus. On both sides there was an ideology of separateness, with the Jews feeling themselves the chosen people, with a special and at times mystic union with God, while the Christians believed in a "new covenant" with the appearance of Jesus, with Jews now seen as covenant breakers. In turn the Jews considered Christians to be idol worshipers, seeing themselves as the upholders of the pure faith.

Meanwhile for much of the time, the existence of the Jews as a community depended upon economic relations with their Christian rulers as well as varying amounts of political protection. While economic relations were important, the underlying religious differences based upon attitudes to the covenant with God remained as the driving force for relations between the faiths with varying intensity, depending upon societal circumstances. While there were periods of discrimination against Jews, there were also relatively peaceful periods, such as between the ninth and eleventh centuries, where, for example, in France and Germany Jews were allowed to transact business almost without any restrictions. Nonetheless Christian and Jewish communities remained virtually two distinct societies, and being in the same economic and political framework this eventually caused many problems.

While it was possible in earlier times for Jewish populations to remain relatively separate from other communities, this was increasingly untenable as a position for those settling in Europe, and Jewish scholars and rabbis found various ways of trying to manage the need for more contact by reinterpreting aspects of Jewish everyday law, for example, acknowledging the Christian deity as having much in common with their own, being the maker of heaven and earth.

The point to make here is that if there is to be toleration, then two sides need to restrain themselves as well as opening up to the other there is then a mutual process of acceptance; that is, there is an *intersubjective* dimension.

I mention this sort of detail as a reminder that in looking to improve inter-faith relationships in our days, a matter of increasing urgency, there is clearly from these examples a need to look at *both* sides. The history of how Jews and Christians struggled with these issues may well be instructive and relevant today.

It was only in 1215, with the Fourth Lateran Council that a new attitude to Jewish contact with Christians came into existence, with the branding of Jews as an inferior social grouping, the compulsory wearing of the Jewish yellow badge (later appropriated by the Nazis) and warnings not to mix freely with Jews. This was also the period when religious inquisitions against heretics and schismatics came to the fore. By then, there was widespread limitation of Jews in social life and active discrimination against them, probably fuelled by the religious crusades, whose aim was to liberate the Holy Land from Islamic rule. One can see here then how religious belief can become intolerant when mixed with military ambitions—a phenomenon visible in, for example, Syria and Iraq in our times.

As I have mentioned, Jews had some tranquillity in the Iberian Peninsula, until they were expelled in 1492 from Spain, in 1497 from Portugal, having already been expelled from England in 1290 and from various European centres in the fourteenth century. The Spanish Inquisition then began as a way of trying to distinguish any heretics in those many Jews and Muslims who had converted to Christianity, though it then widened its scope towards any heretics. The Jews who left had to survive where they could, a haven being the Turkish Ottoman Empire, which had a particularly tolerant attitude to non-Muslims. The barriers between Muslims and non-Muslims were fluid and allowed such a useful cultural and commercial interchange between faiths that the Empire grew in wealth, as evidenced for example in Constantinople where mosques, churches, and synagogues were abundant and often in near proximity to one another.

Such tolerance was in striking contrast to the Habsburg Empire at the time of the Thirty Years War (1618–1648), where cohabitation between those holding different religious beliefs was impossible. Indeed, looking over the broad sweep of history, one could even say that in the last thousand years or so, Islam has been considerably tolerant, often giving hospitality to other faiths, something which can be easily lost sight of in the contemporary context. Indeed, the tolerationist writers of the seventeenth century often pointed to Islamic toleration as an example to be imitated.

It is also worth mentioning the subsequent formation of the Italian ghetto, following the diaspora of Jews after the expulsions from Spain and Portugal, most famously in Venice from 1516, as this represented a new period in Jewish–Christian relations, and one which in a number of ways was quite creative for both sides, in contrast to the derogatory sense that the term ghetto has today, and in marked contrast to how it was used by the Nazi regime as a way station to extermination.

On the one hand the Venetian ghetto was created in 1516 as a compulsory segregated quarter in which all Jews were required to live. Jews had already been reasonably well tolerated, as there was need for their economic help after a period of war with Genoa. The Venetian senate then decided to provide a protected space for the Jewish population. The term ghetto probably arose as there was a foundry (*getto* in Venetian) on this site. While the ghetto separated the Jewish and Venetian populations, there was considerable contact between them, and indeed during the day Jews were permitted to circulate freely throughout Venice. It was really an "open ghetto". While there were restrictions at night, there were several allowable exceptions, such as the passing through the ghetto gates of Jewish doctors attending on Christian patients. The ghetto was also later enlarged to take account of the increasing number of Jewish residents, who had grown considerably due to their increasing prosperity, and it then also included a wave of migrants who had been forcibly converted to Christianity but had retained their faith in secret.

While the ghetto limited the freedom of the Jewish population, it also offered them several benefits. It offered an urban experience in the heart of Venice and in immediate proximity to the Christian population. The boundaries between the ghetto and the rest of the city were porous, and thus created a new sense of intimacy between both sides. From the Jewish side, the ghetto then enhanced Jewish cultural interaction with the outside world, and Jewish culture, the printing industry, music, and architecture flourished. It also gave them a basic sense of security, even with the restrictions; they were not being expelled and their own experience was given some legitimacy. They felt they had a home. Interestingly, doctrinal differences between

Judaism and Christianity in medieval times constituted the "primary demonstration of the existence of a mutual awareness of diversity".[26] The situation in the ghetto became one in which Jews did not define their faith in terms of comparison with Christianity, and polemics against Christianity virtually ceased in the sixteenth century.

From the Christian side, there were benefits from contact with Jewish merchants and professionals, and even the Kabbalah, the Jewish mystical writings, became of great interest and influenced Christian intellectuals. Such writings had already influenced one of the most important of Renaissance philosophers—Pico della Mirandola.

The administration of the ghetto became more formalised as it enlarged, with its own councils, which had in time to take account of different ethnic Jewish populations—the Ashkenazi, Sephardic, and Levantine communities. In short, the ghetto came to function like a small republic at the heart of the larger Venetian republic.[27] This form of ghetto showed how the acceptance of differences can have a reasonable side, if managed well, that if communities are to remain in ghettos or ghetto-like areas, they need to be porous to the world outside the ghetto, and close to administrative centres, as well as open to close cultural exchanges. Assimilation may be preferable, but the fact is, communities of faith and of different cultures do often wish to be close to one another; they do not want to be lost in the general population.

Another feature of the Nazi Imaginary is that they appropriated the notion of the ghetto for their own purposes. Mitchell Duneier in his study of the ghetto idea and its modern versions, calls this the "Nazi deception".[28] They appropriated the ghetto as a way of maintaining the separateness of the Jewish population, but in a different and of course destructive form. Hitler claimed that he was reviving the ghetto of the Middle Ages as a way of legitimising his actions, but this was misleading as it was something entirely new—its express purpose was to destroy its inhabitants though violence and brutality.

As described above, the traditional ghetto was as Duneier describes always a mixed bag, as separation both created disadvantages for the Jews but also allowed their culture to continue and even at times flourish, as in Venice. Napoleon was the first to attempt to demolish the ghettos, but he also liberated the Jews in the name of the Revolution. Most ghettos in Western Europe then slowly fell.

The Nazi ghetto was a new creation, and thanks to the new technology which produced barbed wire, first used by cattlemen in the American West and then by the British in the Boer Wars, containment and effective isolation of those within the ghetto, mainly the Jews of Eastern Europe, was quickly made possible. This enabled Jews to be rounded up and confined separately from the rest of society. It made it easy to create the image of Jews as wild animals needing containment—coaches would be organised so that Germans could peer at them as if in a zoo. Being enclosed and overcrowded, the ghettos were sources of infection, thus reinforcing the image of Jews as dirty and disease-ridden, not only carrying lice but being lice. Ghetto residents were starved of supplies so became increasingly weak and debilitated with a high mortality among the most vulnerable. Their weakened condition again perpetuated the images of Jews as weak and subhuman. And the ghettos were the sites of continuous violence and brutality, and then way stations for the camps. They were also the sites of the residents' economic enslavement—all in the name of the Nazi Imaginary of racial purity.

Duneier also discusses the significant differences between the Nazi ghettos and how the idea of the ghetto has been used for understanding the situation of poor blacks in the US today. The black ghetto in America has always been used to restrict residential space based on race, income, and wealth. It can become a way of perpetuating racial intolerance and disadvantage by allowing ghetto hospitals, schools, and police protection to sink to the lowest level. The presence of the ghetto creates a

> vicious cycle in which space plays a distinctive role. When schools or streets or hospitals are rendered unequal through societal power, they come to symbolize the black way of life. This way of life is made visible through the physical living space that becomes known as the ghetto.[29]

The physical reality of the ghetto becomes a rationalisation for further segregation. There are, one might add, certain similarities in how this vicious cycle plays out and how the Nazi ghetto created a space for further attacks on human life, by creating an environment where Jews would be disease-ridden, they would then be perceived as disease carriers, rather than victims of a diseased ideology.

British–American slavery: social death and yearning for a psychic home

Though having distinct histories there is a resonance between black and Jewish peoples' experiences of dispersal, exile, and slavery. Slavery created a new form of racism based primarily on skin colour, which still provides a poisonous legacy. Sexist attitudes and sexual exploitation of black female slaves has added even more poison to the slavery legacy.[30] Some of the racist attitudes to black slaves by British and then American slave owners in the Caribbean and the US has uncomfortable parallels with some aspects of the Nazi Imaginary. My focus here is on some of the essential elements of the dynamic between slaves and their owners in the British-American context, which have remained a traumatic and still unworked through element in the present.

Slavery has a long history, and the modern slave trade has involved several different European powers and included Arab and African interests. But the transatlantic slave trade had an important part to play in the early development of capitalism in the UK. Goods such as sugar, spices, tobacco, and then cotton, which were not available in European markets, soon became highly prized commodities for consumers, and the ability to employ cheap labour and use large areas of land for cultivation in the New World became highly desirable for British investors. The slave plantations of the Americas not only provided these goods for the European markets but also provided a ready market for the colonists themselves, trading in a variety of goods and textiles. In early modern England and the Americas there was a veritable boom in the different elements of the Atlantic trade. As described in Eric Williams's classic 1944 study of the period, *Capitalism and Slavery*, British capitalism was a cause of the flourishing of the slave trade not a consequence of the slave plantation development; the origins of black slavery were economic not racial, more to do with the cheapness and availability of black labour and the ability of black workers to survive in the heat and to bring agricultural experience with them than the colour of the their skin.[31] But racism soon became a way of justifying the harsh conditions experienced in the slave plantations. Race became a construction created to legitimise inequality and protect the position of the white slaveholder, and it became backed up by legislation and the power of colonial administration.

Hugh Thomas in his comprehensive history of slavery doubts the accuracy of Eric Williams's take on the direct relationship between capitalism and slavery, though accepts that substantial profits from the slave trade were invested in British industry, in particular ship building and textile manufacture as well as various other commodities.[32] Even if Williams went too far in his argument about the direct link between capitalism and slavery, there seems little doubt that the Atlantic slave trade was a key factor in the development of the West European economies.

Keith Thomas in his book, *In Pursuit of Civility*, on the manners and civilisation of early modern England, notes that paradoxically the English were deeply involved in the slave trade at a time when their enthusiasm for personal liberty had never been greater.[33] But that liberty remained at home not abroad. Indeed, Adam Smith explained, "… that the more cultivated the society, and the greater the freedom and opulence of the inhabitants, the worse was the treatment of their slaves".[34]

Underpinned by the economic benefits of the slave trade, Thomas describes how the English then justified black slavery on the grounds that its victims were not Christian, and that their enslavement was necessary if they were to be converted, though conversion would not in fact lead to emancipation. Indeed, it was believed by many that if emancipated the slaves would fall into a life of idleness and crime. There was a belief that Africans were barbaric, lacking ordinary civility, with no knowledge of the arts or of science and hence were unacquainted with what constitutes civilised life. Thus, removal of Africans out of their state of "brutish barbarism" was doing them a favour. It must be said of course that "The West Indian planters … were predictably hostile to any attempts at 'civilizing' their slaves. By the end of the eighteenth century, it was they who had increasingly come to be seen as the barbarians."[35]

Many people in early modern England sincerely believed that the civilising mission was a moral obligation, and that it was good to bring people from a state of barbarism to a civilised way of life. "Even the great abolitionist William Wilberforce believed that 'the arts and sciences, knowledge and civilization,' were never the native growth of any country: 'They have ever been communicated from one nation to another, from the more to the less civilized.'"[36]

There was of course gradually increasing opposition to slavery and the notion of the slave as both barbarous and undeserving of emancipation, and a developing conviction that it was the condition of slavery that was undermining of civilisation. But it took many years for the abolitionists to win their argument, and then it was not only humanitarian considerations that led to the abolition of slavery in the British colonies, but also very likely the reality that the economic arguments for slavery were no longer relevant to a Britain in the throes of massive industrial growth and attendant new international markets.[37] There were other factors too that added to the pressure for reform, such as the Declaration of Independence in the American colonies, the sweeping away of traditional hierarches by the French Revolution and with it the Declaration of the Rights of Man, the interest taken by the British Prime Minister William Pitt in the abolition of slavery, the views of a variety of influential thinkers such as Montesquieu, Thomas Clarkson, William Wilberforce, and Benjamin Constant, and increasing slave revolts, such as in the French colony of Saint Dominigue (later known as Haiti) and led by the ex-slave Toussaint Louverture. But the legacy of the British slave trade remains to this day, with the persistence of overt or covert racist attitudes to non-white citizens, reminiscent of what Keith Thomas described as the eighteenth-century English attitudes to the "barbarous natives" of Africa.

Of course, emancipation did not take place in America, and the Southern states in particular remained wedded to the plantation economy and its use of slaves until the Civil War. Even after that war, black people in the South and elsewhere had to endure at times what one could call a transformed version of slavery—segregation and loss of essential human rights. Slavery remained, as Ira Berlin has described,

> woven into the fabric of American life. For most of its history, the American colonies and then the United States was a society of slaves and slaveholders. From the first, slavery shaped the American economy, its politics, its culture, and its most deeply

held beliefs. The American economy was founded upon the production of slave-grown crops, the great staples of tobacco, rice, sugar, and finally cotton that were sold on the international market and made some men extraordinarily wealthy … Between the founding of the Republic and the Civil War, the majority of presidents … were themselves slaveholders, and generally substantial slaveholders.[38]

The power of the American slaveholding class, many of whom were the nation's leaders, substantially shaped American culture and values. The struggle for freedom was linked to the reality of generations of Americans who spent their lives in captivity.

The history of slavery and the dynamic between freedom and slavery continues to haunt present day America, as it does the UK. There may not be organised segregation but institutionalised conscious or unconscious inequalities have become a way of perpetuating racial intolerance and disadvantage. Racist language and practice remain embedded in the fabric of many institutions such as the police—in the UK where racist and sexist banter can be deemed acceptable because it is banter, and in the US where it is hardly controversial to maintain that at least several US police forces remain racist, given what happened to George Floyd and many other victims of police brutality. The combination of racism and sexism has proved at times both intertwined and malignant, proving deeply traumatic for black women.[39]

Paul Gilroy argues[40] that the politics and social fabric of Western society, reliant as it was on slavery as a foundation of economic wealth, continues to be haunted by the inability to process the harsh reality of slavery and its continuing after-effects. He also argues that the history of slavery is not just confined to the black experience but is integral to Western history and the roots of modernism. The removal of Africans from their homes across the Atlantic in the cruel "middle passage" to the Americas where they became enslaved remains embedded in the Western modern experience. Modernity owes as much to the "catastrophic rupture of the middle passage"[41] as it does to the modern dream of revolutionary transformation.

The middle passage refers to one side of the triangular sailing route taken by British slave traders, the outward passage being the trip to Africa to exchange goods for slaves, and the final passage being the return from the Americas to Britain. During the middle passage, the slaves were packed below the decks of the ship. The men were usually shackled together in pairs using leg irons, or shackles as they were considered dangerous, as they were mostly young and strong and likely to turn on their captors if the opportunity arose, as indeed did happen from time to time. People were packed so close that they could not get to the toilet buckets, and so lay in their own filth. These conditions also encouraged disease, and there was about a 20% mortality rate. The voyage usually took six to eight weeks, but bad weather could increase this to thirteen weeks or more. The middle passage obviously has resonances with the way that Jews were packed together in cattle trucks on their way to the camps, both sets of experiences being the first step in the malignant process of deindividuation and loss of identity.

Gilroy uses the image of the slave ship in motion across the spaces between Europe, America, Africa, and the Caribbean, or what he calls the "Black Atlantic" as a central organising symbol for his enterprise and his starting point.[42] Fundamental to his project is also the concept of "diaspora", or the forced dispersal and scattering of peoples, common to both the black and Jewish experience and an important element in their sense of identity. The metaphors of journey, exile, and a yearning for what I have called a psychic home remain central to the black and Jewish diaspora.

I have proposed that the notion of a psychic home consists of several different and interacting elements, including the physical interior of a home but internalised as a psychic interior.[43] The notion of "personal identity" refers to the development and then maintenance of a person's character, how they put together in some way their various multiple identifications, as well as including wider issues concerning a person's cultural and social influences. I suggest that the basic elements of the psychic home can be seen to provide a way of organising the person's identity or can be seen as intrinsic to any notion of identity. Identity is a term used in many ways and by a variety of disciplines. It has become a central issue of concern in contemporary debates about politics, ethics, and culture. Issues of identity also touch upon the soul territory, that of each person's unique sense of who they are.

Identity is a vitally important but complex and at times elusive or indeterminate concept. There are various fixed or constant elements in the development of our identity, which can become the source of integration and of a sense of permanence, of achievement and coherence, and there are still issues about the nature of identity that challenge our thinking, such as its link with the processes of identification, the question of whether unity is an illusion or a real possibility.

I have proposed that one of the constant elements is that of the psychic home and that this provides a basis for a sense of identity, for crucial questions such as "Who am I? Who do I look and act like? Which religion and nationality am I?" They indicate a search for a place in life, an identity which provides a relatively stable sense of home, and that provides the core of the elusive and precarious notion of identity, whatever its complex vicissitudes, however much the human subject is distributed between other subjects. What contemporary accounts of identity in other disciplines repeatedly focus on is the notion of identity as plural, multiple, merging one with another, rather than as it were facing each other from separate corners. In addition, though identity involves individuals, their identity is formed under multiple influences. Identities involve having a position within our society and in relation to a history, a lineage. Certain markers of identity may be visible or can appear through inquiry—whether that is from a country of origin, race, religion, or ideological standpoint.

One can see an identity as involving the taking up of a particular position, depending upon different social roles or different histories. But taking up a position requires a starting point, or a frame of reference, or at least some scaffolding. This is where I have suggested that the notion of a psychic home comes in, as the starting point for the complex and indeed lifelong task of forming an identity in one's personal or professional life.

Stuart Hall, Gilroy's supervisor, faces similar issues to those of Gilroy in his exploration of visual representations of Afro-Caribbean and Asian "blacks" of the diasporas of the West—the new postcolonial subjects.[44] Such subjects must face complex identity issues. Historically displaced from their homes, they are not able to reclaim their homes, as those living in the colonies could do; they are subjects of a diaspora, dispersal. They have found other homes, and yet still have fundamental connections, through culture, history, myth, narrative, fantasy, and transmitted memories, to their origins. Dispersal and fragmentation are embedded in the history of all enforced diasporas, and clearly involve trauma and loss of identity. Such loss can only begin to be healed when forgotten connections between past and present are brought to light and once more set in place. That is not to say that there can be a return to what was; people's identities have moved on and have a life of their own. There are similarities but also differences between then and now which must be recognised. Hall rethinks the positionings and repositionings of Caribbean cultural identities in relation to at least three "presences"—the African presence, the sight of the repressed; the European presence, which is the site of exclusion and expropriation; and the American presence, the beginning of diaspora, diversity, hybridity, and difference. There is no simple way that these presences can be harmonised or unified in a comfortable identity. Rather, these presences, which represent different discourses, meet at various junction-points; they can become the site of different subjective positions, or sites of temporary attachment to different subject positions.

That is, he argues for a flexible, open-minded notion of identity, which can embrace different cultures and not impose on them from the outside. Such a view contrasts with that of imperialism, which was essentially about acquiring territory and imposing a particular way of life on other cultures, that is, about acquiring *other homes*. Imperialism is the attitude of a dominating metropolitan centre ruling a distant territory. The attitude of those who ruled the colonies, creating an imperial culture in these other homes, reflected the various tensions and injustices in the home culture. There arose a complex relationship between the home culture, which needed to be stable and prosperous, while exploiting overseas territories. Thus, Thomas Bertram's slave plantation in Jane Austen's *Mansfield Park* is shown to be mysteriously necessary to the poise and beauty of Mansfield Park. Imperial possessions are usefully *there*, in some other space, with an unnamed population, whose identity is scratched out, erased; while such places become the site for adventurers, disgraced younger sons, travellers who sow wild oats or collect exotica. Edward Said describes how in the great Victorian novels, "home" and "abroad" became crucial dimensions for analysing the nature of English society. Abroad

> … was felt vaguely and ineptly to be out there, or exotic and strange, or in some way or other "ours" to control, trade in "freely", or suppress when the natives were energized into overt military or political resistance. The novel contributed significantly to these feelings, attitudes, and references and became a main element in the consolidated vision, or departmental cultural view, of the globe.[45]

Said shows how there was in fact considerably more resistance to the imperialist impositions than was openly admitted. He also describes how in the course of time, decolonisation was very much about *reclaiming homes* which had been usurped. In these acts of reclamation, all nationalist cultures become dependent on the concept of a national identity. As necessary as this process is in the act of liberation, there is of course a danger of mirroring the dominating culture from which they wish to be liberated.

Said argues for a new concept of identity, one which respects different cultures, *different homes*, where connections are made between cultures, other languages and geographies, where it is accepted that none today is *one* thing. Identity in this sense is about inclusion not exclusion; what I have called a "home for otherness" is integral to this more open notion of identity.

However, it does seem that currently, with the rise of populist movements, there is far from there being an end to excluding nationalist sentiments, rather there is an increasing tendency globally to look towards the idea of the nation as a way of trying to assert control over what is seen as too much interference from "outside".

As I have mentioned in the introduction, Zygmunt Bauman considered that the reality of the Holocaust means that one must rethink the nature of modernity, but he did not take the legacy of slavery into his account, thus missing the opportunity to deepen his argument. Instead, he considered that it was the rational world of modern civilisation itself that made the Holocaust, the epitome of evil, thinkable, or imaginable, and thus possible. The reality of mass killings of millions on an industrial scale was an event "which disclosed the weakness and fragility of human nature … when confronted with the matter-of-fact efficiency of the most cherished among the products of civilization; its technology, its rational criteria of choice, its tendency to subordinate thought and action to the pragmatics of economy and effectiveness".[46]

Thus he argues that a major lesson of the Holocaust is that such destructiveness remains a permanent possibility of our modern civilisation, in view of the way that modern society tends, for example, to facilitate emotional distance between people, or to depersonalise them, and to treat the human subject as a mere cog in a hierarchical structure dominated by technology. Strong safeguards which recognise the susceptibility of modern society to become genocidal, particularly when a powerful monolithic ideology threatens to dominate political life, are then essential if we are to have a decent society with a reduced risk of unleashing unbridled destructiveness. Without just safeguards, one can see how violence becomes dissociated from moral oversight through the machinery of bureaucracy. I would add that the slave plantations also revealed how the machinery of imperialism and exploitation wedded to racist and sexist attitudes to the slaves was able to distort moral values in the slaveholders, attitudes that have remained embedded in those Western societies unable or unwilling to face their history.

Regarding the internal and external dynamics of slavery, the classic work of Orlando Patterson in his 1982 book *Slavery and Social Death* remains central to the understanding of the experience of both slaves and slave owners. He describes instances of slavery in every type of society where slavery has been found, including medieval Europe, the Islamic kingdoms, the Caribbean islands, and the American South, among many others. He describes three key elements of slavery, intensified in the slave plantations.[47]

The first is the element of power enforced through coercion. Even under disguise, this absolute use of forceful power is always present. Slavery is one of the most extreme forms of domination, with the threat of violence and coercive influence backed by the power of the authorities. Thus, violence towards slaves such as whipping, or sexual control of women, was not just a method of punishment but a way of impressing on the slaves that they were mere slaves, under the control of their master, a technique, one might add, dear to concentration camp guards.

Second is what he calls "natal alienation", which means that the slaves were excluded from the social order and disowned of any rights belonging inherently to other members of that society. Forced out of their native homes, they lost the connections that bind them together in a community or live intersubjective relations. Social ties between slaves were unrecognised and forcibly discouraged. Cut off in time from integrating the experience of their ancestors into their daily lives, the slaves were alienated from their culture, with a

> loss of ties of birth in both ascending and descending generations ... It was this alienation of the slave from all formal, legally enforceable "ties of blood", and from any attachment to groups or localities other than chosen by the master, that gave the relation of slavery its peculiar value to the master.[48]

Natal alienation did not prevent slaves from yearning for their lost homes, which became a major theme of their songs, what W. E. B. Du Bois called "The sorrow songs" in his book *The Souls of Black Folk*. Their themes are permeated by fear and sorrow, as well as hope and yearning for a better life and what I would call a psychic home as a marker of identity. "Mother and child are sung, but seldom father; fugitive and weary wanderer call for pity and affection, but there is little of wooing and wedding; the rocks and the mountains are well known, but home is unknown."[49] Of course, music remains to this day essential to black communities in the US and the UK as an expression of their authenticity. Gilroy explores in detail how the power and significance of music grew in the Black Atlantic, while slaves were denied access to literacy on pain of death. Slaves were forbidden to use drums, as there was a fear they would incite rebellion, but even in contemporary black music the "irrepressible rhythms of the once forbidden drum are often still audible".[50]

Natal alienation did not occur to the Jews during the Holocaust, at least not to the same extent as to the black slaves, and not in previous generations, because even when persecuted and slaughtered in pogroms or by the Nazis, they retained their close relationship to their ancestors and traditions; they did not suffer the complete rupture of an ongoing middle passage. "The Holocaust was not natally alienating ... because the central tenets of Judaism—the defining traditions of Judaism—endured in spite of Hitler's every intention to the contrary."[51]

The power of music to sustain human connections also became an important element of Jewish communities. Music in the synagogue was always integral to worship, with the cantor and the choir performing powerfully evocative melodies to the Hebrew texts. With emancipation in the nineteenth century, one can see an explosion of Jewish musicians, violinists and pianists, etc., which enabled them to join in cultural life and not remain on the margins, and which has lasted to this day.

The third feature common to slavery is the constant dishonouring of the slave by explicit behaviours that communicate to him or her that they are completely powerless. The slave had no honour because he or she had no power and no independent existence as a human subject. They had no name of their own to defend but could only defend their master's worth and name. The Southern slave owners had a sense of themselves as men of honour, fostering gentility and graciousness in their own, while mistreating their slaves, at times with a sado-masochistic intensity. Patterson quotes Frederick Douglas, once a slave, who wrote that, "A man without force is without the essential dignity of humanity. Human nature is so constituted that it cannot honor a helpless man, although it can pity him; and even that it cannot do long, if the signs of power do not arise."[52]

Another major concept introduced by Patterson is that of the "social death" of the slave which follows as a result of the toxic relationship between slaveholder and slave. The slave is violently uprooted from home and community, and is dissocialised and depersonalised. This is the process of social negation, the first phase of enslavement.[53] This is followed by introduction of the slave into the master's community, but they are introduced paradoxically as a non-being, with no live subjectivity, not subject of their experiences but subject to the master's authority, hence socially dead. They will lose their name and might be tattooed to show that they are the master's property. But although the slave might be socially dead, they remained nonetheless an element of society, but on the margins, in a "liminal state", of institutionalised marginality,[54] not an outcast like being a Jew in Nazi Germany, but lacking human rights and living "on the margin between community and chaos, life and death, the sacred and the secular".[55] The slave was to be an integral part of society but as a subordinate and subject to the slave owner. This entailed a form of what Du Bois called "double consciousness",[56] the sense of always looking at oneself through the eyes of the other, feeling a conflict-ridden two-ness in the soul, as American and as black.

Claudia Card has argued that social death is one of the defining features of genocides wherever they may occur. For her social death is central to both the slave experience and the Nazis' Final Solution, "at least as important to what is evil about it as the mass physical murder and physical torture".[57] Furthermore, she maintains, I think convincingly, that the intentional production of social death in a people or community is the central evil of genocide, distinguishing genocide from other mass murders.[58] This use of the notion of social death is close to what I have described as the evil which aims to produce the annihilation of the human subject, where human otherness and agency is psychologically denied and/or physically eliminated.

CHAPTER 6

Shakespeare and evil—a dagger of the mind

It would be difficult to imagine an important and simultaneously evil or intolerant work of art, whether that is in writing, the visual arts, or music. Totalitarian art is usually just boring, as it tends to push one ideology, such as socialist realist portrayals of the benefits of cooperative labour, or the bland sculptures commemorating some heroic endeavour. Or it can be strangely fascinating if sinister, such as Leni Riefenstahl's 1934 film of Hitler's Nuremberg rally, with its beautifully filmed yet obvious promotion of the Nazi ideology. Intolerant art such as this film, however, promotes conflict, while lasting and successful art tries to resolve it. Cartoons and satire can push the boundaries of acceptable taste and even when successful may require a certain element of intolerance, but the accompanying humour usually provides some humanising balance, and intolerance is usually aimed at satirising some absurdity or even injustice. There are of course examples of intolerant cartoons such as those depicting racial stereotypes, but they hardly count as art. In general, the arts are tolerant activities; their practice requires mutual understanding and communication on the part of artists, performers, and audiences for the artist's vision to be fully realised. They may evoke intolerant reactions, particularly when they push the boundaries of human understanding and perception, or challenge current values and beliefs, but their aim is to communicate not dominate; and if they sometimes challenge accepted values, it is to open up to the world a new and usually positive vision, which may nonetheless require examination of the evils of the world and illustration of how goodness is a fragile affair, and how limited are our capacities to modify some of our most irrational impulses.

While there is no perfectly tolerant society, Shakespeare's texts, particularly his Comedies, offer a vision of how different and apparently alien cultures can be tolerated in a world of conflicting desires. His Tragedies, most obviously *King Lear* and *Othello*, often reveal the damage and devastation brought about by intolerance, hatred, and jealousy, as well as encapsulating vividly the way that evil characters can dominate vulnerable people or attempt to destroy the good, which is one way that evil manifests itself. I have already quoted Stuart Hampshire's insight from his work as an intelligence officer dealing with Nazis, how unmitigated evil and nastiness are as natural, it seemed, in educated human beings as generosity and sympathy, a fact that was obvious to Shakespeare but not previously evident to Hampshire.

Shakespeare demonstrates in many of his plays a remarkable ability to tolerate conflicting, strange, and ambiguous elements, which offer us a vision of a respectful and human world, where otherness is to be wondered at, not disavowed, a vision which still stands as a beacon of humanity in dark times. Shakespeare, as Harold Bloom put it, "invented the human as we continue to know it".[1] By this he meant that Shakespeare developed characters that develop rather than unfold, because they reconceive themselves, they overhear themselves as they talk, or show a capacity for self-reflection, and they also appear to be genuinely alive, even if they are still dramatic characters. He was able to invent innumerable ways to represent human change and transformation through his heightened language and multilayered poetry. "The dominant Shakespearean characters—Falstaff, Hamlet, Rosalind, Iago, Lear, Macbeth, Cleopatra among them—are extraordinary instances not only of how meaning gets started, rather than repeated, but also how new modes of consciousness come into being."[2]

That is, Shakespeare has provided us with the vocabulary and complex and inwardly deep scenarios involving human characters, for what we still consider to be definitive aspects of the human condition. Even when conflicts and murders are represented on stage, or when as in *Hamlet* the stage is littered with corpses, the end of the drama leaves one with an enlarged sense of human relations. Hamlet's last words "The rest is silence" reverberate in the soul; it is an almost unbearable reminder of human mortality and frailty.

Shakespeare's texts are rich in ambiguity, antitheses, fundamental metaphors, and in-depth insight into human desires and motivations. "The antithetical style is a powerful means of suggesting the paradox and enigma of the nature of man."[3] The Shakespearean text itself is thus able to incorporate multiple viewpoints, while remaining free from moralistic judgments—which is not to say that Shakespeare does not reveal judgment; evil is never sanctioned in his works, though it may be well represented. Instead, there are numerous injunctions to demonstrate Christian patience; evil is to be punished by God, not men. Justice and mercy were crucial issues for the age, and the constant interaction between what humans may judge on earth and what must be left to God, is particularly well represented in *Measure for Measure*, where several characters who have behaved badly or immorally are shown mercy.[4]

As Shakespeare was able to reveal the inner life of the human subject, both human and "inhuman", on the stage in a powerful way, his evil characters encapsulate how evil can develop and take over a person's inner world, revealing, "a deep, poetic, psychology or metaphysics of the birth of evil",[5] and how people can become "bewitched" by evil into performing or colluding with dreadful actions.

In his classic study on Shakespearean tragedy, A. C. Bradley wrote that in the Tragedies moral evil is the main source of the convulsion which produces suffering and death and violently disturbs the order of the world.

> The love of Romeo and Juliet conducts them to death only because of the senseless hatred of their houses. Guilty ambition, seconded by diabolic malice and issuing in murder, opens the action in *Macbeth*. Iago is the main source of the convulsion in *Othello*; Goneril, Regan and Edmund in *King Lear*. Even when this plain moral evil is not the obviously prime source within the play, it lies behind it; the situation with which Hamlet has to deal has been formed by adultery

> and murder … Evil exhibits itself … as something negative, barren, weakening, destructive, a principle of death. It isolates, disunites, and tends to annihilate not only its opposite but itself.[6]

Evil in the tragic character not only masters the good in them, but eventually destroys other people and themselves, with the overturning of an elemental moral order; their human subjectivity is diminished or destroyed, and lives can end up wasted, as at the end of *Hamlet*, with the stage full of corpses and young lives blighted or cut short.

Macbeth displays many of the basic themes associated with the presence of human evil, its temptations, consequences, and its potentially corrosive impact on the human soul, while also emphasising the ultimate if somewhat fragile triumph of human good. As Peter Hall wrote,

> *Macbeth* is the most thorough-going study of evil that I know in dramatic literature. Evil in every sense: cosmic sickness, personal sickness, personal neurosis, the consequence of sin, the repentance of sin, blood leading to more blood, and that in a way leading inevitably to regeneration … I find it the most metaphysical of Shakespeare's plays—an unblinking look at the nature of evil in the person and in the state and in the cosmos.[7]

Other plays such as *Othello*, *Richard III*, and *King Lear* also reveal the machinations of evil characters and how evil "violently disturbs the order of the world".[8] But *Macbeth* is suffused with the atmosphere of evil, of how it corrupts a once noble person, how, with the influence of unknown "dark powers", ambition can take over and reverse moral values; and how this can lead to the annihilating effect of evil acts on the human subject and how such dark forces can deaden human feeling, or in Lady Macbeth's case cause madness. It also displays the making of a tyrant or dictator as he moves from crime to crime in a cycle of violence and destructiveness. Once the first murder is committed then others follow more easily. By the end, Macbeth is both an absolute and unpopular tyrant, but powerless to prevent the sudden and rapid collapse of his regime and the return of order and relative peace—a common end to dictatorship, as was evident in for example the collapse of the Third Reich and the fall of communism, including the petty dictators of Romania and East Germany.

The fact that Macbeth becomes evil and reveals the details of his imagination through the play's poetry and does so in the context of an intense relationship between himself and his wife, makes him even more terrifying than the villains who start out as evil such as Richard III, Edmund, and Iago. With the Macbeths, we can see how it is possible in certain circumstances to become caught up in evil acts, and how that corrupts the human soul. Shakespeare thus revealed through dramatic means the inhuman as a possibility of the human condition, making the play doubly disturbing to us, portraying not only the manifestations of evil but also the vulnerability of humans to be sucked into evil actions and have their identity distorted.

One of the play's main themes is the influence of the unknown powers on humans and their destiny, what we might now call the dark forces of the unconscious, or uncanny experiences which cause horror and dread. To understand such experiences, Freud's paper on "The Uncanny"—"Das Unheimliche", in German, literally, the "unhomely"—is fundamental. Freud traces these experiences back to what are previously known and familiar, and yet which erupt in unexpected ways. The word *das Heimliche* in German can be traced back to what is home-like, what belongs to the house, but also something that becomes concealed, withdrawn from the eyes of strangers.[9] Typical uncanny experiences include inanimate objects apparently coming to life, a sudden appearance of a double, the appearance of ghosts and spirits and other hauntings, as happens in *Macbeth*. Something becomes uncanny when the distinction between imagination and reality is effaced. Ultimately, the uncanny is something which is secretly familiar and has undergone repression and then returns from it—hence the double feeling of the strange and the familiar that is indicative of an uncanny experience.

Modern audiences do not need to believe in the supernatural to feel the impact of the various uncanny phenomena in the play, as they can also be seen as concrete manifestations of evil, or as externalisations of evil forces created for their theatrical effect. In the theatre we must see and hear on the stage what otherwise would be intangible or difficult to grasp. The horror needs to be made clearly manifest to make an impact on the audience. Evil can bewitch people, through literal or symbolic witchcraft. "The fact that we no longer believe in demons, and that Shakespeare's audience mostly did, does not diminish the dramatic effect for us: for with the fading of belief in the objective existence of devils, they and their operations can still symbolize the working of evil in the hearts of men."[10]

As a prelude to evil, everything in the play seems at first open to questioning. The play's opening scenes are full of questions, adding to the atmosphere of uncertainty about what is real and what imagination. Just to cite a few selections of the many that are in the text, the witches begin the play by asking when they will meet again, Duncan's first words after this scene ask, "What bloody man is that?" seeing a bleeding soldier, various lords ask questions about the recent battle, when the witches return one asks where the other had been, when Banquo and Macbeth enter Banquo asks what kind of beings are the witches that they see before them, and he then asks Macbeth why he looks so startled, and Duncan's reappearance begins with the words, "Is execution done on Cawdor?" etc.

Stanley Cavell[11] writes of an uncanny experience like horror as a human response to the "perception of the precariousness of human identity, to the perception that it may be lost or invaded, that we may be, or become, something other than we are, or take ourselves for; that our origins as human beings need accounting for, are unaccountable".

There is thus an uneasy tension in the soul between feeling at home and feeling estranged. This tension is revealed in uncanny experiences which one might say remind us of the precariousness of our hard-won sense of psychic organisation. Michel de M'Uzan[12] emphasises how uncanny experiences commemorate a crucial phase in the development of psychic functioning, a moment which brings to the fore the indeterminate nature of identity, when the self becomes "strange" to itself.

The latter point resonates with Julia Kristeva's meditation on the stranger—*Strangers to Ourselves*.[13] She writes that with Freud, an uncanny foreignness creeps into the tranquillity of reason. "Henceforth, we know that we are foreigners to ourselves, and it is with the help of that sole support that we can attempt to live with others."[14] That is, *we are our own foreigners*, strangers to ourselves, divided and estranged. Psychoanalysis is a "journey into the strangeness of the other and of oneself, towards an ethics of respect for the irreconcilable. How could one tolerate a foreigner if one did not know one was a stranger to oneself?"[15] One could indeed say that in order to listen psychoanalytically at all requires one to abandon the familiar so as to be receptive to the strange and unfamiliar. Yet it is only with the greatest of efforts at times that we can learn to tolerate both the strange within and the stranger without, providing a "home for otherness".

To return to *Macbeth*, the uncanny pervades the work, accounting for the constant play of fantasy and reality, the doubts about whether phenomena like the witches are real or are mere phantoms, whether objects are real or hallucinations, whether ghosts are figments of a disease or manifestations of evil, boundaries between reality and fantasy are constantly challenged, identities become confused and even lost, dream and reality are often merged, most obviously in Lady Macbeth's sleepwalking scene, and objects may be outside or inside the mind, when for example, Macbeth contemplates Duncan's murder:

> *Macbeth.*
> Is this a dagger, which I see before me,
> The handle toward my hand? Come, let me clutch thee:
> I have thee not, and yet I see thee still.
> Art thou not, fatal vision, sensible
> To feeling, as to sight? Or art thou but
> A dagger of the mind, a false creation,
> Proceeding from the heat-oppressed brain? (Act II, 1, 33–39)

But he soon comes back to reality, and with the ringing of a bell from the outside world:

> I go, and it is done: the bell invites me.
> Hear it not, Duncan; for it is a knell
> That summons thee to Heaven, or to Hell. (Act II, 1, 62–64)

The uncanny contrast between the strange and the familiar is revealed in the short but powerful Porter scene which occurs just after Duncan's murder, when we see the Macbeths' hands stained by Duncan's blood, and which is announced by loud knocking at the castle door, first heard on stage by the Macbeths. This knocking seems to be simply someone wanting entry to the castle (in fact Macduff and Lennox as will soon become evident), but its theatrical timing means that it attracts other meanings, it becomes both a real and a symbolic knocking. The inebriated Porter with grim humour likens himself to the doorkeeper of Hell and imagines various sinners wanting to gain entrance. His speech has the comic formula "Knock, knock, who's there?" embedded in the lines several times as he wonders what sinner is going to come through his doors. At the end he urges the audience to remember the Porter, no doubt reminding them that their turn will come to face him and his gate.

Thomas De Quincey in his famous essay "On the Knocking at the Gate in *Macbeth*", wrote that at this point in the play, the murderers have become taken into "another world", that of the demonic or the world of evil. Lady Macbeth is "unsexed":

> *Lady Macbeth.*
>   Come, you Spirits
> That tend on mortal thoughts, unsex me here,
> And fill me from the crown to the toe, top-full
> Of direst cruelty! (Act I, 5, 40–43)

Macbeth becomes taken into this other world, partly convinced by the visions of the three witches and finally driven by the appeal to his masculinity by Lady Macbeth.

> *Macbeth.*
> I do dare all that may become a man;
> Who dares do more, is none.
> *Lady Macbeth.*
>   What beast was't then,
> That made you break this enterprise to me?
> When you durst do it, then you were a man;
> And, to be more than you were, you would
> Be so much more the man. (Act I, 7, 46–51)

The Macbeths, then, have become increasingly taken over by their evil thoughts and actions, in a sort of bubble of toxicity; they have been taken out of the human world and another evil world has stepped in and they are transfixed by it. De Quincey asks how their devilish world can be conveyed and made dramatically palpable.

In order to account for the role of the knocking at the gate, he writes that the knocking represents the assertion of the *human world* knocking to come in.

> In order that a new world may step in, this world must for a time disappear. The murderers and the murder must be insulated—cut off by an immeasurable gulf from the ordinary tide and succession of human affairs—locked up and sequestered in some deep recess; we must be made sensible that the world of ordinary life is suddenly arrested, laid asleep, tranced, racked into a dread armistice; time must be annihilated, relation to things without abolished … Hence it is that, when the deed is done, when the work of darkness is perfect, then the world of darkness passes away like a pageantry in the clouds; the knocking at the gate is heard, and it makes known audibly that the reaction has commenced; the human has made its reflux upon the fiendish; the pulses of life are beginning to beat again; and the reestablishment of the goings-on of the world in which we live first makes us profoundly sensible of the awful parenthesis that had suspended them.[16]

So, the knocking at the gate reminds us of the presence of both the human and the inhuman world, how they are separate but can easily merge once the gate is opened. The human asserts itself by both external and internal knocking, the latter manifested by the pangs of conscience which Macbeth will in due course suppress but which will drive Lady Macbeth mad. The knocking and the subsequent opening of the gate perhaps also symbolises that a door has been opened into the world of evil, that the human world can no longer keep evil at bay. It also opens the door into Macbeth's internal hell.

One may ask then, where is hell, which side of the gate, where is the boundary? By this time in the play, Macbeth can no longer go back and undo the damage done or does not wish to; another threshold is reached. How can one forget those other gates at Auschwitz and other camps which announced with cruel irony that "Work will free you" (*Arbeit Macht Frei*), a sign that prisoners could see every time they arrived or returned from work assignments; they were truly the gates of hell.

Knocking at a gate or door should usually mark the arrival of a visitor or guest, who should be hospitably welcomed, but instead in *Macbeth* it marks the arrival of those who will soon discover the king's murder, and hence is a marker of the line the Macbeths have crossed and from which Macbeth will not return.

Hospitality is the reverse of the uncanny, when the stranger is welcomed into the home, enjoying the homely; the stranger becomes the guest. This contrasts with those who come uninvited, whether as *gate*crashers, or as ghosts, apparitions, spirits, and hallucinations. I mentioned in the introduction that Susan Neiman describes how evil is a phenomenon that shatters trust in the world. Evil acts to destroy what is vital about being human, our feeling of being at home in the world.[17] In *Macbeth*, home becomes both a refuge and site of banquets and hospitality and a site for betrayal, murder, and the subversion of hospitality.[18]

In fact, from the beginning of the play, we see how everything is not what it seems, language will both reveal and conceal, meaning will be equivocal. As the *Witches* chant:

> Fair is foul, and foul is fair.
> Values will be reversed, what appears fair is foul, and the foul will appear to be fair. (Act I, 1, 11)

Lady Macbeth welcomes Duncan into her castle home as a welcoming hostess but is planning murder. Prior to meeting her, *Duncan* says:

> This castle hath a pleasant seat; the air
> Nimbly and sweetly recommends itself
> Unto our gentle senses. (Act I, 6, 1–3)

This is followed by Banquo's pastoral meditation on the way that the martlet, or house martin, a summer guest, enjoys making its home in the castle's walls, an image of fertile (procreant) nature, contrasting with the murderous and "unnatural" dialogue between the Macbeths that had preceeded the king's arrival, when the possibility of his murder is suggested.

> *Banquo.*
>   This guest of summer,
> The temple-haunting martlet, does approve
> By his loved mansionry, that the heaven's breath
> Smells wooingly here: no jutty, frieze,

> Buttress, nor coign of vantage, but this bird
> Hath made his pendant bed, and procreant cradle:
> Where they most breed and haunt, I have observed
> The air is delicate. (Act I, 6, 4–11)

This speech is then followed by the entrance of Lady Macbeth, appearing as the welcoming hostess, excessively grateful for the honour the king bestows on her and Macbeth.

> *Lady Macbeth.*
>   All our service,
> In every point twice done, and then done double,
> Were poor and single business, to contend
> Against those honours deep and broad, wherewith
> Your Majesty loads our house: for those of old,
> And the late dignities heap'd up to them,
> We rest your hermits. (Act I, 6, 14–20)

We had already just witnessed Lady Macbeth tell her husband to hide murderous feelings behind an innocent-looking front (like an innocent flower, once more a positive image of nature), so we are aware that her offer of hospitality is poisonous.

> *Lady Macbeth.*
>   … bear welcome in your eye,
>   Your hand, your tongue: look like th'innocent flower,
>   But be the serpent under't. (Act I, 5, 64–66)

Again, appearances are deceptive, as in foul is fair and fair is foul. This use of words is similar to the use of ambiguity. Ambiguity in this context refers to a word or grammatical structure that is effective in several ways at once. There may be different interpretations or meanings of various lines of poetry, with no one interpretation being predominant. This means, according to William Empson, that the "machinations of ambiguity are among the very roots of poetry".[19] The director John Barton recommended to his actors that in performing Shakespeare, "… we must look for the deliberate ambiguities and inconsistencies that he delights in. These inconsistencies are the character: flawed, contradictory, human".[20]

The phrase fair is foul clearly means a reversal of values, but also sets the scene for appearances not being what they seem, either consciously as with Lady Macbeth's urging of her husband to dissemble, or more ambiguously with the appearance of ghostly and supernatural phenomena. This is also different from the use of "equivocation", which refers to consciously lying under interrogation while secretly saying the truth inwardly, which as I shall describe below was a central concern of Jacobean England recently reeling from the Gunpowder Plot, and which provided one of the contexts for *Macbeth*'s construction and performance before King James I.

One can also see how hospitality and its violation is a central theme of the play and a driving force of the drama, not only in these early scenes but later, when Macbeth, now king, afraid of the witches' prophecy that Banquo's descendants will become future kings, has him killed. The Macbeths entertain various lords, offering their hospitality with heightened ceremonial language, when the murderers enter to say that Banquo is dead, but his son has escaped. Soon after this troubling news, Banquo's ghost appears to Macbeth who becomes increasingly disturbed:

Macbeth.
Hence, horrible shadow!
Unreal mock'ry, hence! (Act III, 4, 122–123)

Banquo's ghost has gatecrashed the banquet and Macbeth can no longer play the royal host; hospitality is once more disrupted, this time by another appearance of the uncanny. The uncanny, or the "unhomely" and the homely are once more contrasted.

One further uncanny theme concerns how in the play identity becomes ambiguous and put in question. Macbeth never remains secure in his identity as king, not just because of the consequences of the murders, but also because of his obsession with succession, with the fact that he has no children, and that the witches prophesised that Banquo's descendants would be kings but not Macbeth's.

Despite Macbeth's martial prowess, Lady Macbeth as we have seen makes comments about his manliness, implying he would be too effeminate if he did not carry through what needed to be done, again putting his masculine identity in question. He may have been an effective warrior; indeed, according to the narration of a Captain, he showed incredible ferocity in the battle that precedes the action of the play; when facing the rebel Macdonwald, he "unseam'd him from the nave to th' chops and fixed his head upon our battlements," (Act I, 2, 22–22). Anyone who can cut a man from his navel to his throat is exceedingly ferocious. But murdering a man in cold blood and outside the context of war requires a very different mentality.

Even at the beginning of the play there is an apparent ambiguity about Macbeth's identity. He begins as Thane of Glamis, but the witches hail him as Thane of Glamis, Thane of Cawdor and then as King, which provokes, not surprisingly, Macbeth's startled response. Then he is addressed by Rosse as Thane of Cawdor.

> *Macbeth.*
> The Thane of Cawdor lives: why do you dress
> Me in borrow'd robes? (Act I, 3, 107–108)

After Duncan's murder, Macbeth is never secure in his identity as king; the image of borrowed robes resonates through the play. Macbeth continues to be pursued by fears and "scorpions" in the mind (Act III, 2, 36), as well as by insomnia. Lady Macbeth loses her reason and sense of self, remains restless and unable to sleep, unable in her hallucinatory state to erase the stain of blood from her hands, and then imagines hearing knocking at the gate, reminding us of the Porter scene, the internal knocking of conscience and no doubt also alluding to the gates of hell through which she may fear passing through.

The only time Macbeth seems briefly at rest is when, after more murders, he has deadened himself to human feeling, and having heard that his wife is dead, sees life as a walking shadow:

> *Macbeth.*
> It is a tale
> Told by an idiot, full of sound and fury,
> Signifying nothing. (Act V, 5, 26–28)

He has also been lulled into a false sense of security by his second visit to the witches, who prophecy he will not be killed by a man born of woman (Macduff born by caesarean, will kill him) and only when Great Birnam Wood moves to Dunsinane Hill (which it appears to do when Malcolm's troops hide behind branches as protection and camouflage). He is still also persecuted by seeing, by means of the witches' conjuring, Banquo's descendants take the crown over generations and tries in vain to eliminate this potentiality by killing Macduff's family—his son escapes, once again frustrating Macbeth. The traumatic lack of heirs and the failure to guarantee the succession brings the murder of Macduff's wife and children by Macbeth into the area of Bollas's structure of evil. To recall, evil considered as a structure, points to a complex reorganisation of trauma, in which the subject recollects the loss of love and the birth of hate by putting subsequent others through the unconscious terms of a malevolent physical or psychological extinction of the self, or what I have termed the annihilation of the human subject. Macbeth hopes to eliminate his trauma through murdering other subjects.

Thus, in terms of the movement of the drama and the development of Macbeth's character on stage, he begins by being a brave and noble warrior with a sensitive conscience but, yielding to temptation, becomes a superstitious murderer, suffering torments of the mind and imagination as he knows he is doing evil. He is shaken by terrible dreams and visions, manifestations of the uncanny, and then, after his second visit to the witches so that he may "know by the worst means, the worst" (Act III, 5, 133–140), loses his conscience and becomes subjectively dead, "life's but a walking shadow". He moves from a martial hero whom Lady Macbeth fears being too full of the milk of human kindness (Act I, 5, 17), to the man who sees life as having no meaning and loses the sense of being an alive subject. Perhaps only at the end of the play when he is fighting for his life, even knowing that the prophecies have become true, and returns to being a fighting man, do we sense that he retains some human dignity.

This movement of Macbeth's soul, as Henry N. Paul has shown in his book *The Royal Play of Macbeth*, mirrors the contemporary work of King James who in his book on *The Kingly Gift (or Basilikon Doron)*, which he wrote to guide his eldest son Henry in the nature of good morals and the art of kingship, describes the three stages of changes in conscience in possession by the devil—the social conscience, the superstitious conscience, and the cauterised conscience.[21] Macbeth moves from the brave and noble warrior with a sensitive conscience, who yields to temptation and becomes a superstitious murderer suffering torture of the mind and is shaken by terrible dreams, fleeing to the imaginary in order to flee from himself. This stage continues until he revisits the witches, and his conscience is then burnt out and fear disappears.

Indeed, looking at the historical context of *Macbeth* adds an important layer to understanding the play's meaning, even if of course Shakespeare's vision is universal and goes beyond his historical context. The main historical themes which provide the context for the writing and the performance of *Macbeth* are the Catholic led Gunpowder Plot, discovered on 5 November 1605, and its after-effects, including the capture and public execution of the traitors, the general issue of the accession of King James, a protestant Scottish king whose mother, Mary Queen of Scots was a Catholic, and thereafter the legitimacy of the Stuart succession, the contemporary belief in witches emphasised by the king's own book on demonology and his interest in the interrogation of alleged witches, and the role of "equivocation" by the Gunpowder Plot conspirators as a way of managing interrogations. Anxieties about treachery, betrayal, and murder pervaded the court and the establishment by the time *Macbeth* was performed before the king some time in 1606.

The trauma of the Gunpowder Plot, a potential "terrorist attack",[22] must have been very raw in the consciousness of the king and his court. It nearly led to the destruction of much of the establishment. Contemporaries "found themselves searching for the ultimate source of such a hellish crime".[23] The trials and the grim executions of the plotters and close supporters gained considerable publicity and would still have been fresh in those seeing *Macbeth* for the first time.

Treachery is depicted at the beginning of the play with the Thane of Cawdor aiding Norwegian invaders, and that leads to his execution. But Shakespeare is no propagandist and ironically, he replaces one traitor with another—Macbeth. Only at the end of the play is order restored with the defeat of Macbeth and the accession of Malcolm, Duncan's appointed heir.

During the trial of the Jesuit priest Henry Garnet for complicity in the Gunpowder Plot, the issue of equivocation, mentioned above, loomed large; though a concept that was in the culture previously, by the summer of 1606 it had become a burning topic. Needless to say, it proved no defence for Garnet, and he was duly executed. Equivocation had become linked closely to betrayal through concealing the truth under the cover of lies. Indeed, soon after the execution of the conspirators, James introduced an act of the Oath of Allegiance, designed to allow Catholics to demonstrate their loyalty to the crown rather than the Pope, as if to counter the role of equivocation or mental evasion.

There are a few references in *Macbeth* to equivocation. The Porter mentions equivocators in his fantasy about being the gatekeeper to hell, and when Macbeth is confronted by a messenger with the news that the wood was moving to Birnam, he threatens him with hanging, and muses about the devil's role in what has been seen:

Macbeth.
> I pull in resolution; and begin
> To doubt th'equivocation of the fiend,
> That lies like truth. (Act V, 5, 42–44)

Frank Kermode comments on the impact of Garnet's use of equivocation.

> When Father Garnet and his friends defended the practise, they incurred a charge to which Jesuits were anyway liable, that they had placed themselves on the side of the devil. Furthermore, as no man ... can choose an apparent good in preference to a real one unless his will is corrupted by appearance, evil acts imply the constant presence of equivocating factors in the world of moral choice. In other words, no one does an evil act unless the consequences of it appear to him more desirable than the consequences of not doing it; and since they cannot be so in truth, they clearly present themselves to him, as he deliberates up on the issue, in an equivocal manner ... The role of the weird sisters is to represent that equivocal evil in the nature of things which helps deceive the human will.[24]

The witch world of equivocation is different from poetic ambiguity, though there are times when the difference seems to be blurred, once again fair is foul, and foul is fair.

The drama of *Macbeth* portrays a "Scotland under an equivocating Macbeth, a nightmare world where words belie intentions and honest exchange is no longer possible."[25] Such an evil terrain has become familiar to us in the modern world.

Overall, *Macbeth* explores dramatically the nature of evil, its origin, and its effect on the human soul. Though soaked in the contemporary themes of treachery and fears of regicide, it explores the way that evil can appear from the outside but soon eats into the soul inside. That threatening outside can be seen in religious terms as the work of the devil corrupting the sinner or can be seen in secular terms as the temptations of power and ambition. Shakespeare keeps open which sort of explanation is predominant, thereby once more proving himself a universal writer, not bound to one narrow portrayal of human action.

CHAPTER 7

Final comments—resisting evil

I think the first point to make when tackling the issue of resisting evil is the need to confront past evils, and not to let them be forgotten or denied. Working through of past atrocities at a group and societal level is far from easy, and history shows that there are often strong psychological resistances to undertaking such a hard task, as there is to face any major individual or group trauma. But without working through of such collective states of mind there remains the perpetual risk that the factors that led to the atrocities remain unmodified and capable of being reignited in some form.

There is considerable evidence of the great difficulty that many Germans had after the defeat of the Third Reich in coming to terms with the fact that the regime was sustained by the conformity and mobilisation of most of the population.[1] Alexander and Margarete Mitscherlich, in their classic 1967 book, *The Inability to Mourn*, describe in great detail the group and individual psychological factors that led so many Germans to deny or minimise how caught up they had become in what I have described as the Nazi Imaginary, such as the holding of fantasies of Aryan superiority, the belief in the almost superhuman power of Adolf Hitler, and the tacit or active acceptance of the need to eliminate Jews in order to create a new world order.

They suggested that the

> inability to mourn the loss of the Führer is the result of an intensive defence against guilt, shame, and anxiety, a defence which was achieved by the withdrawal of previously powerful libidinal cathexes. The Nazi past was de-realised i.e., emptied of reality. The occasion for mourning was not only the death of Adolf Hitler as a real person, but above all his disappearance as the representation of the *collective ego-ideal*. He was an object on which Germans depended, to which they transferred responsibility … As such, he represented and revived the ideas of omnipotence we all cherish about ourselves from infancy; and his devaluation by the visitors, also implied the loss of a narcissistic object and, accordingly, an ego- or self-impoverishment and devaluation. Avoidance of these traumata must be regarded as the most immediate reason for the general de-realization. Defence against mourning for the countless victims of Hitler's aggression—an aggression which, in their identification with the Führer, the German people had so willingly, so unresistingly shared—came later … The Germans … had received a blow to the very core of their self-esteem, and the most urgent task for their psychic apparatus was to ward off the experience of a melancholy impoverishment of the self.[2]

Instead of working through these traumata, the Germans collectively refused to succumb to melancholia, refused to mourn, lost touch with empathy for the victims of the regime, and used denials, evasions, and a focus on the economic recovery at all costs to refuse to face the reality of the German people's collusion with atrocities.

The Mitscherlichs' analysis of the German denial of their past guilt was one of the pivotal factors in helping Germans come to terms over time with their collusion with the Nazi Imaginary.

One must add too that the conditions at the end of the war were not that conducive to effective mourning. By then, the political system and German society was completely paralysed and had been unable

> to resist the suicidal course of the Nazi leadership, which itself was too deeply committed through the criminal deeds of the regime. This was part of the accelerating process of self-destruction

which led to an increasing atomisation of the governmental process and made the system incapable of ending a war which was evidently already lost. Symptomatic of this was the complete collapse of any authority in Germany after the fictitious unity of Hitler's personal rule disappeared. Neither the organisational stronghold nor its ideology survived the total collapse which accompanied the military defeat and the end of the war.[3]

The division of Germany after the Soviet takeover of the East no doubt was a further complicating factor in delaying any effective mourning for past horrors and indeed the taking of effective action against Nazi criminals, many of whom either got off lightly, or were not prosecuted or melted seamlessly into the institutions of the new regimes, many details of which are described with clear evidence in Mary Fulbrook's comprehensive account of the legacies of Nazi persecution, *Reckonings*.[4]

While the Nuremberg trials were effective at bringing into the public eye some of the horrors of genocide, by focusing on a few elite members of the regime ordinary Germans could pretend to themselves that post war was the time to forget the past, and just get on with the reconstruction of the new Germany. It must be said that the East Germans were apparently more effective in rooting out and prosecuting former Nazis, no doubt encouraged by the Soviets, millions of whom had been slaughtered in the battles against the German army and in the various labour and extermination camps. One should also add that the Allies were also not that keen on continuing prosecution of those responsible for the genocides. There was the pressing need to reconstruct Europe devastated by the war and to face the reality of Soviet aggression and the developing Cold War. One can also wonder about how much guilt for appeasing Hitler early on had a place in limiting the Allies' wish to pursue Nazi criminals, that they had their own share of responsibility for the Holocaust.

It was not only in Germany that people in the aftermath of the war wanted to forget the horrors of the camps. Even in Israel, survivors initially found little immediate sympathy for their stories. The Eichmann trial was probably a turning point in that it gave survivor testimony authority and a space to be registered and heard.

It was important that in that trial justice was seen to be done; just procedures, as Stuart Hampshire emphasised, are a protection against destructive evil.

In order to resist evil, one also needs to face the dark forces of the unconscious, and the power of group processes in facilitating evil acts, much of which has been the topic of Chapter 3, as well as the social psychological forces that can impede human conscience as described in Chapter 2.

Based upon suggestions in my previous book on tolerance,[5] I also suggest that resisting evil requires the development of an active *tolerance process* that can resist the forces that lead to evil practices. Tolerance is not just to be seen as an endpoint but requires time to achieve. The very act of going through a process is potentially tolerance promoting. It goes without saying that for this process to even begin, there would need to be an atmosphere of respectful debate and a wish to examine uncomfortable realities, including a natural ambivalence towards the very process itself. It requires tackling various *obstacles* to tolerance, including irrational states of mind. The tolerant public space needs to be open to all, while being guarded against the destructive forces of intolerance. Tolerance requires a movement from "object" to "subject" tolerance. This form of tolerance requires a *tolerant imaginative internal space*, and it also implies that one respects the other and others as subjects of their experience, with agency and capacity for independent judgment. Seeing the other as a subject, being open to otherness, requires some self-reflection, where otherness in oneself is seen as part and parcel of being human. In Kristeva's words: "How could one tolerate a foreigner if one did not know one was a stranger to oneself?" This attitude contrasts with what Hannah Arendt saw in Adolf Eichmann, an entirely negative quality, not stupidity but the inability to think from the other's standpoint. This was also one of the key issues for many Germans after the war, as the Mitscherlich book described, when empathy for victims was diminished or absent and with a common attitude of holding onto their own sense of victimhood instead.

Tolerance also requires acts of reflective judgment, and a special kind of enlarged mentality, where one takes account of the views and judgment of others, putting oneself in the position of others in the hope of coming to an agreement. This is a form of common human understanding, requiring thought and imagination, but also paying attention to how intolerance and hatred can undermine open communication. This involves a fundamental change in attitude of citizens towards their fellows, an act of *imagination*. One could characterise this shift as providing what I have described as a "home for otherness".

In addition, we have seen that there are occasions when effective and organised resistance to evil is possible, as with the village of Le Chambon-sur-Lignon in southern France, whose strong community links and sense of human value created an environment which provided aid and shelter to persecuted Jews in the Second World War. Christopher Browning has described how a particularly courageous young American, Tracy Strong Jr, became linked up with the village in order to rescue interned young people, including Jews. He played a key role in obtaining the transfer of young prisoners from Vichy internment camps to accommodation in Le Chambon—the Maison des Roches. From there he helped some of these men to escape over the border into Switzerland.[6]

Browning asks what enabled Strong to accomplish these humanitarian actions. His family upbringing was atypical, in that due to his father's job as director of youth activities of the international YMCA, the family moved across various countries, and Strong was educated in Europe and the US, and felt "at home" with different cultures. The family also had a strong progressive tradition, and he became influenced by progressive Christian thought. He began working with the European Student Relief Fund in April 1940, an ecumenical consortium of various Christian faiths which provided humanitarian aid to European students victimised by the war. He initially helped organise constructive activities for POWs at various camps, but in a few months was barred by the Germans from such work and returned to his Geneva base.

Browning comments that Strong kept a journal over this period which recorded his observations and responses to the Nazi regime. He noted that the Germans remained unenthusiastic about the war but broadly supported Hitler and Germany's "righteousness", and that England not Germany was blamed for starting the war. To his surprise Strong found that many Protestant pastors had enlisted and were fatalistic about the war, in opposition to Strong's own position of wanting to better the world.

He was also scathing about the Nazi racist beliefs and was shocked about the indifference to the euthanasia programme, about which there was clear knowledge. In contrast to what he found as typical attitudes, he had a strong belief in helping people in need as the self-evident purpose of life.[7] And he refused to go along with the Nazi categorisation of people as a result of their so-called race, emphasising instead where they came from and what language they spoke.

He was successful in rescuing several internees as he was not only committed to helping others, but was adept at working with others, for example, with the key figures in Le Chambon, and had experience of negotiating or working his way round the Nazi system, as when he visited POWs. As Browning comments: "As dictatorships have long known, and as the story of Tracy Strong illustrates, the presence of individuals willing to challenge government policies is important, but it is the ability of such individuals to work together with others of like mind that is most effective."[8]

I have already cited evidence from some empirical research on "rescuers". One study[9] investigated the extent to which personality variables can be used to discriminate non-Jewish heroes of the Holocaust from bystanders and from a comparison group of pre-war European immigrants who left their countries of origin prior to the Second World War.

> People who risked their own lives to help Jews differed in several ways from those who did not. They scored higher on independence and perceived control, indicating that they were willing to stick with their own beliefs even if others disagreed … They also scored higher on risk-taking … This combination of attributes appears to have given them the confidence to show courage.[10]

Unsurprisingly, the group of helpers also showed more altruism, empathy, and social responsibility. This and other studies paint a picture of a moral rebel as someone who is confident, independent, and altruistic, with high self-esteem and a strong sense of responsibility. One might add from the example of Tracy Strong's relationship with the villagers of Le Chambon, that if there is a community such as this French village, which can promote and sustain such attributes, then there is more likelihood about individuals being able to avoid bystander apathy and act to resist evil.

The Dutch village of Nieuwlande also rescued Jews with a network of rescuers.[11] Le Chambon and Nieuwlande shared a common Protestant Calvinist religious tradition. The latter, unlike Lutheranism, was opposed to anti-Semitism, respected the Hebrew Bible, and had had their own share of persecution as minorities in Catholic societies, and thus could empathise with persecuted Jews.

Overall, in France between 1940 and 1944 about three quarters of Jews escaped deportation and survived, despite the Vichy government's collaboration with the Germans and the Nazi occupation, a much higher percentage than other European occupied countries, bar Denmark. As shown by detailed research by Jacques Semelin,[12] this was not just because of the actions of a few courageous individuals but because of a variety of factors. Despite anti-Semitism and denunciations, there developed widespread sympathy for the plight of the Jews. There were many random acts of solidarity, and refusals to comply with the Vichy and German attempts to round up Jews. At the same time, many Jews learned to adapt to the strained circumstances, blending in with the population to avoid arrest, putting up with poverty and displacement from their homes, shifts in their working environments, and even displaying open defiance, for example refusing to wear the yellow star. The notion that the Jews only survived through being hidden in attics and suchlike was very far from the truth. This of course does not minimise the horror that led to the deportation of 25% of the Jewish population.

There were examples of German resistance to the evil regime during the war, the most famous being that of the failed plot to assassinate Hitler on 20 July 1944, described in detail in, for example, the book *German Resistance to Hitler* by Peter Hoffmann.[13] This was one of several attempts by resistance within the military, but the one that came nearest to achieving success, even if it seemed doomed from the start. There was an absence of ruthlessness and joint purpose, but it was felt that some response to the evil of the regime had to be made.

The persecution and murder of Jews was for many of the 1944 conspirators the most important motive to enter underground opposition, as admitted to the Gestapo interrogations after the failed attempt.[14]

There is also evidence of assistance to Jews inside Nazi Germany; for example, as described in the book *Lives Reclaimed* by Mark Roseman, a group of peaceable idealists, who came together in the early 1920s and who called themselves "the Bund", subsequently gave aid and support to Jews in camps, and sheltered dissidents and Jews on the run.[15] Apart from an element of luck, what helped the group to survive included the fact that they owned a number of buildings they could use as protected living and meeting spaces; to outsiders their dance and gymnastic activities seemed near enough to the regime's own emphasis on physical activity as to escape suspicion; they had networks of participants organised around their lifestyle choice which gave them a sense of unity; they had good and effective leadership; and they were helped by the fact that the Bund had a large number of female members, who were in principle not taken by the regime to be such serious threats as were men. Effective leadership combined with group cohesion, loyalty, and trust enabled the group to act against the regime.[16]

It is also important to emphasise how much resistance has taken place within targeted and oppressed populations. For example, the history of American slavery is rich with many examples of slave rebellions during their transport from West Africa, resistance from black field workers and from white Quaker and black preachers, fugitives, vigilantes, and a variety of activists, as well as the more famous and comprehensive rebellion of Toussaint L'Ouverture. Slaves were not lacking agency, even when every attempt was made to eliminate it as much as possible by the slavery institution.[17]

Similarly, during the Holocaust, as illustrated in considerable detail at a recent exhibition at the Wiener Holocaust Library, Jewish partisan groups and underground resistance networks launched attacks, sabotage operations, and rescue missions, while resistance groups in ghettos organised social, religious, cultural, and educational activities and armed uprisings in defiance of their Nazi oppressors. In death camps, in the most extreme circumstances, resisters gathered evidence of Nazi atrocities and even mounted armed rebellions.[18]

The Warsaw Ghetto uprising was only one of several other instances of armed resistance in other ghettos such as in Białystok, Krakow, Minsk, Vilna, Będzin, Częstochowa, and Kovno, and also in camps such as Sobibor, Treblinka, and Auschwitz-Birkenau. There was also resistance with guerrilla warfare, with urban resistance groups, and with partisan groups in the Soviet states, and thousands of escaped Jews also joined the

Red Army to fight. Such documented evidence provides a counter to the notion that Jews went passively to their death without protest, a view which mirrors how the Nazis refused to accept the human otherness of their victims. Similarly, no one blames the millions of Russians who were taken from their homes and sent to labour camps in the Gulag for being passive victims. One cannot underestimate the power of totalitarian regimes to enforce their practices of control and to rob people of their ability to resist. This is not to underestimate the heroism of individual survivors and the courage of those who are prepared to bear witness to being the victims of genocide.

While the effective resistance to evil and the power of the evil imagination usually requires networks of support, we all have an individual responsibility to see evil where it exists and keep hold of the human, however fragile.

Endnotes

Notes for Chapter 1

1. Taylor, K. (2009, p. 8).
2. Kennedy, R. (1998, pp. 62 ff.).
3. Fulbrook, M. (2018, pp. 4–5).
4. Gilroy, P. (1993).
5. Wilson Knight, G. (1930, p. 137).
6. Kant, I. (1793, p. 77).
7. Kant, I. (1793, p. 105).
8. Dews, P. (2013, pp. 101–102).
9. Tyerman, C. (2019, p. 14).
10. Tyerman, C. (2019, pp. 16–17).
11. Kekes, J. (2005, pp. 27–28).
12. Bernstein, R. (2005, pp. 51–52).
13. Confino, A. (2014, pp. 14 ff.).
14. Buber, M. (1922).
15. Bernstein, R. (2002, p. 180).
16. Stone, M. (2009, p. 22).
17. Kekes, J. (2005, p. 2).
18. Card, C. (2010, p. 4)
19. Morton, A. (2004, p. 13).
20. Neiman, S. (2002, pp. 240 ff.).

21. McGinn, C. (1997, p. 145).
22. Baudelaire, C. (1857, p. 275).
23. Hampshire, S. (1989, p. 8).
24. Hampshire. S. (1989, p. 67).
25. Hampshire, S. (1989, pp. 106 ff.).
26. Zimbardo, P. (2004, p. 3).
27. De Waal, F. (2013, p. 240).
28. Bloom, P. (2013).
29. Baron-Cohen, S. (2011).
30. Sartre, J.-P. (1944, p. 223).
31. Fromm, E. (1974, p. 294).
32. Arendt, H. (1951, pp. 457–458).
33. Burleigh, M. (2010, p. x).
34. Browning, C. (1992, p. 240).
35. Thomas, L. M. (1993, p. 71).
36. Derrida, J. (1997, p. 75).
37. Roseman, M. (2019).
38. Bell, R. (2020).
39. Warnock, B. (2020).
40. Freud, S. (1923b, pp. 40–41).
41. Solomon, R. (2000, pp. 20 ff.).
42. Camus, A. (1942, pp. 27 ff.).
43. Bettelheim, B. (1976, pp. 8–9).
44. Arendt, H. (1963, pp. 49 ff.).
45. Covington, C. (2017, p. 179).
46. Eagleton, T. (2010, p. 85).
47. Shay, J. (1994, p. 19).
48. Shay, J. (1994, p. 34).
49. Shay, J. (1994, p. 152).
50. MacMillan, M. (2020, p. 174).
51. Glover, J. (1999, p. 156).
52. Bourke, J. (2014).
53. Freud, S. (1933b, pp. 210 ff.).
54. Fornari, F. (1966, pp. xvii–xviii).
55. Misterlich, A., & Misterlich, M. (1967).
56. Glover, J. (1999, p. 113).
57. Fussell, P. (1975, p. xv).
58. Fussell, P. (1975, pp. 4–5).
59. Fussell, P. (1975, p. 31).

60. Fussell, P. (1975, p. 207).
61. Lifton, R.-J. (1986, pp. 423–424).
62. Elias, N. (1989, p. 182).
63. Gerwarth, R. (2016, p. 106).
64. Gerwarth, R. (2016, p. 124).
65. Kershaw, I. (2015, p. 2).
66. Kershaw, I. (2015, p. 6).
67. Hobsbawm, E. (1990).
68. Anderson, B. (2006, p. 141).
69. Hobsbawm, E. (1990, p. 144).
70. Hilberg, R. (1985).
71. Bauman, Z. (1989, p. 13).
72. Gilroy, P. (1993, p. 46).
73. Staub, E. (1989, p. 13).
74. Waller, J. (2002, p. 138).
75. Kennedy, R. (2019, p. 142).
76. Kennedy, R. (2019, p. 1).
77. Kennedy, R. (2019, p. 19).
78. Kennedy, R. (2019, pp. 5–6).
79. Browning, C. (1992).
80. Zimbardo, P. (2007).
81. Browning, C. (1992, p. 168).
82. Freud. S. (1921c, p. 115).
83. Perry, G. (2013).
84. Asch, S. E. (1951).
85. Waller, J. (2002, p. 90).
86. Adshead, G., & Horne, E. (2021, p. 11).
87. Alford, C. (1997).
88. Ogden, T. (1989, p. 75).
89. Baumeister, R. (1997, p. 376).
90. Baumeister, R. (1997, p. 377).
91. Baumeister, R. (1997, p. 8).
92. Baumeister, R. (1997, p. 18).

Notes for Chapter 2

1. Sapolsky, R. (2017).
2. Sapolsky, R. (2017, p. 5).
3. Sapolsky, R. (2017, p. 53).

4. Damasio, A., Grabowski, T. et al. (1994).
5. Sapolsky, R. (2017, p. 54).
6. Luria, A. (1973, p. 223).
7. Luria, A. (1963).
8. Luria, A. (1973, pp. 43 ff.).
9. Sapolsky, R. (2017, p. 54).
10. McGilchrist, I. (2009, pp. 27–28).
11. McGilchrist, I. (2009, p. 61).
12. McGilchrist, I. (2009, p. 57).
13. McGilchrist, I. (2009, p. 86).
14. Schore, A. (2003, p. 257).
15. Schore, A. (2003, pp. 135–136).
16. Schore, A. (2012, p. 34).
17. Damasio, A. (1994), Damasio, A. (2010).
18. Baron-Cohen, S. (2011, pp. 65–66).
19. Sapolsky. R. (2017, pp. 158–159).
20. Sapolsky. R. (2017, p. 170).
21. Sapolsky, R. (2017, p. 173).
22. Caspi, A., Mccloy, J. et al. (2002).
23. Motzkin, J., Newman, J. et al. (2011).
24. Gregory, S., Ftche, D. et al. (2013).
25. De Brito, A., Viding, E. et al. (2013).
26. Poeppl, T., Donges,M. et al. (2019).
27. Sapolsky, R. (2017, pp. 31–32).
28. Adolphs, R., Tranel, D., et al. (1994).
29. Adolphs, R., Gosselin, F. et al. (2005),
30. Blair, R. J. R. (2018).
31. Gauthier, N., Methot-Jones, T. et al. (2020, p. 248).
32. Marsh, A., Finger, E et al. (2008), Jones, A., Kristine, R. et al. (2009).
33. Roberts, R., McCrory, E. et al. (2020).
34. Bowlby, J. (1953).
35. Marshall, L. A. and Cooke, D. J. (1999).
36. Baron-Cohen, S. (2011).
37. Baron-Cohen, S. (2011, pp. 170 ff.).
38. Baron-Cohen, S. (2011, pp. ix–x).
39. Baron-Cohen, S. (2011, p. 109).
40. Bloom, P. (2013).
41. Bloom, P. (2013, pp. 5–6).
42. Bloom, P. (2013, p. 26).

43. Bloom, P. (2013, p. 52).
44. Bloom, P. (2013, pp. 105 ff.).
45. Bloom, P. (2013, p. 218).
46. Miller, A. (1983).
47. Adorno, T. W., Frenkel-Brunswik, E. et al. (1950).
48. Kratzer, A. (2019).
49. de Waal, F. (2013).
50. de Waal, F. (2013, p. 43).
51. de Waal, F. (2013, pp. 160–161).
52. de Waal, F. (2013, p. 63 ff.).
53. Rilling, J. K., Scholz, T. M. et al. (2011).
54. de Waal, F. (2005, p. 215 ff.).
55. Winnicott, D. (1964, p. 85).
56. de Waal, F. (2013, pp. 227–228).
57. de Waal, F. (2013, p. 145).
58. de Waal, F. (2013, p. 157).
59. Asch, S. (1951).
60. Asch, S. (1951, pp. 222–223).
61. Hogg, M. A. (2010).
62. Sherif, M., White, B. J. (1955).
63. Tajfel, H. (1970).
64. Reicher, S. and Haslam, S. A. (2006).
65. Zimbardo, P. (2004, pp. 19–20).
66. Card, C. (2010, p. 13).
67. Card, C. (2010, p. 13).
68. Blass, T. (2002).
69. Hilberg, R. (1985, p. 53.)
70. Allport, G. (1954, 1979).
71. Allport, G. (1954, p. 9).
72. Allport, G. (1954, p. 125).
73. Allport, G. (1954, pp. 14–15).
74. Allport, G. (1954, p. 57).
75. Allport, G. (1954, p. 208).
76. Allport, G. (1954, p. 176).
77. Abrams, D. (2010).
78. Tajfel, H., & Turner, J. (1979).
79. Kennedy, R. (2019, p. 1).
80. Abrams, D. (2010, p. 93).
81. Sanderson, C. (2020).

82. Sanderson, C. (2020, pp. 14–15).
83. Reicher, S., Haslam, S. et al. (2006).
84. Sanderson, C. (2020, p. 16).
85. Sanderson, C. (2020, p. 50).
86. Midlarsky, E., Jones, S. et al. (2005).
87. Sanderson, C. (2020, p. 178).

Notes for Chapter 3

1. Freud, S. (1921c, p. 74).
2. Bion, W. R. (1961).
3. Freud, S. (1921c, p. 92).
4. Freud, S. (1921c, p. 143).
5. Sandler, J. (1960, pp. 155–156).
6. Browning, C. (1992).
7. Haynal, A. (2001, p. 115).
8. Money-Kyrle, R. (1978, pp. 160 ff.).
9. Money-Kyrle, R. (1978, p. 165).
10. Money-Kyrle, R. (1978, pp. 165–166).
11. Money-Kyrle, R. (1978, p. 168).
12. Money-Kyrle, R. (1978, p. 175).
13. Main, T. (1975, pp. 101–102).
14. Main, T. (1975, p. 107).
15. Main, T. (1975, p. 106).
16. Adorno, T. (1951, p. 120).
17. Adorno, T. (1951, p. 124).
18. Chasseguet-Smirgel, J. (1985, p. 62).
19. Chasseguet-Smirgel, J. (1985, pp. 62–63).
20. Chasseguet-Smirgel, J. (1990).
21. Chasseguet-Smirgel, J. (1990, p. 167).
22. Chasseguet-Smirgel, J. (1990, p. 167).
23. Chasseguet-Smirgel, J. (1990, p. 169).
24. Chasseguet-Smirgel, J. (1990, p. 171).
25. Bohleber, W. (2010, pp. 162–163).
26. Bohleber, W. (2010, p. 189).
27. Lifton, R. J. (2003).
28. Lifton, R. J. (2003, pp. 28–29).
29. Lifton, R. J. (2003, p. 29).
30. Bollas, C. (1993, pp. 193–217).

31. Orwell, G. (1946, p. 967).
32. Bollas, C. (1993, p. 203).
33. Kennedy, R. (2019, p. 142).
34. Rosenfeld, H. (1987, pp. 22–23).
35. Rosenfeld, H. (1971, p. 174).
36. Sebek, M. (1996, p. 290).
37. Sklar, J. (2019, p. 12).
38. Allport, G. (1954, pp. 342 ff.).
39. Allport, G. (1954, p. 373).
40. Steiner, J. (2016, p. 287).
41. Steiner, J. (2016, p. 289).
42. Parens, H. (2012).
43. Baumeister, R. (1997, p. 8).
44. Baumeister, R. (1997, p. 18).
45. Hyatt-Williams, A. (1998, p. 42).
46. Hyatt-Williams, A. (1998, pp. 34–35).
47. Hyatt-Willams, A. (1998, p. 29).
48. Kennedy, R., & Magagna, J. (1981, pp. 120–135).
49. Bollas, C. (1995, p. 189).
50. Bollas, C. (1995, p. 189).
51. Bollas, C. (1995, pp. 219–220).
52. Bollas, C. (1995, pp. 210–212).
53. Grand, S. (2000, p. 3).
54. Grand, S. (2000, p. 6).
55. Grand, S. (2000, p. 12).
56. Grand, S. (2000, pp. 14–15).
57. Grand, S. (2000, p. 16)
58. Shengold, L. (1989).
59. Poland, W. (2000, p. 21).
60. Felman, S., & Laub, D. (1992).
61. Freud, S. (1915b, p. 281).
62. Freud, S. (1915b, p. 281).
63. Freud, S. (1915b, p. 281).
64. Laplanche, J., & Pontalis, J.-B. (1967, p. 27).
65. Freud, S. (1908d).
66. Freud, S., with Breuer, J. (1895d, p. 305).
67. Marcuse, H. (1956).
68. Freud, S. (1930a, p. 105).
69. Freud, S. (1930a, p. 111).

70. Freud, S. (1930a, pp. 123–124).
71. Laplanche, J., & Pontalis, J.-B. (1967 p. 97).
72. Bernstein, R. (2002, p. 160).
73. Fromm, E. (1964, pp. 18–19).
74. Fromm, E. (1964, p. 74).
75. Fromm, E. (1964, p. 102).
76. Fromm, E. (1964, p. 46).
77. Fromm, E. (1964, pp. 35–36).
78. Aragno, A. (2014, p. 261).
79. Klein, M. (1952, p. 61).
80. Meltzer, D. (1992).
81. De Masi, F. (2003).
82. Migliozzi, A. (2016, p. 1020).
83. Meltzer, D. (1992, p. 152).

Notes for Chapter 4

1. Kant, I. (1784, p. 18).
2. O'Neill, O. (1986, p. 37).
3. Kant, I. (1784, p. 38).
4. Grayling, A. (2019, p. 265).
5. Kant, I. (1790, p. 126, section 41).
6. O'Neill, O. (2015, p. 4).
7. O'Neill, O. (2015, p. 7).
8. O'Neill, O. (2016, p. 208).
9. O'Neill, O. (2015, p. 33, fn. 16).
10. O'Neill, O. (1990, p. 167).
11. Kant, I. (1793, p. 45).
12. Kant, I. (1793, p. 47).
13. Kant, I. (1793, p. 51).
14. Bernstein, R. (2002, pp. 43–44).
15. Kant, I. (1793, p. 77).
16. Kant, I. (1793, p. 105).
17. Kant, I. (1793, p. 106).
18. Arendt, H. (1963, p. 136).
19. Arendt, H. (1963, p. 136).
20. Crick, B. (1970, p. 66).
21. Kohn, J. (2003, p. xx).
22. Machiavelli, N. (1532, p. 91).

23. Machiavelli, N. (1531, p. 200).
24. Machiavelli, N. (1532, p. 130).
25. Crick, B. (1970, p. 56).
26. Hampshire, S. (1989, p. 162).
27. Machiavelli, N. (1531, p. 217).
28. Machiavelli, N. (1531, p. 177).
29. Machiavelli, N. (1531, p. 113).
30. Hampshire, S. (1989, p. 163).
31. Berlin, I. (1979).
32. Berlin, I. (1979, p. 60).
33. Berlin, I. (1979, p. 62).
34. Berlin, I. (1979, p. 66).
35. Berlin, I. (1979, p. 68).
36. Berlin, I. (1979, p. 69).
37. Berlin, I. (1979, pp. 74–75).
38. Berlin, I. (1979, p. 79).
39. Arendt, H. (1951).
40. Arendt, H. (1951, pp. 311–312).
41. Arendt, H. (1951, p. 318).
42. Herbert, U. (2001, p. 95).
43. Arendt, H. (1951, pp. 465–466).
44. Arendt, H. (1951, p. 468).
45. Nisbet, H. (2005, p. 5).
46. Arendt, H. (1970, p. 25).
47. Arendt, H. (1970, p. 27).
48. Arendt, H. (1951, p. 459).
49. Arendt, H. (1951, p. 459).
50. Arendt, H. (1951, p. 447).
51. Arendt H. (1951, p. 451).
52. Arendt, H. (1951, p. 452).
53. Levi, P. (1986, p. 22 ff.).
54. Arendt, H. (1963, p. 276).
55. Arendt, H. (1971a, p. 180).
56. Arendt, H. (1971b, pp. 179 ff.).
57. Hilberg, R. (1985).
58. Lower, W. (2013).
59. Lifton. R. (1986, p. 12).
60. Russell, L. (2020, p. 15).
61. Hampshire, S. (1983, p. 155).

62. Hampshire, S. (1989, p. 51).
63. Hampshire, S. (1983, p. 168).
64. Hampshire, S. (1989, pp. 32–33).
65. Hampshire, S. (1989, pp. 63–64).
66. Hampshire, S. (1989, p. 67).
67. Hampshire, S. (1989, pp. 68–69).
68. Hampshire, S. (1989, p. 75).
69. Hampshire, S. (1989, pp. 75–76).
70. Nussbaum, M. (1986).
71. Hampshire, S. (1989, p. 106).
72. Hampshire, S. (1989, p. 143).
73. Glover, J. (1999, p. 7).
74. Glover, J. (1999, pp. 22 ff.).
75. Buber, M. (1922).
76. Glover, J. (1999, p. 281).
77. Glover, J. (1999, p. 89).
78. Glover, J. (1999, p. 114).
79. Glover, J. (1999, p. 52).
80. Glover, J. (1999, pp. 156 ff.).
81. Glover, J. (1999, p. 199).
82. Glover, J. (1999, pp. 224 ff.).
83. Glover, J. (1999, pp. 128 ff.).
84. Glover, J. (1999, pp. 146–147).
85. Glover, J. (1999, p. 152).
86. Glover, J. (1999, pp. 265 ff.).
87. Glover, J. (1999, p. 327).
88. Glover, J. (1999, p. 337).
89. Glover, J. (1999, pp. 396–397).

Notes for Chapter 5

1. Thomas, L. M. (1993, p. 13).
2. Thomas, L. M. (1993, p. 117).
3. Ferruta, A. (2020, p. 1155).
4. Anderson, B. (2006, p. 141).
5. Hobsbawm, E. (1990, p. 144).
6. Danziger, R. (2021, pp. 2 ff.).
7. Danziger, R. (2021, p 91).
8. Browning, C. (1992), p. 240).

9. Eilenberger, W. (2018, p. 118).
10. Glover, J. (1999, p. 327).
11. Glover, J. (1999, p. 337).
12. Confino, A. (2014, p. 5).
13. Confino, A. (2014, p. 9).
14. Confino, A. (2014, p. 121).
15. Confino, A. (2014, p. 98).
16. Fenichel, O. (1940, p. 37).
17. Fenichel, O. (1940, p. 31).
18. Fenichel, O. (1940, pp. 31–32).
19. Phillips, K. (2015).
20. Phillips, K. (2015, p. 2).
21. Phillips, K. (2015, p. 16).
22. Steiner, G. (1967, pp. 122–123).
23. Arendt, H. (1951, p. 22).
24. Volkov, S. (2011, p. 30).
25. Katz, J. (1961).
26. Katz, J. (1961, p. 134).
27. Lacorne, D. (2016, p. 91).
28. Duneier, M. (2016, pp. 3–25).
29. Duneier, M. (2016, p. 223).
30. hooks, b. (1982, pp. 15 ff.).
31. Williams, E. E. (1944, p. 14).
32. Thomas, H. (1997, p. 795).
33. Thomas, K. (2018, p. 242).
34. Thomas, K. (2018, p. 243).
35. Thomas, K. (2018, p. 244).
36. Thomas, K. (2018, p. 246).
37. Williams, E. E. (1944, pp. 109 ff.).
38. Berlin, I. (2003, pp. 13–14).
39. hooks, b. (1982).
40. Gilroy, P. (1993).
41. Gilroy, P. (1993, p. 197).
42. Gilroy, P. (1993, p. 4).
43. Kennedy, R. (2014).
44. Hall, S. (1990, pp. 51–59).
45. Said, E. (1993, pp. 87–88).
46. Bauman, Z. (1989, p. 13).
47. Patterson, O. (1982, pp. 2–12).

48. Patterson, O. (1982, p. 7).
49. Du Bois, W. E. B. (1903, p. 542).
50. Gilroy, P. (1993, p. 76).
51. Thomas, L. M. (1993, p. 153).
52. Patterson, O. (1982, p. 13).
53. Patterson, O. (1982, p. 38).
54. Patterson, O. (1982, pp. 46 ff.).
55. Patterson, O. (1982, p. 51).
56. Du Bois, W. E. B. (1903, pp. 364–365).
57. Card, C. (2010, p. 265).
58. Card, C. (2010, p. 237).

Notes for Chapter 6

1. Bloom, H. (1998, p. xviii).
2. Bloom, H. (1998, p. xviii).
3. Muir, K. (1951, p. xxxi).
4. Lever, J. (1965, pp. lxiii ff.).
5. Wilson Knight, G. (1930, p. 137).
6. Bradley, A. C. (1904, pp. 47–48).
7. Hall, P. (2005, p. 260).
8. Bradley, A. C. (1904, p. 48).
9. Freud, S. (1919h, p. 225).
10. Muir, K. (1951, p. lxi).
11. Cavell, S. (1979, pp. 418–419).
12. De M'Uzan, M. (2009).
13. Kristeva, J. (1991).
14. Kristeva, J. (1991, p. 170).
15. Kristeva, J. (1991, p. 182).
16. De Quincey, T. (1823 p. 18).
17. Neiman, S. (2002, pp. 240 ff.).
18. Heffernan, J. (2014, pp. 129 ff.).
19. Empson, W. (1930, p. 3).
20. Barton, J. (1984, p. 170).
21. Paul, H. N. (1950, pp. 34–35).
22. Shapiro, J. (2015, p. 10).
23. Shapiro, J. (2015, p. 219).
24. Kermode, F. (1997, p. 1357).
25. Shapiro, J. (2015, p. 182).

Notes for Chapter 7

1. Fulbrook, M. (2018, p. 521).
2. Mitscherlich, A., & Mitscherlich, M. (1967, pp. 23–24).
3. Mommsen, H. (2001, p. 123).
4. Fulbrook, M. (2018).
5. Kennedy, R. (2019, pp. 143–144).
6. Browning, C. (2016).
7. Browning, C. (2016, p. 12).
8. Browning, C. (2016, p. 40).
9. Midlarsky, E. et al. (2005).
10. Sanderson, C. (2020, p. 178).
11. Fabréguet, M. (2013, pp. 447–463).
12. Semelin, J. (2013).
13. Hoffmann, P. (1988).
14. Hoffmann, P. (1988, p. 131).
15. Roseman, M. (2019).
16. Roseman, M. (2019, p. 235).
17. Bell, R. (2020).
18. Warnock, B. (2020).

References

Abrams, D. (2010). Processes of prejudices: theory, evidence and intervention. London: Equalities and Human Rights Commission.

Adolphs, R., Gosselin, F., Buchanan, T. W., Tranel, D., Schyns, P., & Damasio, A. R. (2005). A mechanism for impaired fear recognition after amygdala damage. *Nature*, 433: 68–72.

Adolphs, R., Tranel, D., Damasio, H., & Damasio, A. (1994). Impaired recognition of emotion in facial expressions following bilateral damage to the human amygdala. *Nature*, 372: 669–672.

Adorno, T. (1951). Freudian theory and the pattern of fascist propaganda. In: G. Roheim (Ed.), *Psychoanalysis and the Social Sciences, Vol. 3*. (pp. 279–300). New York: International Universities Press.

Adorno, T. W., Frenkel-Brunswik, E., Levinson, D. J., & Sanford, R. N. (1950). *The Authoritarian Personality*. New York: Harper & Brothers.

Adshead, G., & Horne, R. (2021). *The Devil You Know*. London: Faber and Faber.

Alford, C. (1997). *What Evil Means to Us*. Ithaca, NY: Cornell University Press.

Allport, G. (1954). *The Nature of Prejudice*. New York: Perseus.

Anderson, B. (2006). *Imagined Communities*. London: Verso.

Aragno, A. (2014). The roots of evil: A psychoanalytic inquiry. *Psychoanalytic Review*, *101*(2): 249–288.

Arendt, H. (1951). *The Origins of Totalitarianism*. San Diego, CA: Harcourt, revised edition, 1967.
Arendt, H. (1963). *Eichmann in Jerusalem*. London: Penguin, 1967.
Arendt, H. (1970). *Men in Dark Times*. San Diego, CA: Harcourt.
Arendt, H. (1971a). Thinking and moral considerations. In: *Responsibility and Judgment* (pp. 159–189). New York: Schocken.
Arendt, H. (1971b). *The Life of the Mind*. San Diego, CA: Harcourt.
Asch, S. (1951). *Effects of Group Pressure upon the Modification and Distortion of Judgments in Groups, Leaderships and Men*. Pittsburgh, PA: Carnegie.
Baron-Cohen, S. (2011). *The Science of Evil*. New York: Basic Books.
Barton, J. (1984). *Playing Shakespeare*. London: Bloomsbury.
Baudelaire, C. (1857). *The Flowers of Evil*. A. Martinez (Ed.). London: Alma Classics, 2016.
Bauman, Z. (1989). *Modernity and the Holocaust*. Cambridge: Polity.
Baumeister, R. (1997). *Evil: Inside Human Violence and Cruelty*. New York: A. W. H. Freeman.
Bell, R. (2020). *America's Long Fight against Slavery*. Chantilly, VA: The Teaching Company.
Berlin, Ira (2003). *Generations of Captivity*. Cambridge, MA: Harvard University Press.
Berlin, I. (1979). *Against the Grain*. London: Hogarth.
Berlin, I. (2001). *The Roots of Romanticism*. H. Hardy (Ed.). Princeton, NJ: Princeton University Press, 2014.
Bernstein, R. (2002). *Radical Evil*. Cambridge: Polity.
Bernstein, R. (2005). *The Abuse of Evil*. Cambridge: Polity.
Bettelheim, B. (1976). *The Uses of Enchantment*. London: Penguin, 1978.
Bion, W. R. (1961). *Experiences in Groups*. London: Tavistock.
Blair, R. J. R. (2018). Traits of empathy and anger: implications for psychopathy and other disorders associated with aggression. *Philosophical Transactions of the Royal Society, B 373*: 20170155.
Blass, T. (2002). Perpetrator behavior as destructive obedience: An evaluation of Stanley Milgram's perspective, the most influential social-psychological approach to the Holocaust. In: L. S. Newman & R. Erber (Eds.), *Understanding Genocide*. Oxford: Oxford University Press.
Bloom, H. (1998). *Shakespeare, The Invention of the Human*. New York: Riverhead.
Bloom, P. (2013). *Just Babies. The Origins of Good and Evil*. New York: Broadway.
Bohleber, W. (2010). *Destructiveness, Intersubjectivity and Trauma*. London: Routledge.

Bollas, C. (1993). *Being a Character*. London: Routledge.
Bollas, C. (1995). *Cracking Up*. London: Routledge.
Bourke, J. (2014). *Wounding the World*. London: Virago.
Bowlby, J. (1953). *Child Care and the Growth of Love*. London: Penguin.
Bradley, A. C. (1904). *Shakespearean Tragedy*. London: Penguin, 1991.
Browning, C. (1992). *Ordinary Men*. New York: Harper.
Browning, C. (2016). From humanitarian relief to Holocaust rescue, and the Maison des Roches in Le Chambon. *Holocaust and Genocide Studies*, 30(2): 211–246.
Buber, M. (1922). *I and Thou*. W. Kaufmann (Trans.). Edinburgh, UK: T&T Clark, 1970.
Burleigh. M. (2010). *Moral Combat*. New York: Harper.
Camus, A. (1942). *The Myth of Sisyphus*. J. O'Brien (Trans.). London: Penguin, 2005.
Card, C. (2010). *Confronting Evils*. Cambridge: Cambridge University Press.
Caspi, A., McClay, J., Moffitt, T. E., Mill, J., Martin, J., Craig, I. W., Taylor, A., & Poulton, R. (2002). Role of genotype in the cycle of violence in maltreated children. *Science*, 297(5582): 851–854.
Cavell, S. (1979). *The Claims of Reason*. Oxford: Oxford University Press.
Chasseguet-Smirgel, J. (1985). *Creativity and Perversion*. London: Free Association.
Chasseguet-Smirgel, J. (1990). Reflections of a psychoanalyst upon the Nazi biocracy and genocide. *International Review of Psycho-Analysis*, 17: 167–176.
Confino, A. (2014). *A World without Jews*. New Haven, CT: Yale University Press.
Covington, C. (2017). *Everyday Evil*. London: Routledge.
Crick, B. (1970). *Introduction to Machiavelli: The Discourses*. London: Penguin, pp. 13–71.
Damasio, A. R. (2010). *Self Comes to Mind*. London: William Heinemann.
Damasio, H., Grabowski, T., Frank, R., Galaburda, A. M., & Damasio, A. R. (1994). The return of Phineas Gage: Clues about the brain from the skull of a famous patient. *Science*, 264(11): 1102–1105.
Danziger, R. (2021). *Radical Revenge*. London: Free Association.
De Brito, S. A., Viding, E., Kumari, V., Blackwood, N., & Hodgins, S. (2013). Cool and hot executive function impairments in violent offenders without antisocial personality disorder with and without psychopathy. *PLOS ONE*, 8(6): e65566.
De Masi (2003). *The Sadomasochist Perversion*. London: Karnac.

De M'Uzan, M. (2009). The uncanny. In: D. Birksted-Breen, S. Flanders, & A. Gibeault (Eds.), *Reading French Psychoanalysis* (pp. 201–209). London: Routledge.

De Quincey, T. (1823). On the knocking at the gate in *Macbeth*. In: S. Schoenbaum (Ed.), *Macbeth: Critical Studies* (pp. 15–19). London: Routledge.

Derrida, J. (1997). *Of Hospitality*. R. Bowlby (Trans.). Stanford, CA: Stanford University Press, 2000.

De Waal, F. (2005). *Our Inner Ape*. London: Granta.

De Waal, F. (2013). *The Bonobos and the Atheist*. New York: W. W. Norton.

Dews, P. (2013). *The Idea of Evil*. Oxford: Blackwell.

Du Bois, W. E. B. (1903). *The Souls of Black People*. New York: Library of America, 1986.

Duneier, M. (2016). *Ghetto*. New York: Farrar, Straus and Giroux.

Eagleton, T. (2010). *On Evil*. New Haven, CT: Yale University Press.

Eilenberger, W. (2018). *Time of the Magicians*. S. Whiteside (Trans.). London: Allen Lane, 2020.

Elias, N. (1989). *The Germans*. E. Dunning & S. Mennell (Trans.). Cambridge: Polity, 1996.

Empson, W. (1930). *Seven Types of Ambiguity*. London: Hogarth, 1984.

Fabréguet, M. (2013). Nieuwlande, Land of Rescues (1941/2–1945). In: *Resisting Genocide*. Oxford: Oxford University Press.

Felman, S., & Laub, D. (1992). *Testimony*. London: Routledge.

Fenichel, O. (1940). Psychoanalysis of antisemitism. *American Imago, 1B*(2): 24–39.

Ferruta, A. (2020). Genocides and processes of subjectification. *International Journal of Psychoanalysis, 101*(6): 1148–1161.

Fornari, F. (1966). *The Psychoanalysis of War*. A. Pfeifer (Trans.). Bloomington, IN: Indiana University Press, 1975.

Freud, S., with Breuer, J. (1895d). *Studies on Hysteria. S. E., 2*: 3–251. London: Hogarth.

Freud, S. (1908d). "Civilized" sexual morality and modern nervous illness. *S. E., 9*: 179–204. London: Hogarth.

Freud, S. (1915b). Thoughts for the times on war and death. *S. E., 14*: 274–307. London: Hogarth.

Freud, S. (1919h). The uncanny. *S. E., 17*: 217–256. London: Hogarth.

Freud, S. (1921c). *Group Psychology and the Analysis of the Ego. S. E., 18*: 67–143. London: Hogarth.

Freud, S. (1923b). *The Ego and the Id. S. E., 19*: 3–63. London: Hogarth.

Freud, S. (1930a). *Civilization and Its Discontents. S. E., 21*: 59–145. London: Hogarth.

Freud, S. (1933b). Why war? *S. E.*, *22*: 197–215. London: Hogarth.
Fromm, E. (1964). *The Heart of Man*. New York: Harper & Row.
Fromm, E. (1974). *The Anatomy of Human Destructiveness*. London: Jonathan Cape.
Fulbrook, M. (2018). *Reckonings*. Oxford: Oxford University Press.
Fussell, P. (1975). *The Great War and Modern Memory*. Oxford: Oxford University Press.
Gauthier, N., & Methot-Jones, T. (2020). Psychopaths and the neurobiology of evil. In: S. Itkowitz & E. Howell (Eds.), *Psychopathy and Human Evil* (pp. 244–261). London: Routledge.
Gerwarth, R. (2016). *The Vanquished*. London: Allen Lane.
Gilroy, P. (1993). *The Black Atlantic*. London: Verso.
Glover, J. (1999). *Humanity: A Moral History of the Twentieth Century*. London: Jonathan Cape.
Grand, S. (2000). *The Reproduction of Evil*. Hillsdale, NJ: Analytic Press.
Grayling, A. (2019). *The History of Philosophy*. London: Viking.
Gregory, S., ffytche, D., Simmons, A., Kumari, V., Howard, M., Hodgins, S., & Blackwood, N. (2012). The antisocial brain: psychopathy matters. *Archives of General Psychiatry*, *69*(9): 962–972.
Hall, P. (2005). Directing *Macbeth*. In: J. Russell Brown (Ed.), *Focus on Macbeth*. Chapter 11. London: Routledge.
Hall, S. (1990). Cultural identity and diaspora. In: K. Woodward (Ed.), *Identity and Difference* (pp. 51–59). London: Sage.
Hampshire, S. (1983). *Morality and Conflict*. Oxford: Basil Blackwell.
Hampshire, S. (1989). *Innocence and Experience*. London: Penguin.
Haynal, A. (2001). Groups and fanaticism. In: E. Person (Ed.), *On Freud's Group Psychology and the Analysis of the Ego* (pp. 111–128). Hillsdale, NJ: Analytic Press.
Heffernan, J. (2014). *Hospitality and Treachery in Western Literature*. New Haven, CT: Yale University Press.
Herbert, U. (2001). Ideological legitimization and political leadership of the National Socialist secret police. In: H. Mommsen (Ed.), *The Third Reich: Between Vision and Reality* (pp. 95–108). Oxford: Berg.
Hilberg, R. (1985). *The Destruction of the European Jews*. New York: Holmes & Meier.
Hobsbawm, E. (1990). *Nations and Nationalism since 1780*. Cambridge: Cambridge University Press.
Hoffmann, P. (1988). *German Resistance to Hitler*. Cambridge, MA: Harvard University Press.

Hogg, M. A. (2010). Influence and leadership. In: S. T. Fiske, D. T. Gilbert, & G. Lindzey (Eds.), *Handbook of Social Psychology* (5th edn., Vol. 2, pp. 1166–1207). New York: Wiley.

hooks, b. (1982). *Ain't I A Woman?* London: Pluto.

Hyatt-Williams, A. (1998). *Cruelty, Violence, and Murder*. Northvale, NJ: Jason Aronson.

Jones, A. P., Laurens, K. R., Herba, C. M., Barker, G. J., & Viding, E. (2009). Amygdala hypoactivity to fearful faces in boys with conduct problems and callous–unemotional traits. *American Journal of Psychiatry*, 166(1): 95–102. https://doi.org/10.1176/appi.ajp.2008.07071050.

Kant, I. (1784). What is enlightenment? In: M. J. Gregor (Ed.), *Practical Philosophy*. Cambridge: Cambridge University Press, 1996.

Kant, I. (1790). *Critique of Judgment*. J. C. Meredith (Trans.). Oxford: Oxford University Press, 2007.

Kant, I. (1793). *Religion within the Boundaries of Reason*. A. Wood (Trans.). Cambridge: Cambridge University Press, 1998.

Katz, J. (1961). *Exclusiveness and Tolerance*. Millburn, NJ: Berman House.

Kekes, J. (2005). *The Roots of Evil*. Ithaca, NY: Cornell University Press.

Kennedy, R. (1998). *The Elusive Human Subject*. London: Free Association.

Kennedy, R. (2014). *The Psychic Home*. London: Routledge.

Kennedy, R. (2019). *Tolerating Strangers in Intolerant Times*. London: Routledge.

Kennedy, R., & Magagna, J. (1981). The aftermath of murder. In: S. Box (Ed.), *Psychotherapy with Families* (pp. 120–135). London: Routledge.

Kermode, F. (1997). Macbeth. In: G. Evan & J. Tobin (Eds.), *Riverside Shakespeare* (pp. 1355–1359). New York: Houghton Mifflin.

Kershaw, I. (2015). *The Nazi Dictatorship*. London: Bloomsbury Academic.

Klein, M. (1952). The mutual influences in the development of the ego and the id. *Psychoanalytic Study of the Child*, 7(1): 51–68.

Kohn, J. (2003). Introduction. In: H. Arendt, *Responsibility and Judgment* (pp. vii–xxix). New York: Schocken.

Kratzer, A. (2019, January 4). Harsh Nazi parental guidelines may still affect German children of today. *Scientific American*.

Kristeva, J. (1991). *Strangers to Ourselves*. New York: Columbia University Press.

Lacorne, D. (2016). *Les Frontières de la Tolerance*. Paris: Gallimard.

Laplanche, J., & Pontalis J.-B. (1967). *The Language of Psychoanalysis*. D. Nicholson-Smith (Trans.). London: Hogarth and Institute of Psychoanalysis, 1980.

Lever, J. (1965). Introduction. In: *Measure for Measure* (pp. xi–xcviii). Arden Shakespeare. London: Methuen.

Levi, P. (1986). *The Drowned and the Saved*. R. Rosenthal (Trans.). London: Michael Joseph, 1988.
Lifton, R. J. (1986). *The Nazi Doctors*. New York: Basic Books.
Lifton, R. J. (2003). *Superpower Syndrome*. New York: Basic Books.
Lower, W. (2013). *Hitler's Furies*. London: Vintage.
Luria, A. (1963). *Restoration of Function after Brain Injury*. New York: Macmillan.
Luria, A. (1973). *The Working Brain*. New York: Basic Books.
Machiavelli, N. (1531). *The Discourses*. B. Crick (Ed.). London: Penguin, 1970.
Machiavelli, N. (1532). *The Prince*. G. Bull (Trans.). London: Penguin, 1961.
MacMillan, M. (2020). *War: How Conflict Shaped Us*. London: Profile.
Main, T. (1975). Some psychodynamics of large groups. In: J. Johns (Ed.), *The Ailment and Other Psychoanalytic Essays* (pp. 100–122). London: Free Association, 1989.
Marcuse, H. (1956). *Eros and Civilization*. London: Routledge.
Marsh, A. A., Finger, E. C., Mitchell, D. G. V., Reid, M. E., Sims, C., Kosson, D. S., Towbin, K. E., Leibenluft, E., Pine, D. S., & Blair, R. J. R. (2008). Reduced amygdala response to fearful expressions in children and adolescents with callous–unemotional traits and disruptive behaviour disorders. *American Journal of Psychiatry*, 165(6): 712–720. https://doi.org/10.1176/appi.ajp.2007.07071145.
Marshall, L. A., & Cooke, D. J. (1999). The childhood experiences of psychopaths. *Journal of Personality Disorder*, 13(3): 211–255.
McGilchrist, I. (2009). *The Master and His Emissary*. New Haven, CT: Yale University Press.
McGinn, C. (1997). *Ethics, Evil and Fiction*. Oxford: Clarendon.
Meltzer, D. (1992). *The Claustrum*. Strath Tay, UK: Clunie.
Midlarsky, E., Jones, S. F., & Corley, R. P. (2005). Personality correlates of heroic rescue during the Holocaust. *Journal of Personality*, 73(4): 907–934.
Migliozzi, A. (2016). The attraction of evil and the destruction of meaning. *International Journal of Psychoanalysis*, 97: 1019–1034.
Miller, A. (1983). *For Your Own Good*. New York: Farrar, Straus & Giroux.
Mitscherlich, A., & Mitscherlich, M. (1967). *The Inability to Mourn*. B. Placzek (Trans.). New York: Grove, 1975.
Mommsen, H. (2001). The Indian summer and the collapse of the Third Reich. In: H. Mommsen (Ed.), *The Third Reich: Between Vision and Reality* (pp. 109–127). Oxford: Berg.
Money-Kyrle, R. (1941). The psychology of propaganda. *British Journal of Medical Psychology*, 19(1): 82–94.

Money-Kyrle, R. (1978). *The Collected Papers of Roger Money-Kyrle*. D. Meltzer (Ed.). Strath Tay, UK: Clunie.

Morton, A. (2004). *On Evil*. London: Routledge.

Motzkin, J. C., Newman, J. P., Kiehl, K. A., & Koenigs, M. (2011). Reduced prefrontal connectivity in psychopathy. *Journal of Neuroscience, 31*(48): 17348–17357.

Muir, K. (1951). Introduction. In: *Macbeth* (pp. xi–lxxiv). Arden Shakespeare. London and Cambridge, MA: Methuen and Harvard University Press, 1984.

Neiman, S. (2002). *Evil in Modern Thought*. Princeton, NJ: Princeton University Press.

Nisbet, H. (2005). Introduction. In: *Lessing: Philosophical and Theological Writings*. Cambridge: Cambridge University Press.

Nussbaum, M. (1986). *The Fragility of Goodness*. Cambridge: Cambridge University Press.

Ogden, T. (1989). *The Primitive Edge of Experience*. London: Routledge.

O'Neill, O. (1986). The public use of reason. In: *Constructions of Reason*. Cambridge: Cambridge University Press, 1989.

O'Neill, O. (1990). Practices of toleration. In: J. Lichtenberg (Ed.), *Democracy and the Mass Media* (pp. 155–185). Cambridge: Cambridge University Press.

O'Neill, O. (2015). *Constructing Authorities*. Cambridge: Cambridge University Press.

O'Neill, O. (2016). *Justice across Boundaries*. Cambridge: Cambridge University Press.

Orwell, G. (1946). Politics and the English language. In: J. Carey (Ed.), *Essays of George Orwell*. London: Everyman Library, 2002.

Parens, H. (2012). Attachment, aggression, and the prevention of malignant prejudice. *Psychoanalytic Inquiry, 32*(2): 171–185.

Patterson, O. (1982). *Slavery and Social Death*. Cambridge, MA: Harvard University Press.

Paul, H. N. (1950). *The Royal Play of Macbeth*. New York: Macmillan.

Perry, G. (2013). Deception and illusion in Milgram's account of the Obedience Experiment. *Theoretical and Applied Ethics, 2*(2): 79–92.

Phillips, K. (2015). Mass nakedness in the imaginary of the Nazis. *Literature and the Arts, 27*: 1–19.

Poeppl, T. B., Donges, M. R., Mokros, A., Rupprecht, R., Fox, P. T., Laird, A. R., Bzdok, D., Langguth, B., & Eickhoff, S. B. (2019). A view behind the mask of sanity: meta-analysis of aberrant brain activity in psychopathy. *Molecular Psychiatry, 24*(3): 463–470.

Poland, W. (2000). Witnessing. *Journal of the American Psychoanalytic Association*, 48: 17–35.

Reicher, S., & Haslam, S. A. (2006). Rethinking the psychology of tyranny. *Journal of Social Psychology*, 45(13): 1–40.

Rilling, J. K., Scholz, J., Preuss, T. M., Glasser, M. F., Errangi, B. K., & Behrens, T. E. (2011). Differences between chimpanzees and bonobos in neural systems supporting social cognition. *Social and Affective Neuroscience*, 7(4): 369–379.

Roberts, R., McCrory, E., Bird, G., Sharp, M., Roberts, L., & Viding, E. (2020). Thinking about other minds: mental state inference in boys with conduct problems and callous–unemotional traits. *Journal of Abnormal Child Psychology*, 48: 1279–1290.

Roseman, M. (2019). *Lives Reclaimed*. New York: Henry Holt.

Rosenfeld, H. (1971). A clinical approach to the psychoanalytic theory of the life and death instincts. *International Journal of Psychoanalysis*, 52: 169–178.

Rosenfeld, H. (1987). *Impasse and Interpretation*. London: Tavistock.

Russell, L. (2020). *Being Evil*. Oxford: Oxford University Press.

Said, E. (1993). *Culture and Imperialism*. London: Chatto & Windus.

Sanderson, C. (2020). *The Bystander Effect*. London: William Collins.

Sandler, J. (1960). On the concept of the superego. *Psychoanalytic Study of the Child*, 15: 128–162.

Sapolsky, R. (2017). *Behave*. London: Bodley Head.

Sartre, J.-P. (1944). *In Camera (Huit Clos)*. S. Gilbert (Trans.). London: Penguin, 1982.

Schore, A. (2003). *Affect Regulation and the Repair of the Self*. New York: W. W. Norton.

Schore, A. (2012). *The Science and Art of Psychotherapy*. New York: W. W. Norton..

Sebek, M. (1996). The fate of the totalitarian object. *International Forum of Psychoanalysis*, 5(4): 289–294.

Semelin, J. (2013). *The Survival of the Jews in France 1940–44*. C. Schoch & N. Lehrer (Trans.). London: C. Hurst, 2018.

Shapiro, J. (2015). *William Shakespeare and the Year 1606*. London: Faber and Faber.

Shay, J. (1994). *Achilles in Vietnam*. New York: Charles Scribner's Sons.

Shengold, L. (1989). *Soul Murder*. New York: Fawcett Columbine.

Sheriff, M., White, B. J., & Harvey, O. J. (1955). Status in experimentally produced groups. *American Journal of Sociology*, 60(4): 370–379.

Sklar, J. (2019). *Dark Times*. Oxford: Phoenix.

Solomon, R. (2000). *No Excuses: Existentialism and the Meaning of life*. Chantilly, VA: The Teaching Company.
Staub, E. (1989). *The Roots of Evil*. Cambridge: Cambridge University Press.
Steiner, G. (1967). *Language and Silence*. London: Faber and Faber.
Steiner, J. (2016). Man's inhumanity to man: confrontation and prejudice. *Psychoanalytic Inquiry*, 36: 285–294.
Stone, M. (2009). *The Anatomy of Evil*. New York: Guilford.
Tajfel, H. (1970). Experiments in intergroup discrimination. *Scientific American*, 223(5): 96–103.
Tajfel, H., & Turner, J. (1979). The social identity theory of intergroup behaviour. In: M. Hatch & M. Schalz (Eds.), *Organizational Identity: A Reader* (pp. 276–293). Oxford: Oxford University Press.
Taylor, K. (2009). *Cruelty*. Oxford: Oxford University Press.
Thomas, H. (1997). *The Slave Trade*. London: Picador.
Thomas, K. (2018). *In Pursuit of Civility*. New Haven, CT: Yale University Press.
Thomas, L. M. (1993). *Vessels of Evil*. Philadelphia, PA: Temple University Press.
Tyerman, C. (2019). *The World of the Crusades*. New Haven, CT: Yale University Press.
Volkov, S. (2011). Antisemitism as a cultural code. In: M. Marras (Ed.), *The Origins of the Holocaust* (pp. 307–328). Munich, Germany: K. G. Saur.
Waller, J. (2002). *Becoming Evil*. New York: Oxford University Press, 2007.
Warnock, B. (2020). *Jewish Resistance to the Holocaust*. London: Weiner Holocaust Library.
Williams, E. E. (1944). *Capitalism and Slavery*. 3rd edn. Chapel Hill, NC: University of North Carolina Press, 1994.
Wilson Knight, G. (1930). *The Wheel of Fire*. London: Routledge Classics, 2001.
Winnicott, D. W. (1964). *The Child, The Family and the Outside World*. London: Penguin.
Zimbardo, P. (2004). A situationist perspective on the psychology of evil. In: A. Miller (Ed.), *The Sociology of Good and Evil* (pp. 494–523). New York: Guilford.
Zimbardo, P. (2007). *The Lucifer Effect: How Good People Turn Evil*. New York: Random House.

Index

Abrams, Dominic, 199
Abu Ghraib prison, 146
abuse, 1, 2, 34, 39, 40, 44, 60, 85, 89, 90, 91, 92, 93
adolescence, 39, 40
Adolphs, Ralph, 198
Adorno, Theodor, 51, 75
Adshead, Gwen, 32
Africa, 2, 3, 14, 26, 130, 154, 155, 156, 157, 158, 160, 192
aggression, 12, 36, 39, 43, 44, 45, 51, 54, 55, 60, 61, 64, 69, 72, 83, 84, 96–98, 112, 137, 186, 187
Alford, Fred, 33, 90
Allport, Gordon, 62–64, 83–84
ambivalence, 85, 94, 98, 188
amygdala, 38, 39, 40, 41–44, 46, 54
Anderson, Benedict, 24–25, 138
annihilation of the human subject, 1, 7, 11, 77, 80, 89, 90, 92, 100, 117, 124, 135, 137, 165, 180

anti-Semitism, 24, 77, 78, 79, 83, 133, 134, 144, 145, 147–148, 191
antisocial personality, 35, 36, 40–44
apocalyptic violence, 7, 12, 13, 80, 83, 137
Aragno, Anna, 202
Arendt, Hannah, 12, 16, 101, 109, 110, 114–121, 137, 147, 188
Aristotle, 16, 122
Asch, Solomon, 32, 56–57, 63
attachment, 18, 39, 45, 48–49, 51, 54, 99, 119, 160, 163
Augustine, Saint, 6, 16
Auschwitz, 2, 22, 133, 135, 175, 192
authoritarianism, 51, 60, 136
Austen, Jane, 160
autism, 46

banality of evil, 16, 119, 120, 121
Baron-Cohen, Simon, 11, 45–47
Barton, John, 177
Bartsch Jürgen, 51

Baudelaire, Charles, 9, 95
Bauman, Zygmunt, 25–26, 161
Baumeister, Roy, 33, 85
BBC Study, 60, 136
Będzin ghetto, 192
Bell, Richard, 196
Berlin, Ira, 156, 157
Berlin, Isaiah, 113, 123
Bernstein, Richard, 18, 108
Bettelheim, Bruno, 15–16
Białystok ghetto, 192
Bion, Wilfred, 70–71
Black Atlantic, 158, 163
black experience, 63, 132, 154, 157, 158, 163, 165
Blair, Rachel, 198
Blass, Thomas, 61
Bloom, Harold, 168
Bloom, Paul, 47–50
Bohleber, Werner, 78, 145
Bollas, Christopher, 79–80, 89–90, 180
bonobos, 10–11, 35, 52–54
Bourke, Joanna, 19
Bowlby, John, 45
Bradley, Andrew, 169
brain injury, 34, 36–38
Browning, Christopher, 28, 31, 72, 91, 189–190
Buber, Martin, 8, 125
Bund, the, 13, 192
Burleigh, Michael, 12
bystanders, 7, 13, 26, 65–67, 190

Cambodia, 2, 61, 165
callous-unemotional children, 11, 43–45
Camus, Albert, 15
Card, Claudia, 8, 61, 165
Caspi, Avshalom, 198

Cassel Hospital, 74–75, 134
Cavell, Stanley, 172
Chasseguet-Smirgel, Janine, 76–78, 80
child abuse, 1, 2, 34, 39, 40, 44, 85, 89, 90, 91, 92, 93
child development, 11, 33, 35, 39, 40, 47–52, 54, 85, 180
chimpanzees, 10–11, 36, 52–53
Christianity, 4, 6, 110, 129, 142, 144, 148, 150, 151, 152
civilisation, 25, 94–97, 98, 113, 142, 155–156, 162
Clarkson, Thomas, 156
Clinton, Hillary, 139
communism, 128, 170
community, 3, 5, 8, 12, 13, 24, 25, 67, 74, 78, 90, 94, 96, 97, 104, 105, 106, 107, 109, 112, 125, 129, 138, 140, 141, 142, 149, 163, 164, 165, 189, 190
Confino, Alan, 142–143
conformity, 29, 32, 36, 57, 60–61, 185
Covid-19, 6
Covington, Coline, 16
Crick, Bernard, 111
criminals, 8, 12, 32, 33, 37, 37, 41, 86, 117, 118, 187
Croatians, 128
cruelty, 1, 15, 19, 32, 45, 46, 47, 86, 94, 101, 111, 114, 122, 125, 126, 174
Crusades, 6, 150
Częstochowa Ghetto, 192

Damasio, Antonio, 39, 42
Dante, 145
Danziger, Renée, 139
death, 2, 7, 14, 15, 19, 22, 79, 86–90, 94, 98–99, 100, 101, 117,

118, 125, 127, 137, 146, 154, 162, 163–165, 169, 170, 186, 192, 193
   social, 162, 164–165
De Brito, Stephanie, 198
delusion, 30, 72, 80, 139, 140
De M'Uzan, Michel, 172
De Masi, Franco, 100
De Quincey, Thomas, 174–175
Derrida, Jacques, 13
destructiveness, 2, 11, 13, 15, 19, 25, 26, 52, 54, 69, 76, 98, 101, 123, 124, 125, 126, 136, 137, 162, 170
devil, 14, 15, 17, 33, 111, 114, 172, 174, 180, 182, 183
De Waal, Frans, 10, 52–55
Dews, Peter, 5
diaspora, 26, 151, 158, 159, 160
discrimination, 27, 56, 59, 63, 65, 134, 150
double consciousness, 165
doubling, 22, 23
Douglas, Frederick, 164
Dresden, 127
Du Bois, William, 163, 165
Duneier, Mitchell, 152–153

Eagleton, Terry, 196
Eichmann, Adolf, 29, 109–110, 119–120, 187, 188
Eilenberger, Wolfram, 205
Elias, Norbert, 197
Eliot, Thomas Stearns, 77
empathy, 7, 11, 12, 17, 20, 38, 40, 41, 43, 44, 45–47, 50, 52, 53, 67, 86, 89, 186, 188, 190
empathy circuit, 11, 46–47
Empson, William, 177

Enlightenment, 95, 103–104, 116, 148
equivocation, 178, 181–182
Eros, 71, 96, 98, 99
evil
   banality, 16, 119, 120, 121
   characters, 4, 69, 85–101, 119, 168, 169, 170
   definition, 7
   dispositions, 10, 55, 98, 112, 132
   and group processes, 70–85
   imagination, 1, 2, 4, 132, 137, 193
   levels of, 14–34, 85–81
   moral, 4, 6, 132, 169
   natural, 6, 9, 123, 168
   philosophy of, 3, 9, 17, 70, 101, 103–130
   psychoanalysis of, 34, 54, 69–101
   radical, 5, 98, 103–108, 114–117
   resisting, 2, 3, 14, 50, 132, 185–194
   science of, 3, 11, 12, 34, 35–67
   and social psychology, 56–67
   spectrum of, 7
evolution, 10–12, 34, 47, 49, 50, 53, 54
extermination camps, 133, 135, 187

Fabréguet, Michelle, 207
fanaticism, 6, 122
fairy tales, 15–16
Faust, 17, 23
fascism, 60, 80, 128, 136
fear, 24, 27, 29, 34, 39, 41–44, 48–50, 53, 55, 65, 66, 73, 74, 75, 84, 85, 87, 88, 100, 127, 128, 129, 136, 138, 142, 145, 146, 163, 179, 180, 181, 183
Felman, Shosha, 93
Ferruta, Anna, 204

Final Solution, 109, 120, 143, 165
First World War, 23, 24, 115, 124, 132, 139
Floyd, George, 157
Fornari, Franco, 19
Frank, Hans, 110
freedom, 5, 11, 56, 96, 104–105, 107, 108, 109, 112, 116, 117, 125, 132, 145, 151, 155, 157
Freud, Sigmund, 15, 19, 31, 70–71, 75, 76, 94–98, 99, 100, 122, 171, 172
Fromm, Erich, 99–100
frontal lobes, 36–37, 39, 40
Fulbrook, Mary, 3, 187
fundamentalism, 79
Fussell, Paul, 20–22

Gage, Phineas, 36
Garnet, Henry, 181–182
Gauthier, Nathalie, 198
gender, 85
genes, 11, 35, 40, 46, 54, 115
genocide, 1, 2, 3, 4, 25, 26, 32, 62, 64, 69, 79, 90, 91, 98, 115, 120, 121, 126, 135, 142, 165, 187, 193
Genovese, Kitty, 66
Germans, 3, 12, 13, 23, 51, 62, 73, 78, 138, 140, 141, 142, 145, 146, 153, 185, 186, 187, 188, 189, 191
Gerwarth, Robert, 197
ghetto, 14, 26, 31, 81, 151–153, 192
Gilroy, Paul, 4, 26, 157–158, 159, 163
Glover, Jonathan, 19, 125–130
Goebbels, Joseph, 73, 140
Golding, William, 58
Goethe, Johann von, 17

good, 4, 5, 9, 11, 13, 14, 15, 16, 17, 22, 31, 47, 48, 51, 61, 89, 94, 98, 99, 100, 107, 108, 110–114, 118, 119, 120, 123, 124, 145, 148, 170, 180, 182
Göring, Hermann, 140
Grand, Sue, 90–91, 92
Gray, Dorian, 9
Grayling, Anthony, 202
Greek tragedy, 15
groups, 3, 5, 7, 11, 14, 24, 27, 28, 30, 42, 47, 51, 52, 56–59, 64, 65–69, 70–85, 97, 98, 99, 101, 109, 116, 118, 125, 131, 139, 140, 144, 146, 163, 192
guilt, 20, 41, 43, 82, 83, 84, 95, 97, 121, 127, 186–187
Gunpowder Plot, 178, 181

Hall, Peter, 170
Hall, Stuart, 159–160
Hamlet, 169, 170
Hampshire, Stuart, 9, 112, 121–125, 168, 188
Hardy, Thomas, 21
Harlow, John, 36
harm, 7, 8, 10, 12, 19, 27–28, 33, 41, 47, 54, 61, 62, 63, 65–66, 81, 85–86, 103, 108, 119, 123, 136, 139
hatred, 66, 72, 73, 76, 83–85, 111, 128, 129, 139, 142, 144, 147, 168, 169, 189
Haynal, André, 200
Heffernen, James, 206
Hegel, Georg Wilhelm, 5, 8
Heidegger, Martin, 141
Heimat, 77, 143
Herbert, Ulrich, 203

INDEX

Hess, Rudolf, 140
Hilberg, Raul, 25, 121, 135
Himmler, Heinrich, 9, 122, 140
Hitler, Adolf, 24–25, 51, 66, 72–73, 76–77, 79, 84, 100, 110, 129, 138, 140, 146, 152, 164, 167, 185–187, 189, 191
Hobsbawm, Eric, 24–25, 138
Hoffmann, Peter, 191
Hogg, Michael, 199
Holocaust, 3, 14, 25, 28, 46, 56, 61, 62, 67, 93, 114, 116, 130, 131, 132–153, 162, 187, 190, 192
home, 2, 5, 9, 13, 22, 23, 27, 30, 43, 49, 54, 65, 77, 78, 81, 91, 106, 127, 133, 143, 145, 151, 154, 155, 157, 159, 160, 161, 163, 164, 171, 172, 173, 176, 178, 189, 191, 193
  for otherness, 2, 13, 27, 81, 161, 173, 189
  psychic, 27, 65, 154, 158, 159, 163
hooks, bell, 154, 157, 205
Huntington's Chorea, 36
Huis Clos, 11
Hyatt-Williams, Arthur, 86–88

Iago, 17, 168, 169, 171
Ibn Rushd, 148
idealisation, 76, 82, 83, 84–85
identification, 27, 31, 38, 65, 71, 72, 74, 76, 80, 83, 87, 88, 158, 159, 186
identity, 6, 19, 27, 59, 61, 64–66, 72, 73, 74, 78, 83, 85, 118, 119, 125–129, 132, 137, 141, 143–145, 147, 158, 159–161, 163, 171, 172, 178–179

ideology, 5, 7, 12, 24, 26, 31, 33, 44, 69, 75, 76, 77, 78, 80, 115, 128, 130, 131, 132, 137, 138, 141, 142, 149, 153, 162, 167, 187
imagination, 11, 17, 23, 25, 81, 128, 137, 145, 171, 189, 193
  evil, 1, 2, 4, 132, 137, 193
imagined community, 24, 25, 138
infants, 48, 49, 53, 54, 123
intersubjectivity, 7, 34, 39, 86, 163
intolerance, 27–28, 80–81, 104, 107, 117, 148, 153, 157, 167, 168, 188, 189

Jekyll and Hyde, 9
Jews, 7, 12, 13, 23, 25, 31, 51, 62, 64, 67, 73, 77, 79, 84, 109, 116, 118, 120, 129, 131, 132–153, 158, 163, 185, 189–192
judgment, 26, 27, 38, 47, 57–58, 73, 75, 81, 99, 105, 110, 120, 124, 169, 188
Julius Caesar, 16
justice, 9, 11, 39, 47, 49, 50, 52, 112, 115, 122, 123, 124, 125, 139, 169, 188

Kant, Immanuel, 4, 5, 8, 12, 50, 103–110, 114, 117, 125, 140
Katz, Jacob, 148
Keats, John, 95
Kekes, John, 9
Kennedy, John F., 128
Kermode, Frank, 182
Kershaw, Ian, 23–24
Khrushchev, Nikita, 128
King James I, 178, 180, 181
King Lear, 169, 170

Klein, Melanie, 101
Kohn, Jerome, 202
Kovno Ghetto, 192
Krakow Ghetto, 192
Kratzner, Anne, 199
Kristeva, Julia, 172, 188
Kurlander, Eric, 146

Lacorne, Denis, 205
Lanzmann, Claude, 8
Laplanche, Jean, 201, 202
Laub, Dori, 93
Le Chambon sur-Lignon, 13, 67, 109, 189, 190, 191
Lever, John, 206
Levi, Primo, 119, 145
Levinas, Emmanuel, 8
Lifton, Robert Jay, 22, 32, 79, 80, 121
limbic circuits, 38, 39, 41, 46
Livy, 112
L'Ouverture, Toussaint, 156, 192
Luria, Alexander, 37, 39

Macbeth, 16, 168, 169, 170–183
Macmillan, Harold, 111
MacMillan, Margaret, 19
Machiavelli, Niccolò, 110–114, 117, 123
Maimonides, Moses, 148
Main, Tom, 74–75
Marcuse, Herbert, 96
Marsh, Abigail, 198
Marshall, Lisa, 198
Marxism, 15, 128–129
maternal care, 11, 45, 54
McGilchrist, Iain, 38
McGinn, Colin, 196
Meltzer, Donald, 100, 101
memory, 12, 20, 37, 39–40, 91, 92

Mephistopheles, 17
Middle East, 128
Midlarski, Elizabeth, 200
Migliozzi, Anna, 100–101
Milgram experiments, 28–32, 60, 61, 65, 110
Milgram, Stanley, 28, 29–32, 59–61, 65, 119
Mill, John Stuart, 27
Miller, Alice, 51
Minsk Ghetto, 192
Mitscherlich, Alexander, 185–186, 188
Mitscherlich, Margarete, 185–186, 188
modernism, 9, 143, 157
Mommsen, Hans, 206
Money-Kyrle, Roger, 72–74, 75
Montesquieu, Charles, 156
monoamine oxidase, 40
moral evil, 4, 6, 132, 169
morality, 5, 11, 12, 15, 17, 18, 19, 20, 32, 47–52, 56, 71, 95, 96, 97, 110, 113, 122, 124, 125, 126, 130, 148
Morton, Adam, 8
Moscovici, Serge, 57–58
Motzkin, Julian, 41
Muir, Kenneth, 206
murder, 9, 11, 16, 18, 19, 32, 41, 44, 66, 69, 79, 80, 86–89, 92, 100, 118, 121, 165, 169, 170, 173, 175, 176–181, 191
music, 151, 163, 164, 166
Muslims, 64, 148, 150
Mỹ Lai massacre, 18

narcissism, 78, 80, 82, 85, 87, 99, 139
natal alienation, 163
nationalism, 23, 24, 25, 83, 128, 138, 137

natural evil, 6, 9, 123, 168
Nazis, 3, 9, 12, 13, 17, 24, 29, 46, 62,
    72, 73, 76, 77, 79, 110, 115,
    118, 122, 123, 124, 126, 129,
    138, 139, 140, 141–148,
    150, 163, 165, 168, 187, 193
Nazi doctors, 22–23, 32, 115, 121
Nazi Imaginary, 3, 78, 132–138, 139,
    140, 142, 143, 144, 146, 152,
    153, 154, 185, 186
Neiman, Susan, 9, 176
neuroscience, 3, 12, 35, 36–47
Nietzsche, Friedrich, 17
Nisbet, Hugh, 203
Nieuwlande, 191
Northern Ireland, 128
Nussbaum, Martha, 124

Ogden, Thomas, 33
Oedipus complex, 77
O'Neill, Onora, 106
Orwell, George, 80, 107
otherization, 1
otherness, 1, 2, 3, 7, 13, 16, 27, 76, 81,
    93, 93, 101, 102, 135, 137,
    161, 165, 168, 173, 188,
    189, 193
    home for, 2, 13, 27, 81, 161, 173, 189
Othello, 17, 168, 169, 170

paranoia, 20, 73, 74, 128
Parens, Henri, 85
Patterson, Orlando, 162–164
Paul, Henry, 180–181
perpetrators, 26, 32, 34, 86, 90, 91, 145
Perry, Gina, 197
Phillips, Kathy, 145–146
Pico della Mirandola, Giovanni, 152
Pitt, William, 156

Plato, 16
pluralistic ignorance, 66
Poeppl, Timm, 198
Poland, Warren, 201
Pontalis, Jean-Bertrand, 201, 202
post-traumatic stress, 18, 20, 39
prejudice, 7, 27, 29, 36, 51, 56, 59,
    62–65, 83–85, 104, 105,
    128, 131, 134, 144, 145,
    147–148
projection, 55, 70, 71, 74, 76, 79, 83,
    84, 85, 144
projective identification, 74, 80
psychic home, 27, 65, 154, 158,
    159, 163
psychopaths, 37, 40, 41, 43, 47, 52,
    69, 86, 119

Quakers, 14, 192

race, 17, 63, 76, 78, 85, 124, 129, 138,
    141, 142, 143, 145, 153, 154,
    159, 190
racism, 2, 50, 75, 76, 78, 116, 129,
    132, 138, 141, 142, 147,
    154, 157
radical evil, 5, 98, 103–108, 114–117
rape, 1, 10, 19, 41, 84
Reicher, Stephen, 199, 200
religion, 4, 5, 6, 85, 103, 107, 109,
    110, 116, 128, 159
resisting evil, 2, 3, 14, 50, 132,
    185–193
respect, 3, 8, 19, 26–28, 76, 81, 93,
    101, 104–105, 124, 125,
    129, 137, 141, 161, 168, 172,
    188, 191
revenge, 6, 21, 24, 87, 117, 124,
    139–140

Richard III, 170, 171
Riefenstahl, Leni, 76, 167
Rilling, James, 199
Roberts, Rita, 198
Roseman, Mark, 191–192, 196
Rosenfeld, Harold, 81–82, 85, 99, 101
Russia, 2, 16, 24, 115, 135, 144, 193
Russell, Luke, 203
Rwanda, 128

Said, Edward, 160–161
Sandler, Joseph, 71, 76
Sanderson, Catherine, 65–66
Sapolsky, Robert, 35–36, 40, 46
Sartre, Jean-Paul, 11
Sassoon, Siegfried, 21
Schopenhauer, Arthur, 95
Schore, Alan, 39
Sebek, Michael, 82
Second World War, 9, 13, 20, 24, 37, 51, 67, 115, 122, 128, 132, 144, 189, 190
Semelin, Jacques, 207
Serbs, 128
serial killers, 7, 32, 33, 51, 69, 89–90, 137
sexism, 157
sexuality, 88, 95–97
Shakespeare, William, 4, 9, 16, 17, 167–183
Shapiro, James, 206
Shay, Jonathan, 18
Sherif, Muzafer, 58
Shelley, Percy Bysshe, 95
Shengold, Leonard, 92
Shoah, 8, 135 (*see also* Holocaust)
Sklar, Jonathan, 83
slavery, 1, 2, 3, 4, 14, 26, 69, 123, 127, 130, 131, 132, 154–165, 192

Socrates, 17
social death, 154, 162, 164–165
social identity theory, 59, 64
social psychology, 3, 12, 29, 35, 36, 56–67, 101, 125, 136
Solomon, Robert, 15
soul murder, 92
Soviet Russia, 16, 52, 114, 128–129, 187, 192
Stalin, Joseph, 15, 114, 124, 126, 128
Staub, Erwin, 26
Steiner, George, 146
Steiner, John, 84–85
Stone, Michael, 8
Stanford Prison experiment, 10, 28, 30–32, 60–61, 62, 65, 119, 136
stranger anxiety, 48–49
strangers, 13, 26–27, 47–49, 53, 65, 85, 171, 172
Strong, Tracy, 189–190
subject (human), 1, 5, 7, 8, 10, 25, 26, 27, 29, 31, 34, 39, 59, 60, 62, 63, 78, 80, 81, 82, 86, 89, 90, 103, 104, 106, 107, 108, 112, 118, 119, 120, 121, 122, 124, 126, 129, 130, 132, 135, 136, 137, 142, 149, 159, 160, 162, 163, 164, 165, 169, 170, 180, 188
subject relations, 1, 7
superego, 31, 71, 76, 78, 82, 97
survivors, 34, 56, 90, 93, 132, 145, 187, 193

Tajfel, Henri, 59, 63, 64
Taylor, Kathleen, 1
terrains of evil, 1–35, 69, 90, 94, 101
terrorism, 79

INDEX 227

Thanatos, 98
theodicy, 4, 103
theory of mind, 38
Thomas, Hugh, 155–156
Thomas, Keith, 155
Thomas, Lawrence Mordechai, 131–132
tolerance, 26–28, 80–81, 83, 104, 106–107, 114, 116, 117, 148–149, 188–189
torture, 9, 10, 12, 33, 90, 97, 146, 165, 181
totalitarianism, 16, 28, 30, 76, 82–83, 107, 114–119, 120, 136, 138, 167
totalitarian object, 82–83
transference, 30, 32, 92, 97
trauma, 3, 7, 13, 18, 20, 24, 33, 34, 36, 38, 39, 40, 48, 51, 82, 85, 87, 88, 89, 90–93, 101, 128, 136, 141, 144, 154, 157, 160, 180, 181, 185, 186
Trump, Donald, 19, 75, 139
Twin Towers, 2
Tyerman, Christopher, 195
uncanny, 133, 144, 171, 172–173, 176, 178, 180
unconscious, 19, 25, 31, 51, 70, 73, 74, 78, 84, 88, 89, 130, 138, 144, 145, 157, 171, 180
Ukraine, 2, 20
Urbache-Wiethe Disease, 42
United States Capitol riot, 2, 19, 75, 125

Vichy, 189, 191
Vietnam, 18
Vilna Ghetto, 192
violence, 2, 4, 6, 11, 12, 13, 19, 25, 26, 28, 30–33, 36, 40, 43–44, 47, 60, 62–64, 70, 72, 73, 78, 79, 80, 90, 100, 111, 112, 137–140, 143, 145, 148, 152, 153, 162, 170
Volkov, Shulamit, 147
Volksgemeinschaft, 12, 141
Waller, James, 26
war, 2, 4, 6, 9, 13, 18–24, 29, 37, 51, 62, 63, 67, 72, 73, 91, 94, 100, 110, 115, 122, 124, 126, 127, 128, 132, 135, 139, 144, 146, 150, 151, 153, 156, 157, 179, 186, 189, 190, 191
Warnock, Barbara, 196, 207
Wilberforce, William, 155
Williams, Eric, 154–155
Wilson Knight, George, 195
Winnicott, Donald, 55
witchcraft, 16, 172, 173, 174, 176, 178, 179, 180, 181
witnessing, 34, 87, 93, 100

Yad Vashem, 133

Zimbardo, Philip, 10, 28, 30–32, 59–61, 62